CW01262584

Friendship in the Hebrew Bible

THE ANCHOR YALE BIBLE REFERENCE LIBRARY is a project of international and interfaith scope in which Protestant, Catholic, and Jewish scholars from many countries contribute individual volumes. The project is not sponsored by any ecclesiastical organization and is not intended to reflect any particular theological doctrine.

The series is committed to producing volumes in the tradition established half a century ago by the founders of the Anchor Bible, William Foxwell Albright and David Noel Freedman. It aims to present the best contemporary scholarship in a way that is accessible not only to scholars but also to the educated nonspecialist. It is committed to work of sound philological and historical scholarship, supplemented by insight from modern methods, such as sociological and literary criticism.

John J. Collins
General Editor

THE ANCHOR YALE BIBLE REFERENCE LIBRARY

Friendship in the Hebrew Bible

SAUL M. OLYAN

Yale UNIVERSITY PRESS

NEW HAVEN AND LONDON

"Anchor Yale Bible" and the Anchor Yale logo are registered trademarks of Yale University.

Copyright © 2017 by Yale University.
All rights reserved.
This book may not be reproduced, in whole or in part, including illustrations, in any form (beyond that copying permitted by Sections 107 and 108 of the U.S. Copyright Law and except by reviewers for the public press), without written permission from the publishers.

Yale University Press books may be purchased in quantity for educational, business, or promotional use. For information, please e-mail sales.press@yale.edu (U.S. office) or sales@yaleup.co.uk (U.K. office).

Set in Adobe Caslon type by Newgen North America.
Printed in the United States of America.

Library of Congress Control Number: 2016943626
ISBN: 978-0-300-18268-2 (hardcover : alk. paper)

A catalogue record for this book is available from the British Library.
This paper meets the requirements of ANSI/NISO Z39.48-1992 (Permanence of Paper).

10 9 8 7 6 5 4 3 2 1

For Lorne Sabsay, my oldest friend

Contents

Acknowledgments, ix

List of Abbreviations, xi

Introduction, 1

1. Friends and Family, 11
2. Failed Friendship, 38
3. Friendship in Narrative, 61
4. Friendship in Ben Sira, 87

Conclusion, 104

Notes, 117

Index of Passages, 171

Index of Subjects, 185

Acknowledgments

It is a great pleasure to acknowledge the contributions of friends, colleagues, and institutions to the development of this book. I am indebted to David Konstan and Nathaniel Levtow for reading individual chapters and providing valuable critical and bibliographic suggestions. I also thank Michael Satlow, Matthew Rutz, Jacob L. Wright, and Susan Harvey for providing additional bibliographic references, and John Huehnergard, Zackary Wainer, and Nathaniel DesRosiers for suggestions regarding aspects of the book's content or argument. I am grateful to John J. Collins for the helpful suggestions he made while editing the manuscript for Yale University Press. This is a better book as a result of his efforts. In addition to the contributions made by these individuals, I have also benefited from the feedback of the press's anonymous referees. Needless to say, all errors of fact or judgment that remain are my responsibility alone.

Brown University awarded me a fellowship at the Cogut Center for the Humanities during the spring semester of 2014, during which I was able to write several chapters of the book. I am grateful to the university for this opportunity, as well as for sabbatical time during the fall semester of 2010 when I began to work in earnest on this project. Some of the content in Chapter 1 appeared in a different form in my essay "The Roles of Kin and Fictive Kin in Biblical Representations of Death Ritual," in *Family and Household Religion: Toward a Synthesis of Old Testament Studies, Archaeology, Epigraphy, and Cultural Studies* (ed. Rainer Albertz et al.; Winona Lake, IN: Eisenbrauns, 2014), 251–63. I thank James Eisenbraun for permission to reproduce this material in this volume. Finally, I am immensely grateful to my husband, Frederik Schockaert, for his unwavering support at every stage of the writing of this book.

Abbreviations

AnBib	Analecta biblica
AYB	Anchor Yale Bible
b.	Babylonian
BASOR	Bulletin of the American Schools of Oriental Research
BDB	*A Hebrew and English Lexicon of the Old Testament.* Edited by Francis Brown, S. R. Driver, and Charles A. Briggs. Boston: Houghton, Mifflin, 1906.
Beentjes	*The Book of Ben Sira in Hebrew: A Text Edition of All Extant Hebrew Manuscripts and a Synopsis of All Parallel Hebrew Ben Sira Texts.* Pancratius C. Beentjes. VTSup 68. Atlanta: Society of Biblical Literature, 2006.
BJS	Brown Judaic Studies
BKAT	Biblischer Kommentar Altes Testament
BO	*Bibliotheca orientalis*
BWL	*Babylonian Wisdom Literature.* W. G. Lambert. Oxford: Clarendon, 1960.
BZAW	Beihefte zur Zeitschrift für die alttestamentliche Wissenschaft
CAT	*The Cuneiform Alphabetic Texts from Ugarit, Ras Ibn Hani and Other Places* (KTU: second, enlarged edition). Edited by Manfried Dietrich, Otto Loretz, and Joaquín Sanmartín. Münster: Ugarit-Verlag, 1995.
CBQ	*Catholic Biblical Quarterly*
EA	*El Amarna.* According to the numbering of the Amarna letters in *Die el-Amarna-Tafeln: Mit*

	Einleitung und Erläuterungen. J. A. Knudtzon. Leipzig: Hinrichs, 1915.
FAT	Forschungen zum Alten Testament
GKC	*Gesenius' Hebrew Grammar.* Edited and enlarged by E. Kautzsch. Second English edition by A. E. Cowley. Oxford: Clarendon, 1910.
HALOT	*The Hebrew and Aramaic Lexicon of the Old Testament.* Ludwig Koehler, Walter Baumgartner, and Johann Jakob Stamm. Translated and edited under the supervision of M. E. J. Richardson. 5 vols. Leiden: Brill, 1994–2000.
Hi	Hiphil
Hit	Hitpael
HSM	Harvard Semitic Monographs
JAJSup	Journal of Ancient Judaism Supplements
JBL	*Journal of Biblical Literature*
Joüon	*Grammaire de l'hébreu biblique.* Paul Joüon. Rome: Institut Biblique Pontifical, 1923.
KAI	*Kanaanäische und aramäische Inschriften.* H. Donner and W. Röllig. 2nd ed. Wiesbaden: Harrassowitz, 1966–1969.
LXX	Septuagint
LXX[B]	Codex Vaticanus
MT	Masoretic Text
Ni	Niphal
NIDOTTE	*New International Dictionary of Old Testament Theology and Exegesis.* Edited by Willem A. VanGemeren. 5 vols. Grand Rapids, MI: Zondervan, 1997.
NJPS	*Tanakh: The Holy Scriptures: The New JPS Translation According to the Traditional Hebrew Text.* New York: Jewish Publication Society, 1985.
NRSV	New Revised Standard Version
OCD	*The Oxford Classical Dictionary.* Edited by Simon Hornblower and Antony Spawforth. 3rd ed. New York: Oxford University Press, 1996.
OTL	Old Testament Library
Pi	Piel

RSV	Revised Standard Version
TDOT	*Theological Dictionary of the Old Testament.* Edited by G. J. Botterweck, H. Ringgren, and H.-J. Fabry. Translated by J. T. Willis, G. W. Bromily, and D. E. Green. 15 vols. Grand Rapids, MI: Eerdmans, 1974–2006.
TLOT	*Theological Lexicon of the Old Testament.* Edited by Ernst Jenni with assistance from Claus Westermann. Translated by Mark E. Biddle. 3 vols. Peabody, MA: Hendrickson, 1997.
Vg.	Vulgate
VT	*Vetus Testamentum*
VTSup	Vetus Testamentum Supplements
Williams	*Hebrew Syntax: An Outline.* Ronald J. Williams. 2nd ed. Toronto: University of Toronto Press, 1976.
W.-O.	*An Introduction to Biblical Hebrew Syntax.* Bruce K. Waltke and M. O'Connor. Winona Lake, IN: Eisenbrauns, 1990.
y.	Jerusalem

Introduction

What is friendship? At first blush, the answer seems obvious: Friendship is a voluntary association between people who enjoy one another's company and care, at least to some degree, about one another's welfare. But this definition, which would probably elicit few objections from most present-day Europeans and North Americans, does not address a number of contested issues in contemporary Western friendship. For example, is it possible for men and women to be friends? Must friends be peers in every respect, or is there room for age differences, or inequality of income, social status, or power? Can parents and children be friends? Might sexual relations play a role in friendship? Does friendship necessarily involve emotional intimacy? Are there contrasting male and female, gay and straight, working-class and middle-class friendship patterns? Each of these questions would very likely stimulate debate among the people I know, and the answers would probably depend on some combination of the generation, gender, sexual orientation, class, and cultural background of the respondent. Apart from agreeing that friends associate voluntarily, like one another, and take an interest in one another's well-being, there might not be much consensus among my friends, neighbors, colleagues, students, and family members about the contested aspects of friendship that I have mentioned. Were we to go beyond speculation about the views of the people I encounter in my life, and conduct research on the beliefs about friendship held by a larger population of contemporary North Americans or other Westerners, I would expect to find even less agreement about what constitutes friendship. In short, friendship as we know it in contemporary Europe and North America is shaped by a variety of socio-cultural influences and is understood differently by different people. If I cannot assume that my own preferred configuration of what constitutes friendship is normative for everyone in my own community or society, let alone Western cultures, then I certainly cannot presuppose much about friendship in ancient societies, given their cultural, linguistic, and chronological distance from us.[1] Thus, I begin this study of friendship in the Hebrew Bible without presuming that the Hebrew Bible's authors necessarily share many (or any) of our ideas about what might constitute a friendship. What is important is that the texts be permitted to speak and that we strive to understand their explicit and implicit communication critically and contextually, allowing our contemporary perspective to formulate the questions we ask but not to presuppose any answers. As a result, friendship configurations in the Hebrew Bible will gradually come into focus, permitting comparison with patterns of friendship in other contexts, ancient and modern.

Friendship is a topic that has mainly been ignored by scholars of the Hebrew Bible, possibly on account of its complexity and elusiveness. The vocabulary of biblical friendship is frequently ambiguous; only a few texts represent particular friendships in any kind of depth (e.g., that of Jonathan and David, or Job and his three comforters), and these are literary creations that may or may not have any basis in the lives of historical people.[2] Perhaps it is not a surprise, then, that no monograph on friendship in the Hebrew Bible has been published, and aside from a number of dictionary articles and brief review essays, the scholarly literature is quite limited and often topic-specific (e.g., the friendship of Jonathan and David, or friendship in wisdom literature).[3] Yet friendship in the Hebrew Bible warrants the kind of thorough, detailed exploration that friendship has received or is presently receiving from specialists in related areas such as classics and New Testament studies and in any number of other fields (e.g., contemporary legal studies, sociology, social anthropology, developmental psychology, philosophy, medicine, and public health).[4] The data of the Hebrew Bible, though often a challenge to interpret, are nonetheless rich and intriguing, raising many questions about the nature of biblical friendship, some not unlike the questions about contemporary European and North American friendship I mentioned above, and some quite different. Among the questions that I explore in this book are the following: What are the basic expectations of friendship, or put differently, what are the characteristics of the ideal friend? What exactly is the relationship between friends and family members, given that biblical texts often classify friends with relatives implicitly and compare friends to family members both implicitly and explicitly? Are there differences between the set of obligations owed to family members and those owed to friends? Must friendship necessarily have a formal, contractual dimension as it sometimes appears to have (e.g., as indicated by the treaty language in the David/Jonathan narratives), or can it be thoroughly informal? Can relatives also be friends? Must friends be peers in every respect? Can women be friends with one another and with men? Might friendships have an erotic dimension, or are they by definition nonsexual, as in the classical world?[5] What might cause the failure of a friendship? And finally, is there evidence in biblical texts—either explicit or implicit—for the classification of friendship into different types or gradations (cf. Aristotle's three types of friendship in the *Nicomachean Ethics* 8.3–4)?

In order to explore these questions, I begin with a detailed examination of the vocabulary and idioms of friendship in the Hebrew Bible. Then I consider the following topics in succeeding chapters: (1) the link between friends and family members (e.g., shared classification, common obligations of kin and friends, differing expectations); (2) failed friendship, including the topos of the disloyal friend in the psalms of individual complaint; and (3) friendships in narrative such as those of Ruth and Naomi and Jonathan and David, including the relationship of friendship and covenant. In the final chapter, I compare the configurations of friendship evidenced in Ben Sira, a second-century BCE Hebrew wisdom composition likely influenced to some degree by Greek notions of friendship, with representations of friendship in earlier texts of the Hebrew Bible.[6] Finally, in my conclusion, I compare the representation of friendship in different types of biblical literature, explore the evidence suggesting an emotional component to biblical friendship, consider the relationship of friendship and covenant, compare women's friendships with those of men, reflect upon why extant evidence does not bear witness to friendships between men and women, explore the axes of equality and inequality evidenced in biblical representations of friendship, entertain what a diachronic dimension can contribute to our understanding of biblical friendship, and consider the friend as a distinct social actor. I also reflect upon what this study might contribute to the larger, incipient, cross-disciplinary theorization of friendship in the contemporary academy as well as what it might contribute to cross-cultural theorizing of friendship from the perspective of a single discipline.[7]

A few caveats: The focus of this study is friendship as it is represented in biblical texts. I make no claim to reconstruct particular historical friendships that once existed in specific settings, a task that is unhappily beyond our ability given the state and nature of the extant evidence.[8] Because the data are scattered broadly throughout the Hebrew Bible and the dating of many texts relevant to this study is contested, one cannot avoid a significant synchronic emphasis. Nonetheless, comparison of the representation of friendship in earlier materials with that of friendship in demonstrably later sources such as Ben Sira will provide a welcome diachronic dimension to the discussion, and comparison of friendship in pre-Hellenistic wisdom sources such as Proverbs and Job to its representations in prose narrative, prophetic texts, the psalms of individual complaint, and other materials will give added depth to the study. I devote most of the remainder of this introduction to the vocabulary of biblical friendship, the study of which provides an initial glimpse into biblical presuppositions about friendship and allows me to develop a preliminary working definition of the phenomenon. I end with a brief consideration of the range of biblical literature in which material relevant to this study is evidenced.

The Hebrew Bible's vocabulary and idioms of friendship are complex and often challenging and require careful analysis in order to set the stage for the larger project I am undertaking here.[9] Although the biblical text has no word for "friendship," there are a number of words for "friend."[10] Most common is *rēaʿ* and related nouns such as *rēʿâ*, *raʿyâ*, *rēʿeh*, and *mērēaʿ*, each apparently derived either from a root *rʿh* or a root *rʿʿ*, both meaning something like "to associate with" or "to affiliate with," suggesting a voluntary dimension to friendship.[11] Other words and expressions for "friend" include *ʾōhēb*, literally "one who loves" or "lover";[12] *ʾallûp*, which may be related to an adjective of the same form meaning "gentle" (BDB) (Jer 11:19);[13] *ʾîš / ʾĕnôš šālôm* or *šōlēm*, probably best rendered "one with whom I enjoy good relations";[14] *mĕyuddāʿ*, "one who is known (to me)";[15] and likely *yōdēaʿ*, "one who knows (me)."[16] Occasionally, two words meaning "friend" are apparently combined in a hendiadys construction intended to communicate a single, complex notion: *ʾōhăbay wĕrēʿay*, "my loving friends" (Ps 38:12; cf. 88:19), and *ʾallûpî ûmĕyuddāʿî*, "my gentle intimate" (Ps 55:14), are but two examples.[17]

In addition to these words and expressions, a variety of verbal forms and idioms are associated with the friend, and these provide us with additional insight into biblical presuppositions about friendship: *dbq*, "to cling (to)," an idiom of loyalty used of the friend in Prov 18:24 and Ruth 1:14; *bṭḥ*, "to trust," associated with friendship in Ps 41:10 (cf. Mic 7:5; Jer 9:3);[18] *šlm*

(Pi), *śym*, or *gml ṭôb/ṭôbâ*, "to pay back that which is good" instead of what is evil, a norm of friendship by implication in Ps 7:5; 35:12; 38:21 (by implication because the actual, extant idiom is *šlm* [Pi], *śym*, or *gml rāʿâ/raʿ* [*taḥat ṭôbâ*], "to pay back that which is evil [instead of what is good]"); and *himtîq sôd*, literally "make sweet fellowship" (Ps 55:15), interpreted by Koehler and Baumgartner to mean "to keep close company" or "conduct confidential business," in either case an idiom of intimacy.[19] Deuteronomy 13:7, characterizing the particularly intimate friend, refers to him as "your friend who is as yourself" (*rēʿăkā ʾăšer kĕnapšĕkā*); 1 Sam 18:1 speaks of the "self" or "life" (*nepeš*) of Jonathan "bound" (*nikšĕrâ*) to the "self" or "life" of David, another idiom for intimate personal connection, as Gen 44:30, regarding the close attachment of Jacob to his youngest son Benjamin, makes clear.[20] The potential intimacy of friendship as expressed through communication is articulated in Exod 33:11, which describes the manner in which Yhwh communicates with Moses: "Yhwh would speak to Moses face to face, as a man speaks to his friend." In addition, the friend is described in Ps 41:10 as *ʾôkēl laḥmî*, "one who eats my food," suggesting a role for hospitality, including commensality, as a component of friendship. In Ps 35:27, a context of adversity, friends are characterized as "they who delight in my vindication" (*ḥăpēṣê ṣidqî*). Finally, one's friends, in contrast to one's enemies, are expected to pursue one's well-being (lit. "pursue what is good" [*rdp ṭôb*], Ps 38:21).[21]

On the basis of only a survey of biblical nouns often rendered "friend," we can say that ideally friendship is a relationship between people who choose to associate or affiliate with one another[22] and that it involves positive feelings described by texts as "love."[23] A degree of personal knowledge of the other is assumed, as is mutual goodwill. Gentleness (of interaction?) may also be characteristic of friendship if our understanding of the meaning of the noun *ʾallûp* is correct.[24] Verbal forms and other idioms add to this composite portrait. The friend is loyal, a quality prized especially in times of adversity: she "clings" (*dbq*) to her friend; he desires justice for his friend; he does not abandon his friend or his father's friend (Prov 27:10). The friend is hospitable, offering table fellowship; he is trustworthy; and he might be on particularly intimate terms with one (e.g., "your friend who is as yourself," Deut 13:7; "there is a friend who clings more closely than a brother," Prov 18:24). Friendship is assumed to be reciprocal: friends share personal knowledge (*mĕyuddāʿ*, "one who is known [to me]"; likely also *yōdēaʿ*, "one who knows [me]"), and the friend is expected to repay beneficence with comparable treatment (see, explicitly, Ps 35:13–14, where the petitioner details his previous benevolent acts on behalf of his now disloyal friends). The latter example also suggests that friendship is a social relationship not without obligations. Needless to say, this composite, synchronic characterization is oversimplified, ignoring the diachronic perspective and potential differences due to literary type or authorial preference. It is also idealized, for biblical texts themselves acknowledge and even bring into relief the failings of friends.[25] Finally, it does not address a number of important questions about biblical friendship (e.g., can relatives be friends? must friends be peers in all respects?).[26] Nonetheless, this composite portrait provides me with a starting point for my analysis; it will be subject to complication and gain nuance as the study proceeds.

The vocabulary of biblical friendship, for all its richness, is not unproblematic. First and foremost, there is the challenge of ambiguity. Simply put, a number of the Hebrew words for "friend" can mean other things as well, and therefore we must depend upon their contextual usage to help us determine their meaning.[27] A primary example is the noun *rēaʿ*, the most common word for "friend" in the Hebrew Bible. Though *rēaʿ* appears to mean "friend" in passages such as Prov 17:17 ("At all times the friend loves") or Prov 27:10 ("Do not abandon your friend or your father's friend"), its meaning in other contexts evidently includes "neighbor" (Deut 19:14, "You shall not move your neighbor's landmark"); "peer" or "fellow" who belongs to the same subgroup (1 Kgs 20:35 [a fellow prophet]; Zech 3:8 [fellow priests]; 2 Sam 2:16 [a fellow soldier]); "peer who is a rival" (1 Sam 15:28; 28:17; 2 Sam 12:11, all concerning rivals for the throne);[28] or simply "another person," "someone other than you" (Gen 11:3).[29] Another word, *mērēaʿ*, clearly means "friend" in some contexts, as in Prov 19:7, which states that the friends of the poor man reject him. Yet it can also evidently mean something like "assigned companion" as in Judg 14:11, 20; 15:2, 6, where it is used of male strangers chosen by Samson's Philistine hosts to keep Samson company.[30] To further complicate matters, the rhetoric of friendship—including the words *ʾōhēb*, *rēaʿ*, and *mērēaʿ*—is used of political relations, as in 1 Sam 30:26; 2 Sam 3:8; Isa 41:8; and Lam 1:2, as are idioms of kinship such as "brother" and "father," yet treaty partners neither are kin nor are likely to be personal friends.[31]

Thus, each occurrence of an ambiguous word such as *rēaʿ* or *mērēaʿ* must be examined carefully in its context to determine its relevance to this study.

In a text such as Exod 33:11, which describes Yhwh speaking to Moses face to face "as a man speaks to his friend," it is evident from the comparison that *rēaʿ* must mean "friend" rather than "neighbor," "peer" or "fellow," or "another," given the text's emphasis on intimacy and singularity of communication between two individuals. Translations of the Hebrew Bible often ignore this problem, with the result that passages pertinent to the study of friendship are sometimes unintentionally obscured, while other texts are rendered in a manner that suggests a relevance that they do not really have. An example of the former tendency is the NJPS translation of Exod 33:11, the text mentioned above: "The Lord would speak to Moses face to face, as one speaks to another" (*rēʿēhû*). The idea the text is trying to communicate is the singularity and intimacy of Moses's encounter with Yhwh, and the phrase "as one speaks to another" does not capture that sense of singularity and intimacy in the way that "as a man speaks to his friend" does.[32] An example of the latter tendency is the RSV translation of Zech 3:8: "Hear now, O Joshua the high priest, you and your friends who sit before you, for they are men of good omen." In this case, the context suggests that the meaning of *rēaʿ* is not "friend," as the RSV renders it, but rather "colleague" (NRSV), "peer," or "fellow" (see NJPS), as the people with Joshua are fellow priests. In contrast to Exod 33:11, a text that is relevant to a study of friendship, Zech 3:8 is not.[33]

Another manifestation of the ambiguity of the vocabulary of friendship is its extensive overlap with the terminology of covenanting. Words such as *ʾōhēb* ("lover" or "friend"), *rēaʿ* ("friend"), *ṭôb/ṭôbâ* ("that which is good"), and *ʾîš/ʾĕnôš šālôm* ("one with whom I enjoy good relations"), all associated with friendship, occur as technical terms in treaty settings, carry political overtones when used in such contexts, and may or may not tell us anything at all about the personal dispositions of the parties involved in treaty-making.[34] Familial terms, such as "brother" and "father," also frequently used of treaty partners, have similar political nuances in a covenantal setting.[35] Thus, parties to a treaty may have no genuine affection or concern for one another in the manner of friends or family members. The rhetoric of friendship and family relations is likely marshaled in treaty contexts in order to emphasize expectations of loyalty to treaty stipulations. So when we read that Hiram king of Tyre "had always been a lover [or "friend," *ʾōhēb*] of David" (1 Kgs 5:15), we ought to understand the statement in its treaty context: that Hiram had always been loyal to his parity treaty with

David.³⁶ The claim in 1 Sam 18:16, that "all Israel and Judah loved David for he led them in battle" ought to be understood similarly: the army was loyal to their successful commander. This is rather different in meaning from the statement of Prov 17:17 mentioned earlier, that "at all times the friend loves [*ʾōhēb*]." All three statements may presuppose loyalty as a component of loving, but otherwise their assumptions probably differ. Where Prov 17:17 seems to presume an emotional bond, there is no evidence that 1 Kgs 5:15 and 1 Sam 18:16 share this assumption. In fact, covenant love, in contrast to emotional love, "can be commanded," in the words of William L. Moran, as in Deut 6:5: "You shall love Yhwh your god with all your heart, with all your self, and with all your might."³⁷ Thus, each occurrence of a term associated both with friendship and with covenanting must be assessed carefully to determine its potential resonances. A term such as "lover" (*ʾōhēb*) or "friend" (*rēaʿ*), when used in a treaty setting, likely does not presuppose the existence of an emotional bond, affection, or personal concern between the parties (e.g., 1 Sam 18:16; 1 Kgs 5:15); however, outside of a context of covenant, it seems likely that such a term does (e.g., Prov 17:17).

Given these complexities, interpretation becomes particularly challenging when a friendship is structured unambiguously as a treaty as in 1 Sam 18:1–4. On the one hand, demonstrably nontreaty idioms of emotional intimacy are used of Jonathan's relationship to David in that text, suggesting a friendship with emotional dimensions (e.g., his "self" or "life" was "bound" to David's "self" or "life," an idiom of emotional intimacy without evident treaty associations, as I have discussed). On the other hand, typical covenant rhetoric is used in the passage: Jonathan loved David as himself (*kĕnapšô*), and they cut a covenant (*bĕrît*) together.³⁸ Thus, a text such as 1 Sam 18:1–4 suggests that it is possible to formalize an emotionally intimate friendship with treaty rites and stipulations, at least in the world of the text. Psalm 55:14–15, 21 is likely a second example of a friendship formalized through covenantal rites, as I shall discuss in Chapter 3.

The use of friendship vocabulary for sexual intimates further complicates our attempt to understand the phenomenon of friendship in the Hebrew Bible. Though *ʾallûp* is appropriately translated "friend" in a text such as Mic 7:5 or Ps 55:14, its use for a woman's husband in Prov 2:17 and for Yhwh as Israel's husband in Jer 3:4 (with *ʾāb*, "father") suggests a different kind of relationship than friendship as conceived in a text such as Ps 55:14 and Mic 7:5. The same is true of the use of *rēaʿ* in a text such as Song 5:16 in reference to the male lover: "This is my beloved, this is my friend."³⁹

Jeremiah 3:20 compares Israel's deceiving (*bgd*) of Yhwh to an adulterous wife's treachery (*bgd*) against her "friend" (*rēaʿ*), obviously a reference to her husband. Furthermore, the term *raʿyâ* ("companion") is used frequently in the Song of Songs of the female lover, though, like *rēaʿ* and *ʾallûp*, it appears also to have nonsexual connotations elsewhere (Judg 11:37, *kĕtîb*, used of Jephthah's daughter's female companions).[40] The use of friendship vocabulary for sexual intimates raises interesting questions. Could it be that biblical constructions of friendship might potentially include a sexual dimension? Or is the friendship language used of husbands, wives, and lovers to be understood simply as metaphorical, intended to enrich the poetic imagery of the text in some way? A point in favor of the metaphorical interpretation is the fact that familial language is also marshaled in the rhetoric of the Song of Songs to describe the lovers. Not only is the female lover a "beloved," a "bride," and a "companion" (*raʿyâ*); she is also described as the male lover's "sister" in a number of contexts (Song 4:9, 10, 12; 5:1, 2). A comparable simile is used of the male lover in Song 8:1: "Would that you were like a brother to me, one who sucks at the breast of my mother." Given this simile, it seems likely that the sibling language used of the female lover is not intended to be taken literally, but functions rather as a metaphor intended to enrich the text's poetic rhetoric by adding yet another axis of emotional intimacy to the portrait of the relationship. If I am correct about the metaphorical nature of the familial rhetoric, the same is likely true of the vocabulary of friendship when used of sexual intimates. It makes the portrayal of the relationship between the lovers more emotionally complex without suggesting anything about the nature of friendship per se. Thus, one ought not to assume that biblical constructions of friendship include the possibility of sexual relations between friends without clearer and more cogent evidence. The strongest case that can be made for the possibility of eroticized friendship in biblical materials is to be found not in the Song of Songs, but in 2 Sam 1:26, a verse of David's Lament over Saul and Jonathan, a text that I address in Chapter 3.

Some comments about the types of biblical literature that evidence the vocabulary and idioms of friendship and bear witness to its literary representation round out this introduction. A variety of texts are relevant to the study of biblical friendship. These include prose narratives such as the stories of David and Jonathan, Ruth and Naomi, and Job and his three comforters; prophetic texts such as Jer 9:3 or Mic 7:5–6; legal materials (e.g., Deut 13:7); a number of the psalms, including psalms of individual complaint; nonpsalmic lyrical texts, such as David's Lament over Saul and Jonathan (2 Sam 1:19–27); pre-Hellenistic wisdom collections—both traditional and skeptical—such as Proverbs and the poetic dialogues of the book of Job; and the Hellenistic-era wisdom book Ben Sira.[41] Some of these materials are poetic in nature, and others are prose. Some are precisely dated (e.g., Ben Sira), but most are not easily datable. In some texts the friends in question are complex and richly evoked (e.g., David, Naomi, or Jonadab [2 Sam 13]); in others they are less individuated and more idealized and predictable (Ruth, Job's three comforters in the Job prologue); in still others they are at best flat, one-dimensional types without individuality who display stereotypical behaviors (e.g., the nameless, unfaithful friends of the psalms of individual complaint and the Job dialogues). At various points throughout this study, I compare the representation of friendship and friendship's idioms and technical vocabulary in two or more literary types, and in Chapter 4, I compare Ben Sira's usages to those of earlier wisdom and nonwisdom texts.

1 Friends and Family

After considering the vocabulary of friendship and its complexities, I move on now to an exploration of the relationship between friends and family members as it is represented in biblical texts. Friends and family are an appropriate place to begin a detailed investigation of friendship in the Hebrew Bible, as biblical texts compare friends and relatives and even suggest implicitly that they enjoy a common classification as intimates. Such comparison suggests that friends and family members share, or ought to share, certain characteristics, behaviors, and obligations in common. I query these not infrequent comparisons and shared taxonomies in order to ask what specific expectations family members and friends are assumed to have in common by our sources and how differing obligations set friends and family members apart as distinct social actors.[1] I also compare the idioms of familial intimacy to those used of friends and consider the evidence for gradations of friendship, how such gradations compare to gradations of familial intimacy, and whether familial gradations of intimacy might have served as a model for such gradations in friendship. I begin with a consideration of family members as intimates par excellence in order to set the stage for comparison of friends to them.

Family Members as Paradigmatic Intimates

Biblical texts and other West Asian materials typically represent primary familial relationships as paradigmatically close, at least in theory if not in practice. Idealized ties between parents and children and brothers and sisters, characterized by intimacy, harmony, loyalty, support (particularly in times of need), and respect for hierarchy, serve as a model for relationships, both voluntary and involuntary, that extend beyond the immediate family circle and the larger kin group. Ties between a deity and his or her worshipers, a king and his people, human treaty partners, members of professional classes, and friends are all shaped, at least in part, by the rhetoric and/or presuppositions of idealized familial relations according to our texts. Yhwh, a father to Israel his firstborn son (Exod 4:22–23), ought to be honored as a father is honored by his son (Mal 1:6). As king, Saul is David's "father," and each party in their relationship is expected to treat the other appropriately (*gāmal haṭṭôbâ*, "pay back that which is good") (1 Sam 24:17–18; cf. 26:17). Political allies describe their relations as loving and address one another as "brother" (1 Kgs 5:15; 9:13; Amos 1:9). The leader of a professional group (e.g., of prophets) is a "father" to its members (1 Sam 10:12), who are often described as "sons of the prophets" (e.g., 2 Kgs 9:1).[2] Friends, though rarely if ever described using familial terminology, are often compared to intimate kin, implicitly and explicitly, as I shall demonstrate (e.g., Prov 17:17; 18:24). Thus, I begin this chapter with an exploration of gradations of familial intimacy, its idioms, and the expectations of family members before going on to consider the relationship of friends and family.

Gradations of Familial Intimacy

A hierarchy of family relationships may be discerned from extant texts, and these suggest gradations of intimacy and responsibility within familial circles. Leviticus 21:1–4 concerns the family members for whom a priest may defile himself through corpse contact. These relatives include his mother, father, son, daughter, and brothers, each of whom is characterized as "his flesh, the one who is close to him [*šěʾērô haqqārōb ʾēlāyw*]." His virgin sister, also described as "the one who is close to him [*haqqěrôbâ ʾēlāyw*]," is included in this group because she has no husband.[3] But his wife is explicitly excluded, and uncles, aunts, and cousins go unmentioned, suggesting their omission as well. Thus, according to Lev 21:1–4, the priest's obligation to bury familial dead extends only to certain blood relations, whom we might characterize as his closest family members; it does not extend to the spouse, who is not a blood relation, nor to other family members, whom the text classifies implicitly as more distant by not including them among those characterized as "his flesh" and/or "close to him." The law regarding the high priest in Lev 21:11 supplies additional information about familial hierarchies of intimacy and obligation. In this text, the high priest, in contrast to the priest, may not pollute himself for anyone in his family, "even for his father or mother." The mention only of parents here suggests a level of intimacy and obligation incumbent upon a child that goes beyond that which a man might have for his own children or brothers or unmarried sisters. Thus, even within the group of family members characterized as "close" in Lev 21:2–3, 21:11 suggests that there is a hierarchy of obligation and intimacy.

Other texts support the idea that a man's closest relations are his parents, children, and siblings. Numbers 27:8–11 provides an order of inheritance from most intimate family members to less close relations. According to this text, when a man dies, his landed property goes to his son; if he has no son, it goes to his daughter; if he lacks a daughter, it is inherited by his brothers; if he has no brothers, it goes to his paternal uncles; and if there are no paternal uncles, the patrimony is to be given to "his flesh, the one who is close to him from his clan," an expression similar to that of Lev 21:2 but here a designation for more distant relations (e.g., cousins). If Ruth 3:12 is any indication, there is a hierarchical order of closeness among these more distant relations as well. Presumably, Num 27:8–11 assumes that the parents of the dead man have predeceased him, leaving only children and siblings among his closest relatives. But he, too, is a parent, and his children are his primary potential heirs, suggesting the closeness of parents to children and vice versa. It is notable that in Num 27:8, the man's daughter inherits before his brothers do, suggesting that being a child of the dead man trumps gender status in this one case, even though gender is the primary organizing principle of such a patrilineal system of inheritance.[4] At all events, Num 27:8–11 assumes a hierarchy of familial intimacy not much different from that of Lev 21:1–4, 11, though it does not include unmarried sisters in the order of inheritance and speaks explicitly of paternal uncles and other, more distant male relations of the clan. Leviticus 25:48, concerning the redemption of indentured kin, is similar, mentioning brothers, paternal uncles, uncles' sons, and more distant relations of the clan as potential redeemers, presumably in a hierarchy of obligation.

Where do wives fit in this schema? Although texts such as Lev 21:2–4; 25:48 and Num 27:8–11 suggest either explicitly or by their silence that wives do not share the same status (they are not "flesh" or "close"), obligations (e.g., redemption), or privileges (e.g., inheritance) as blood relatives, not a few texts speak of the relationship between husband and wife in intimate terms. The most notable of such passages is probably Gen 2:24: "Therefore a man leaves his father and his mother and clings [*dābaq*] to his wife and they become one flesh [*bāśār 'eḥād*]." Becoming "one flesh" through marriage is not exactly the same as being a man's "flesh, the one who is close to him" (Lev 21:2), a birth-ascribed status, though the two idioms are similar and both of them communicate intimacy of some kind. Other idioms of intimacy used of close relatives are also used of spouses, as in Prov 31:11, where the "woman of strength" is said to be trusted by her husband (cf. Jer 9:3, which implies that trust is an expectation of brothers). Given the evidence, the wife appears to be understood as an emotional and sexual intimate ("one flesh") in contrast to close relatives, whose intimacy is of an entirely different order: it is nonsexual and its emotional component probably overlaps with that of the husband and wife only partially. In addition, the obligations and privileges of the wife both differ from and overlap with those of intimate blood relations. Overlapping obligations appear to include such qualities as loyalty and trust, as we shall see, while among differing obligations one might mention the wife's exemption from the requirements of redemption. As I shall show, the friend, like the wife, shares some obligations and privileges with close family members while being exempt from or excluded from others. In contrast to the wife, however, the friend's intimacy overlaps to some degree with that of the close relative, in that it is generally represented as nonsexual. I shall have more to say about these configurations at the end of this chapter.

Expectations of Kin

I now turn to the behaviors and attitudes that characterize ideal familial relations, many of which are brought into relief through an examination of particular idioms of intimacy extant in the Hebrew Bible. Some of the behaviors and attitudes expected of kin are also expected of wives, treaty partners, and, as we shall see, friends, according to biblical texts. I begin with love, a basic expectation of familial relations that may have both emotional and behavioral resonances in the setting of the family and is expressed through several idioms, including the verb "to love" (*'āhēb*) and its derivatives. According to Gen 22:2, Abraham is ordered to sacrifice Isaac, his "only son" whom he loves, as a burnt offering to Yhwh. A father's love for his son is also mentioned in Gen 25:28, where Isaac is said to love Esau, and in Gen 37:3–4, where Israel/Jacob is said to love Joseph more than all his (other) sons, who are offended by Joseph's favored status and privileges (e.g., his special garment).[5] A mother's love for her son is a theme of Gen 25:28, where Rebecca is said to love Jacob; she favors him in the story that follows, just as Isaac favors Esau. Many other texts speak of the love of parents for children using idioms other than the verb "to love" and its derivatives. Perhaps most interesting is Gen 44:30–31, in which the "self" or "life" (*nepeš*) of Jacob is said to be "bound" to the "self" or "life" of Benjamin, his youngest son; were Benjamin to die, says his brother Judah, his father Jacob would die of grief.[6] The binding together of two selves or lives in this context is clearly an emotion-laden idiom of parental love, as the claim that Jacob would die of grief were Benjamin to die suggests. A comparable idiom of love, *kmr* (Ni) *raḥămîm ʿal-*, with a meaning something like "to be overcome with emotion toward," is used once of a mother with respect to her infant child under mortal threat (1 Kgs 3:26).[7]

In these examples, parental love, whether expressed through the verb "to love" and its derivatives or through another, unrelated idiom, appears to be an emotional state of close attachment not infrequently characterized by behavioral dimensions of some kind, as in the stories of Jacob and Esau and of Joseph, each of whom is favored in concrete ways by a parent who is said to love him. Narratives describing the reactions of inconsolable parents to the death—or assumed death—of a child bring this emotional resonance into relief (e.g., Gen 37:35; 2 Sam 19:1, 5). Oddly, love idioms are rarely used of a child's disposition toward parents, though Ruth 4:15 speaks of Ruth's love for Naomi, her mother-in-law. The love of Joseph for his younger brother Benjamin is expressed through the use of the idiom "to be overcome with emotion toward [*kmr* (Ni) *raḥămîm ʾel-*]" in Gen 43:30, suggesting that brotherly love might be emotionally intense. At all events, it is likely that reciprocal love was expected between close family members, even if surviving texts say little about this, given the emphasis on familial reciprocity evidenced through the examination of other idioms of familial intimacy, as we shall see.[8] Hatred of the relative, the antitype of familial love, is cast as undesirable: "Do not hate your brother in your heart" (Lev 19:17). Its potential emotional resonance is well captured by the reactions of Joseph's brothers to his dreams of domination and to their father's favoritism: "When his brothers saw that their father loved him more than all his brothers, they hated him and could not say anything positive to him."[9]

In contrast to the use of the verb "to love" in the family context, which has both emotional and behavioral components according to biblical texts, the same verb and its derivatives have what appears to be a primarily or exclusively behavioral meaning in settings of treaty-making or covenant. Here, love means conformity to treaty stipulations and its antitype, hate, means nonconformity, as in Exod 20:5–6; Deut 5:9–10; 6:5–9; and 2 Sam 19:6–7.[10] In the latter text, David's feelings toward his loyal army are clearly not in question when his nephew and commander Joab accuses him of "loving those who hate you and hating those who love you"; rather, it is David's behavior that is at issue, for he has treated his faithful soldiers disloyally, shaming them and seemingly rejecting them.[11] Similarly, the hatred or love of Yhwh mentioned in the Ten Commandments is behavioral: Those who serve other gods are "haters" of Yhwh while those who keep his commandments are his "lovers" (Exod 20:5–6; Deut 5:9–10).[12] That love in treaty contexts is assumed to be reciprocal is well illustrated by Joab's castigating words to David in 2 Sam 19:6–7: Even a suzerain must love his vassals. A third type of love is also evidenced in biblical sources, a love that we might refer to as sexual-emotional in character (e.g., Gen 34:3; 2 Sam 13:1, 4, 15; 1 Kgs 11:1–2). This love is not infrequently portrayed as volatile and intense. Its antitype, too, is hatred, described in highly charged emotional terms, as in 2 Sam 13:15, where the hatred of Amnon for Tamar, his half sister, is said to be greater than the love with which he had loved her before he raped her. Clearly, these are three different types of love, each with its own distinct resonances. The love of family members for one another may be distinguished from the love of treaty partners for one another as well as from the love of one who is sexually/emotionally attracted to another person.

Like love, loyalty (*ḥesed*) characterizes ideal familial relations. Loyalty is owed to a father by a son (Gen 47:29), by brothers to brothers (Job 6:14–15), by a wife to her husband (Gen 20:13; Ruth 1:8), and by a wife to her mother-in-law (Ruth 1:8).[13] What constitutes such loyalty within the family circle according to these texts? In Job 6:14–15, it is reliability and not acting with the intent to deceive; according to Gen 47:29, it is keeping an oath to one's father; in Gen 20:13, it is speaking in a misleading way to protect a husband from harm (see Gen 20:12).[14] In each of these contexts, loyalty seems to mean acting reliably and in the best interests of the family member. Loyalty (*ḥesed*), like love, is also a term native to treaty discourse; in covenant contexts, it means conformity to treaty stipulations, as in Exod 20:6; Deut 5:10; Jer 2:2; and numerous other texts, and is conceived as reciprocal (e.g., 2 Sam 10:2; Ps 32:10).[15] It has been suggested that the use of the term "loyalty" (*ḥesed*) in covenant contexts is a secondary development from its familial usage, which may well be the case.[16] In any event, it is likely that in the family context, loyalty is thought to be reciprocal, just as it is in treaty contexts.

Another idiom used to express loyalty in family settings is the verb *dābaq*, literally "to cling to," and its derivatives, one of which is used to characterize the loyalty of brothers to one another in Prov 18:24.[17] Like the noun "loyalty" (*ḥesed*), the "clinging" idiom is not uncommon in treaty contexts, and its use in such settings may also be a secondary development. The root describes the loyalty of the people of Judah to David at a time of rebellion against him (2 Sam 20:2) and the loyalty expected of Israelites to their divine suzerain Yhwh (e.g., Deut 4:4; 11:22; Josh 22:5). Other usages of the verb "to cling to" that have a clear physical connotation (e.g., Ruth 2:8, 21, 23) suggest that a sense of physical proximity as well as loyalty may be implied in a passage such as Prov 18:24. A third, sexual-emotional meaning for the verb "to cling to" that is not unlike the sexual-emotional meaning of the verb "to love" is attested in texts such as Gen 2:24; 34:3; and 1 Kgs 11:2. As with the verb "to love," it is important to be clear about the range of the verb "to cling to" and its derivatives and understand that each type of "clinging" has its own distinct features. While "clinging" in a treaty setting is very likely wholly or mainly behavioral (conformity to stipulations) and "clinging" in a marriage or analogous contexts is sexual-emotional as well as behavioral (staying physically close), "clinging" among family members is likely both behavioral (remaining in close proximity) and emotional but not sexual.

Several texts speak of support for family members as an obligation incumbent on kin. Psalm 38:12 castigates family members (*qĕrôbay*) who keep their distance from a relation who is in trouble, as does Job 19:13–15, which mentions both relatives and brothers (*qĕrôbay* and *ʾaḥay*).[18] By stating that these relatives "stood at a distance from," "were far away from," or "forgot" the sufferer, the texts suggest that the ideal is the opposite: to offer support by not abandoning kin and staying physically close to them when they are suffering.[19] That such appropriately loyal behavior constitutes at least part of what texts call "good things" (*ṭôbôt*) is suggested by Jer 12:6, which condemns the deceitful behavior of brothers and other kin, though their words are appropriate: "Do not believe them, though they say good things [*ṭôbôt*] to you." Psalm 38:21, which likely refers to disloyal relatives as well as disloyal friends, suggests that family members are expected actively to pursue the welfare of their relatives, "to pay back" loyal, supportive treatment ("what is good," *ṭôbâ*) with the same rather than with ill treatment ("that which is evil," *rāʿâ*), and not to play the part of an adversary (*śāṭān*).[20] The idioms *drš ṭôb* and *dbr šālôm* also occur as expressions of loyal, supportive familial behavior. In Esth 10:3, Mordecai is described as "one who seeks that which is good on behalf of his people [*dōrēš ṭôb lěʿammô*]" and "one who says the right thing with regard to all his kin [*dōbēr šālôm lěkol zarʿô*]."[21] A different manifestation of familial support is mentioned in Ruth 4:15. Here, the neighboring women say of Naomi's grandson Obed that he will support Naomi materially (*kilkēl*) in old age. The Joseph story is similar, with Joseph volunteering to support his father, brothers, and their dependents in Egypt while the famine persists in Canaan (Gen 45:11; 50:21). In Ahiqar, fraternal support includes maintenance of the brother at one's own expense and is assumed to be reciprocal: "Thereupon, I took you to my house. There, I supported you [*msbl*] as a man does his brother . . . Now, what I did for you, thus do for me."[22] It is not difficult to imagine that an expectation that kin provide material support is assumed by biblical texts, even if it is not typically stated explicitly as it is in Ahiqar.

Honesty and trustworthiness are qualities expected of family members. Kin ought to be honest with one another, as honesty is the basis for trust, and those kin who deceive should not be trusted (Jer 12:6). Jeremiah 9:2 speaks of a context in which falseness (*šeqer*) rather than trustworthiness (*ʾěmûnâ*) prevails in the land, with Yhwh forgotten and inappropriate acts the norm. As a result of this, brothers should not be trusted (*wěʿal kol ʾāḥ ʾal tibṭāḥû*) and friends should be watched, evidently a reversal of what is expected (Jer 9:3). That trust is a normal expectation in the household is suggested by Num 12:7. In this text, Yhwh speaks of his household (*bayit*), in which Moses is said to be most trusted (*běkol bêtî neʾěmān hûʾ*). By implication, others in the household are also trusted, though not to the degree that Moses is.[23] Finally, Prov 31:11, which lists the good qualities of the "woman of strength," speaks of her husband's trust of her.

Respect for generational hierarchy in the family setting is evidenced as an expectation in not a few texts, and such respect is frequently articulated through idioms of honor and reverence. It is the norm that a son honors (*kbd*) his father according to Mal 1:6, just as a servant honors his master and the priesthood ought to honor Yhwh. "Honor your father and your mother" says Exod 20:12 and Deut 5:16, whatever the exact meaning of this statement.[24] According to Lev 19:3, a man must show reverence (*yrʾ*) for his mother and his father, and in v. 32, the acts of standing before one with white hair and honoring an old man are compared implicitly to reverencing God.[25] In a society whose norms have been reversed, old men are not honored (Lam 5:12) and the youth treats the elder with disrespect (Isa 3:5).

Among Jerusalem's transgressions according to Ezekiel is the diminishment (*qll*) of parents who are, implicitly, worthy of honor (Ezek 22:7).[26] Whoever diminishes (*qlh*) his father and mother is cursed according to Deut 27:16, and anyone who curses his parents shall be executed (Lev 20:9). Though the conferral of honor is reciprocal in a number of passages (e.g., 1 Sam 2:30), texts that speak of the relationship of children to parents consistently emphasize the honor owed to parents by children.[27] This may simply be the result of the text's strong accenting of respect for generational hierarchy. Curiously, no text states explicitly that brothers are bound to honor one another, although allies in treaty contexts, who often make use of fraternal rhetoric to refer to one another, assume this to be the case.[28]

The avoidance by kin of sexual liaisons understood to be unacceptable is represented as a norm according to any number of passages. Sexual relations with close female relatives is forbidden by texts such as Leviticus 18 and 20, as is intercourse with the wives of close male kin.[29] Women who are themselves close kin may not be "taken" together by Israelite men (Lev 18:17, 18; 20:14). Though adultery, whether with the wife of a kinsman or that of another man, is consistently condemned by biblical texts, some passages suggest a more tolerant view of brother-sister marriage than one finds in Lev 18:9 and 20:17 (e.g., Gen 20:12; 2 Sam 13:13). At all events, forbidden sexual liaisons not infrequently involve close family members, and these, along with nonfamilial sexual violations, are condemned in a variety of ways (e.g., as polluting abominations in Lev 18:27).

Brothers living together harmoniously is presented as a familial ideal in Ps 133:1: "How good and how pleasant it is when brothers dwell together." Such is compared to other attractive things: good oil upon the head and the dew of Mt. Hermon. The Babylonian text referred to as the Marduk Prophecy, like Ps 133:1, represents harmony between family members as normative; violence in the family circle, like other social reversals, is exceptional and paradigmatic of a society's dissolution. At the time of social decline, brother fights brother; once normal relations are restored, brother will love brother according to this text.[30] What might contribute to the achievement of such a vision of familial harmony? Very likely the observance of familial expectations such as loyalty, support, honesty and trustworthiness, respect for generational hierarchy, and avoidance of forbidden sexual entanglements.

A number of specific familial duties, often with ritual dimensions, are represented as normative by biblical texts. These include the obligation of an agnatic relative to play the role of redeemer if called upon to do so; the expectation that certain male kinsmen will serve as Levir if required; and the duty of a broader range of family members, in some cases even including spouses, to function as mourners and take on other, death-related responsibilities such as burial, observance of ancestral rites, and care for the family tomb. Redemption is mentioned on a number of occasions in biblical texts. Close male kin on the father's side are obligated to play the role of redeemer (*gōʾēl*), buying back landholdings that have been sold to nonfamily members by relatives with financial difficulties (Lev 25:25–28). The same obligation to redeem applies when kin who are in debt become indentured servants of their creditors (Lev 25:47–49). A third obligation of one playing the role of redeemer is to put to death the murderer of his close kinsman: "The redeemer of blood himself shall kill the murderer; when he encounters him he shall kill him."[31] If the relative's death was an accident, the one responsible for the manslaughter may find refuge from the "redeemer of blood" in one of the cities of refuge established for this purpose according to several texts (Num 35:12, 22–28; Deut 19:1–10). Though close paternal kinsmen such as brothers or uncles have the primary obligation to play the redeemer role, other, more distantly related kin from the patrilineage may also be called upon to do so if necessary (Lev 25:48–49; Ruth 2:1, 20).

A second duty expected of close male kinsmen on the father's side is to play the role of Levir when the need arises. According to Deut 25:5–10, it is a brother specifically who is to fulfill this obligation: "When brothers dwell together and one of them dies without a son, the wife of the dead man shall not become wife to an outsider. Her brother-in-law shall come to her, she shall become his wife, and he shall perform the duty of the Levir for her.[32] The first born son whom she bears will be his dead brother's heir, that his name should not be blotted out from Israel." If the living brother refuses to marry his brother's widow and provide him with an heir, he is to be ritually humiliated by the widow in a public setting. A worse outcome for an uncooperative brother is narrated in Gen 38:8–10. Here, Onan, ordered by his father Judah to perform the role of Levir with Tamar, his sister-in-law, refuses, on the grounds that the child will not be his, and takes action to be sure that she will not be impregnated by him.[33] The story ends with Onan struck dead by Yhwh for his refusal to impregnate his brother's widow and provide him with an heir.[34] After Onan dies, Judah eventually plays the role of Levir unknowingly, a scenario not imagined by Deut 25:5–10, which speaks only of a man's brother who resides with him as a potential Levir. Though referred to as "the redeemer," it is the appropriate Levir whose identity is at issue in Ruth 3:9, 12–13, and he is a kinsman from the wider clan rather than a brother specifically. In Ruth 4:1–13, the roles of Levir and redeemer of landed property are both assumed by Boaz after a closer relation who is said to be the closest "redeemer" declines to exercise his rights.[35] Thus, levirate practices as represented in extant biblical texts vary in their details, as does the technical vocabulary used to refer to the Levir, though in every case a male kinsman—whether a brother, a father, or a more distant agnatic relation—plays the role of Levir and is expected to produce an heir for the deceased.

Close relatives bear a number of death-related responsibilities in the family. They are obliged to bury the dead, play the role of mourner, observe ancestral rites, and care for the family tomb. Texts suggest that burial and related activities are an essential obligation of immediate kin. Children inter their parents (Gen 47:30; 49:29–32; 50:1–11, 12–14; Lev 21:2), parents bury their children (Lev 21:2), siblings inhume one another (Lev 21:2–3; Judg 16:31), and husbands lay to rest their wives (Gen 49:31). Some texts mention the participation of other relatives of the patrilineage, including the uncle, in burial (Amos 6:9–10; Judg 16:31). The ideal interment takes place in the family tomb, likely located on or near the ancestral landholding (*naḥălâ*).[36] According to at least one text, a funeral procession precedes the burial, with the corpse carried on a bier and followed by mourners (2 Sam 3:31). Several texts suggest that family members might exhume relatives interred elsewhere and rebury them in the family tomb, possibly to improve their afterlife, though the reasons for transportation and reburial are uncertain (Gen 50:25–26; Exod 13:19; Josh 24:33).[37] Protecting the integrity of an exposed corpse is a high priority according to the narrative in 2 Sam 21:10–11, which speaks of a mother's actions to defend the corpses of two of her sons, and possibly other relatives, from the depredations of wild beasts and birds. This is not surprising, given the casting of corpse mutilation as a paradigmatic curse in a variety of biblical texts (e.g., Deut 28:26; 1 Kgs 14:11; 2 Kgs 9:10; Jer 16:4) and the possibility that the unburied are thought to suffer in the afterlife, as they do according to cuneiform sources (e.g., Gilgamesh XII.151).[38]

Mourning for a fixed period of time—usually seven days—is represented as an essential duty of family members in any number of texts.[39] Mourners tear their garments, manipulate head or beard hair, cast dirt or ashes upon their heads, weep, fast, wear sackcloth, and sit or lie on the ground, very likely in order to foster close identification with the dead, as Gen 37:35 suggests. In this text, Jacob, who believes his son Joseph is dead, refuses to cease mourning him, saying, "I will descend to my son, to Sheol, in mourning."[40] Psalm 35:14 speaks of the mourning of a son for his mother as paradigmatic, and Jer 16:7 mentions the mourner drinking from a "cup of consolation" at the time of a father's or mother's death. In Gen 27:41, Esau anticipates the coming of the mourning period for his father, Isaac. Brothers weep for their dead brother (2 Sam 13:36). Husbands mourn wives and wives husbands (Gen 23:2; 2 Sam 11:26; Ezek 24:16–17). Parental mourning for a dead child is often represented as profoundly bitter (e.g., Gen 37:34–35; 2 Sam 19:1–5), especially the mourning for an only son (Jer 6:26; Amos 8:10; Zech 12:10). Relatives outside of the immediate family circle or friends and allies might play the role of "comforter" (*měnaḥēm*), a participant in mourning rites who joins with mourners in their ritual actions, consoles mourners, and is responsible for ending the mourning period according to some texts, though most passages that mention "comforters" speak of nonkin rather than kin (e.g., Job's friends in Job 2:11–13). Finally, supporting a mourning petitioner at a time of illness by enacting mourning rites is very likely assumed to be an obligation of kin, as it clearly is of friends in a text such as Ps 35:13.[41] If this is the case, the family members who are said to keep their distance from the suffering petitioner in texts such as Ps 38:12 and Job 19:13 have effectively rejected this obligation.

Second Samuel 18:18 suggests that the invocation of a dead father's name by his son is a ritual norm: "As for Absalom, in his lifetime he had taken and set up for himself a stela in the Valley of the King, for he had said, 'I have no son to invoke my name.'" How widely such a rite was to be observed in the view of the text's author is unclear. It is possible that the text assumes it to be a royal ancestral rite rather than a more generally diffused ritual practice although a more broadly embraced practice is equally possible. It is also unclear whether the text is suggesting that the erection of a stone monument is an exceptional thing, because Absalom has no son to invoke his name, or a standard practice that goes along with filial invocation.[42] Nor does the text suggest how frequently the invocation is to occur. In any case, 2 Sam 18:18 bears witness either to one ancestral cultic observance (invocation of the father's name) or to two such rites (invocation and the erection of a stela) incumbent upon a royal son—perhaps on nonroyal sons as well—but leaves many questions unanswered. Several other biblical texts mention providing food for the dead, sometimes at the tomb, though none speaks explicitly of the involvement of family members in this activity (Deut 26:14; Tob 4:17; Sir 30:18). Nonetheless, it seems likely that it is relatives who are normally responsible for such alimentary maintenance of the spirits of the dead, given the evidence of cuneiform cultures.[43] The "sacrifice of the clan" or "yearly sacrifice" mentioned in 1 Sam 20:6, 29 may well be a patrilineal ancestral observance, as Karel van der Toorn has argued.[44] If van der Toorn's interpretation is correct, a meat sacrifice is offered to the dead by the male members of the clan once a year, presumably in a local sanctuary in the clan's central settlement. Finally, there is the charge to "honor your father and your mother" (Exod 20:12; Deut 5:16). This has been interpreted to refer to acts of reverence for dead parents, possibly including the provision of offerings and other ancestral rites, though the commandment is as easily understood to refer to honoring living parents, as Mal 1:6 suggests.[45] Thus, the evidence for familial ancestral observances is quite limited, though 2 Sam 18:18, the one text about which one can speak with some confidence, does suggest that a son, whether in royal contexts or more generally, is obligated to invoke the name of his dead father and may also be required to erect a memorial stela for him. It may be that in some social settings, such rites took place at the tomb, while in others, they took place elsewhere.[46] Unfortunately, the relationship of rites of invocation and stela erection for the dead to feeding the dead remains unclear.

The obligation of kin to maintain and, if necessary, restore the family tomb is attested in Neh 2:3, 5, a narrative in which Nehemiah asks leave from the Persian king Artaxerxes to go to Jerusalem to rebuild it and, presumably, repair the tombs of his ancestors: "Why should I not be sad, when the city of the house of the tombs of my ancestors is a ruin and its gates destroyed by fire? . . . Send me to Judah, to the city of the tombs of my ancestors, that I might rebuild it." Though only rebuilding the city is discussed explicitly in this text, restoring the tombs seems to be an implicit aim and priority of Nehemiah as he is portrayed in the "Nehemiah Memoir," given that the tombs are mentioned twice in his speech to the king and are inextricably linked to the city itself, described as "the city of the (house of the) tombs of my ancestors."[47] The reasons for Nehemiah's concern about the condition of the tombs of his ancestors is not entirely clear, though two possibilities seem particularly plausible. First, tombs in ruin could well have been a source of humiliation for surviving family members, not unlike unburied and mutilated corpses of relatives. Second, a depopulated city and ruined tombs would have made it difficult for ancestral cultic rites to take place with any regularity at the tomb or in the city, if such rites are an implicit concern to the narrator. And it may be that the dead in the underworld were assumed by the author to fare worse if they lacked a family member providing for them at the tomb or near it, though about this we can only speculate. In any case, Neh 2:3, 5 give the impression that it is incumbent upon kin—most likely close, paternal relatives—to maintain and refurbish the family tomb.

Finally, an ongoing relationship between the living and their dead kin, indicated by such practices as proper burial, invocation of the name of the dead, and care for the family tomb, is also suggested by several idioms used in biblical texts in association with death. In a number of texts, those who die are said to "lie down with" their "ancestors" (*škb ʿim ʾăbôt-*; e.g., Gen 47:30; Deut 31:16; 2 Sam 7:12); other texts speak of a person's death using the idiom "to be gathered to" one's "people" (*ʾsp* [Ni] *ʾel ʿamm-*; e.g., Gen 25:8, 17; Deut 32:50).[48] These idioms may suggest that dying family members were thought to join their dead kin in the afterlife, and each may also intimate an original association with burial in the family tomb, though one can only speculate about these possibilities, as much remains unclear.[49] Whatever the exact nuances of each of these idioms, they suggest that the relationship of the dying and their dead kin continues in some way after death.

Friends and Family Compared and Classified

After considering the ways in which familial intimacy and the expectations of kin are represented in biblical texts, I now examine the comparison of friends and family members. Though friends and, in the political sphere, allies are distinguished in a number of ways from family members, a few texts compare friends and relatives explicitly, suggesting that they share, or ought to share, certain characteristics, behaviors, and obligations in common. Other passages suggest implicitly that friends and family members share a common classification, and therefore at least some common expectations must apply to both. I turn first to explicit comparisons of friends and relatives.

Explicit Comparisons

Several texts present explicit comparisons of friends to family members. An example of this is Prov 18:24: "There are friends for friendly exchanges, / And there is a friend who clings more closely than a brother [*wĕyēš ʾōhēb dābēq mēʾāḥ*]."[50] This verse not only suggests the possibility of gradations of friendship, but also compares the exceptional friend to the brother, using an adjective derived from the verb "to cling to" (*dābēq*), an idiom of familial and treaty loyalty as well as an idiom of physical proximity, as I have observed. The text suggests implicitly an ideal that brothers "cling" closely, that they are in fact paradigmatic intimates to which others (e.g., friends) might be compared. Yet according to this verse, the possibility exists that an exceptional friend might be even more loyal, closely bonded, and perhaps more often physically present than a brother.[51] Thus, the idiom "to cling" is used in this verse to suggest not only that brothers "cling" to one another, but that a close friend might share this characteristic and might even exceed the brother's "clinging." As for other friends, described as "friends for friendly exchanges," the verse assumes that they do not share the same degree of loyalty and closeness, for they are explicitly contrasted with the exceptional friend and implicitly distinguished from the brother. This comparison of the exceptional friend to the brother is typical of texts in which family members are cast as paradigmatic intimates to whom friends or allies might be compared.[52] In contrast, the comparison of relatives to friends, as if friendship were the paradigmatic relationship, a phenomenon familiar to some contemporary Westerners—"my brother/sister/child/parent/cousin is my best friend"—is unattested in biblical texts.[53]

A second example of explicit comparison of friends and family members is also found in Proverbs, although it deals not with ideal behavior, but rather with the failure to meet normal expectations. Proverbs 19:7 reads: "All the brothers of a poor man despise him, / How much more so are his friends far from him [$rḥq$]." According to this verse, poverty results in rejection both by family members and by friends, a reversal of behavioral norms in both cases. But the bad behavior of the poor man's friends is presented as less surprising under the circumstances than that of his relatives, suggesting the idea that the friendship bond is weaker than the family bond.[54] In contrast, the psalms of individual complaint, which speak frequently of disloyal friends and relatives and use similar idioms of distance and detachment (e.g., $rḥq$) about the behavior of both, do not suggest that there is or ought to be a difference of expectations with respect to the behavior of family members and friends. Rather, disloyal friends and family members are cast as equally blameworthy (e.g., Ps 38:12–13).

Implicit Shared Classifications

More common than explicit comparisons of friends to family members are implicit shared classifications. One example is Deut 13:7, a legal text that suggests an implicit common classification shared by an intimate friend and a person's closest family members. "If," says the text, "your brother the son of your mother, or your son, or your daughter, or the wife of your bosom, or your friend who is as yourself, misleads you in secret as follows: 'Let us go and serve other gods . . . ,' you shall not listen to him nor shall your eye pity him nor shall you spare or protect him. You shall certainly slay him." These potential offenders are clearly to be understood as a man's closest intimates, and they are mentioned because even they must be executed should they tempt an Israelite to worship gods other than Yhwh. According to this text, aside from family members such as the brother who is the mother's son, the son, the daughter, or the wife, this intimate circle includes the exceptional, intimate friend, described as "your friend who is as yourself [*rēʿăkā ʾăšer kĕnapšĕkā*]."[55] Clearly distinguished from other friends by the way in which the text describes him, this friend is implicitly classified with intimate family members as part of the circle of people closest to the addressee, those the addressee would be most likely to shield from the consequences of their actions (v. 9). The shared, implicit classification of the intimate friend with closest family members is created through the use of a list that includes both close family members and the intimate friend. Interestingly, though the intimate friend is included in the circle of closest intimates, the brother who is the father's son—but not the mother's—and sisters—married or unmarried, the daughter of the mother or the father—go unmentioned. It is difficult to know what to make of this. On the one hand, the text might be giving several examples of intimate family members without intending to be comprehensive; on the other, it might imply that the unmentioned family members are less close than those who are listed and, consequently, less close than the intimate friend. The former reading seems to me to be the more likely, given that other texts which list close family members such as Lev 21:2–3 include all brothers and at least some sisters—in the case of Lev 21:3, it is unmarried sisters—among those who make up the most intimate family circle.

Several other examples of implicit shared classification of friends and close relatives occur in the Psalms and in wisdom texts such as the book of Job and Proverbs. In these texts, in contrast to Deut 13:7, the common class is suggested not by a list of intimates that includes friends along with family members, but by poetic parallelism. Psalm 15:1–3 speaks of the person who is most worthy:

> Yhwh, who may dwell in your tents?
> Who may reside on your holy mountain?
> He who walks uprightly,

> Who does righteousness,
> And who speaks truth in his heart;
> Who does not speak slander,
> Who does not do wrong [*rāʿâ*] to his friend [*rēʿēhû*],
> And has not borne reproach (for acts against) his relative [*qĕrōbô*].[56]

The implicit shared classification of the friend and relative is indicated by the parallelism of "his friend" and "his relative." This suggests that the two share the same class: intimates whom the worthy person does not wrong. Such parallelism is commonplace in biblical poetry, and often it is the same paired terms that occur over and over again together (e.g., "day/night").[57] As James Kugel suggests, "fixed pairs" of terms "strongly establish the feeling of correspondence between A and B."[58] Though it may be too much to claim that the specific terms "friend" (*rēaʿ*) and "relative" (*qārôb*) are a fixed pair, given that "friend" is often paired in poetry with other familial terms such as "brother," the very fact of frequent poetic pairing of a familial term with a term for a friend is itself not insignificant, as it suggests implicitly a relationship between the friend and family members—what I am calling a shared classification.

Additional examples of the implicit classification of friends with family members by means of poetic parallelism are worthy of note. One such instance is Prov 17:17: "At all times the friend loves, / And a brother is born for distress." Here, the friend is paired with the brother, and the implication of the verse is that both friend and brother will be loyal, even in times of adversity. The text and its parallelism suggest that together, friend and brother constitute a single class of people on whom one can rely even in tough circumstances. A second text of interest is Ps 38:12: "My loving friends [*ʾōhăbay wĕrēʿay*] stand at a distance from my affliction, / My relatives [*qĕrôbay*] stand far off."[59] Here, both friends and relatives are castigated for keeping their distance from the suffering petitioner of Psalm 38. In effect, they have failed to be loyal to the complainant by not offering support. The text suggests that they belong to a single class of people from whom one ought to be able to expect help at times of trouble, as Prov 17:17 also suggests, albeit from a confident angle. Job 19:13–14 is yet another text that implies through its parallelism that friends and family members share a single classification: those who are expected to be loyal in troubled times. But as with Ps 38:12, the friends and relatives of Job 19:13–14 fail to live up to expectations, though in this case Yhwh is blamed for causing their alienation:

>He made my brothers be far from me,
>Those who know me [*yōdě ʿay*] are estranged from me,
>My relatives [*qěrôbay*] are nowhere to be found,
>Those known to me [*měyuddāʿay*] have forgotten me.⁶⁰

Psalm 122:8 pairs "brothers" and "friends" as intimates about whom the psalmist cares. The context is a prayer for Jerusalem's welfare: "For the sake of my brothers and friends, / I call for peace in you."⁶¹ Finally, several poetic texts from the prophetic corpus attest to a pairing of friend and relative that suggests that they share a common classification. Jeremiah 9:3 states that a man should beware of his friend and trust no brother, suggesting that friend and brother belong to the same class of intimates one would normally trust. Micah 7:5–6 is similar in its warning not to trust family intimates or friends.

A prose narrative that is characterized by parallelism and which suggests that friends share an implicit classification with relatives is Exod 32:27. Like Deut 13:7, this text addresses what is presented as a serious crime against Yhwh and commands the punishment of its perpetrators. Those who worshiped the golden calf are to be slain by the Levites, who are told: "Thus says Yhwh, god of Israel: 'Let each man set his sword upon his thigh. Then pass and return through the camp, from end to end, slaying each his brother, each his friend [*rēʿēhû*], each his relative [*qěrōbô*]."⁶² As in Deut 13:7, the friend is classified implicitly with family members, and together, these constitute a group of intimates the addressee would be most likely not to want to kill. Here, however, it is the parallelism of the verse that suggests a common classification rather than the presence of close friend and family members together in a single list of intimates.⁶³ As in Deut 13:7, Exod 32:27 suggests that there can be no mercy for those disloyal to Yhwh, even for those closest to the agents of execution.⁶⁴ Interestingly, Exod 32:29 seems to speak of the Levite commissioning himself to Yhwh's service "at the cost of his son and at the cost of his brother,"⁶⁵ leaving the friend unmentioned and adding explicit mention of the son. Like the presence of the friend in a list of relatives, this is likely yet another indication of the privileging of the close family member as paradigmatic intimate to whom the exceptional friend might be compared.

Though friends are not infrequently compared to family members explicitly and classified with them implicitly, it is not usual for them to be called "brother," "sister," or any other familial term. In fact, such usage is exceedingly rare.⁶⁶ Yet interestingly, political allies are routinely addressed as "brother," a suzerain typically refers to his vassal as his "son," and a vassal commonly calls his suzerain "father." Prose examples of this usage include 1 Kgs 9:13, where Solomon addresses his ally Hiram of Tyre as "my brother"; 1 Sam 24:17, where Saul refers to David as "my son David"; and 1 Sam 24:12, where David calls Saul "my father." Furthermore, in contrast to kin, allies are also commonly referred to as "friends," as in Lam 1:2, where two words for friend are used to describe the abandonment of a personified Jerusalem by her allies at the time of the Babylonian conquest:

> She has no comforter of all her friends [lit., "her lovers" (*ʾōhăbêhā*)],
> All her friends [*rēʿêhā*] have treated her deceitfully,
> They have become her enemies.[67]

It would seem that political allies are treated both as fictive kin *and* as fictive friends, and the manner in which they are addressed or described reflects this duality.[68] The ally can be both "brother" and "friend," as the example of Hiram of Tyre illustrates. In 1 Kgs 9:13, Hiram is Solomon's "brother"; in 1 Kgs 5:15, it is said that he had always been a "friend" (lit., "lover") of David. In contrast, friends are compared to family members and may even share a common classification with them, but they are not typically cast as fictive kin themselves, just as kin are not commonly described as friends.[69] Thus, the distinction between friends and family members is maintained, even if friends and relatives are thought to share a common classification as intimates and at least some common expectations such as loyalty are thought to apply to both. Similarly, a distinction between friends and allies is established by contrasting usages. The ally is called a friend, and loyalty is expected of him, but he is also routinely called a brother, unlike the friend. Furthermore, it seems highly unlikely that any kind of emotional dimension is assumed of the relationship of allies with one another, in contrast to familial relations and many types of friendship, which are represented as having emotional dimensions, as I have argued.

Shared Expectations, Distinct Obligations

Though many of the expectations of family members are shared by friends, friends are exempt from some familial duties, suggesting a set of obligations distinct from those of relatives. I begin with shared expectations, of which there are a number. Like relatives, friends are expected to "love" their friends. Some texts present friends fulfilling this expectation; others emphasize their failure to do so; still others speak of friends who fulfill expectations and friends who do not. To love in the context of friendship appears to have both an emotional and a behavioral resonance, as it does in the context of the family. Proverbs 17:17, bringing the ideal into relief, puts it simply: "At all times the friend loves." In this context, "to love" means, at least in part, to be loyal in times of need. The setting of adversity is implicit in the statement that a friend loves "at all times" and explicit in the mention of "distress" in the parallel colon ("and a brother is born for distress"). Job 19:19, describing friends who have turned against Job in his time of trouble, states that "all the men of my council abominate [*t*ʿ*b*] me, / Those whom I have loved [*'hb*] have turned against me." This verse accents a lack of behavioral parity between friends, something that is also emphasized not infrequently in the psalms of individual complaint (e.g., Ps 35:13–14). Once again, loyalty seems to be at issue, as the verse brings into relief the disloyalty of Job's friends—they reject him utterly—and suggests implicitly his loyalty to them when they were in trouble ("those whom I loved"). Not surprisingly, the friend can be referred to as "lover" (*'ōhēb*), as in Pss 38:12; 88:19 and Prov 18:24, and allies are called the same (e.g., 1 Kgs 5:15; Lam 1:2). In all of these examples, the behavioral aspect of love in friendship—loyalty particularly—is emphasized rather than the emotional dimension, though other texts communicate the emotive aspect of the love of friends quite clearly.

In 1 Sam 18:1, the "self" or "life" (*nepeš*) of Jonathan is "bound" to the "self" or "life" of David, just as the "self" or "life" of Jacob is "bound" to that of his youngest son Benjamin according to Gen 44:30–31.[70] As mentioned earlier, this idiom is highly charged emotionally, given the claim in Gen 44:30–31 that Jacob would die of grief if Benjamin were to die. An emotional resonance, perhaps intense, is therefore likely for the idiom in 1 Sam 18:1, especially given the fact that it is never used of treaty partners, unlike other idioms used to describe the relationship of Jonathan and David that are best explained as treaty language in the contexts in which they occur (e.g., "to love *x* as oneself," used in 1 Sam 18:3 with "to cut a covenant").[71] Thus, the binding of selves or lives in 1 Sam 18:1, an idiom of emotional love used in Gen 44:30–31 of parent and child, points to the potential for an emotional bond—possibly intense—between male friends, a phenomenon that may also be supported by other texts, including Deut 13:7; Exod 32:27; and Prov 17:17.[72] In these passages, the emotional dimension of love is less easily established than it is in 1 Sam 18:1, though it does seem likely that it is at issue. Deuteronomy 13:7 focuses on the circle of people most likely to be shielded from harm by the addressee even though they deserve to die in the view of the author. The text seems to be suggesting that one's feelings toward one's intimates have the potential to get in the way of "just" punishment and cannot be allowed to do so. Though no love idiom is used in this verse, the emotional commitment of the addressee to relatives and the close friend is in focus. Similarly, Exod 32:27 suggests that the friend, along with the brother and relative (*qārōb*), are among the people one would be most reluctant to kill for committing a serious transgression against Yhwh. In the case of Prov 17:17, it seems likely that the loyalty of the friend who "loves" at all times is driven by emotions, though this is difficult to demonstrate conclusively.

Loyalty, a quality communicated by the love idiom in texts such as Prov 17:17 and Job 19:19, is also expressed through the use of the word *ḥesed*, though this is quite rare in friendship contexts, in contrast to its more common use in treaty settings and in the family.[73] A primary example of its usage for friends is Job 6:14–15. Though the text is somewhat difficult, its sense is fairly clear: Just as a friend spurns loyalty (*ḥesed*) and abandons the fear of Shadday, Job's brothers act deceitfully toward him.[74] The text suggests that friends owe friends loyalty (*ḥesed*) as brothers owe loyalty to brothers, a manifestation of behavioral parity. It also suggests that acting loyally entails avoiding deception and is buttressed by reverence for the deity. If Ps 109:16 refers to a disloyal friend, he is condemned because he "did not remember to be loyal [lit., "to perform loyalty," *ʿăśôt ḥesed*], / And pursued a poor, afflicted man," evidently a reference to the petitioner himself (see v. 22).[75] Here, pursuit (*rdp*) constitutes disloyalty.

The "clinging" idiom is also used to express loyalty between friends, just as it is in familial and treaty contexts. Proverbs 18:24 not only compares explicitly the loyalty of the exceptional friend to that of the brother using an adjectival form of the root *dbq*, but also contrasts the exceptional friend to other friends: "There are friends for friendly exchanges, / And there is a friend who clings more closely than a brother." Thus, according to this text, not all friends "cling" in the manner of the exceptional friend. It is not clear whether the friends "for friendly exchanges" are thought to "cling" less than the exceptional friend or not to "cling" at all, even though they are called "friends" (*rēʿîm*). Ruth's "clinging" to Naomi in Ruth 1:14, even after she has fulfilled all expectations toward her mother-in-law and is free to go back to her home of origin in Moab, suggests loyalty that goes beyond that required of a daughter-in-law.[76] I believe that it indicates that a new, voluntary association between Naomi and Ruth is in view, a relationship best described as friendship, as I shall argue in Chapter 3. It is a relationship characterized by absolute loyalty and unaffected by circumstances, in contrast to the mother-in-law, daughter-in-law relationship of Ruth and Naomi, which clearly has an endpoint once all obligations are fulfilled, as the text takes pains to emphasize. Ruth's speech in 1:16–17 details just what her clinging to Naomi will entail: no separation, even in death. If this reading of Ruth's clinging is correct, it suggests the possibility of female friendship in the world of the text, friendship characterized by loyalty and described using the verb "to cling to." In other words, it is a friendship that is not unlike an exceptional male friendship as it is represented in a text such as Prov 18:24.[77] Just as there is a male friend who clings more closely than a brother, there is Ruth, who exceeds familial obligations in her relationship with Naomi.

Support for friends, particularly in times of difficulty, is another expectation that parallels the obligations of family members to one another. Psalm 88:19 mentions friends who withhold support from a suffering petitioner: "You are far from me, loving friend [*'ōhēb wārēaʻ*]."[78] In v. 9 the text speaks of friends who stand at a distance and treat the petitioner as if he were an abomination. Similarly, Ps 38:12 censures friends who keep their distance from the anguished petitioner, just as it condemns relatives who do the same. Like the unsupportive family members, the disobliging friends are said to "pay back that which is evil instead of what is good" and "act as an adversary" to the petitioner instead of pursuing his welfare (v. 21). Psalm 35:12 uses similar rhetoric in its condemnation of friends, as does Ps 109:4–5, which may also refer to friends when it states that "in exchange for my love, they acted as adversaries toward me." The perspective of Job 19:13–14, 19, 21–22 is similar to that of these psalms of individual complaint, in that these verses criticize disloyal friends who have forgotten Job, act as if they are strangers to him, abominate him, and pursue him. Implicit in these statements from both the psalms of individual complaint and the book of Job is the assumption that friends are obligated to reciprocate loyal, supportive treatment (*ṭôbâ*) that they themselves have received and never to take up the role of adversary. Supportive treatment includes not standing at a distance from a suffering friend or treating the friend as a stranger or worse, but actively supporting the friend (e.g., delighting in his vindication, as in Ps 35:27).[79]

Trustworthiness and honest dealings are expectations of friends, as they are of relatives. Jeremiah 9:3 speaks of both friends and brothers who are unworthy of one's trust:

A man should watch his friend,
And do not trust any brother.
For every brother acts aggressively,
And every friend is untrustworthy.[80]

As I have mentioned previously, the larger context of this verse is a time of trouble in Judah when deceit and falseness prevail in the land, evils are multiplied, and the people "do not know" Yhwh (v. 2; see also v. 4). That one must watch friends because they are untrustworthy suggests what the norm ought to be: trustworthy friends. Micah 7:5–6 is similar in its characterization of a corrupt society in which normative expectations are reversed. Here, too, one ought to be able to trust one's friend and rely on one's other intimates for appropriate behavior, but this is impossible: the friend is not to be trusted, the female lover is not worthy of one's confidences, the son treats his father as if he were a fool, the daughter rises up against her mother and the daughter-in-law against her mother-in-law. In short, "the enemies of a man are the people of his household."

In contrast to the expectations that friends share with family members, there are duties incumbent upon only relatives. Friends are not required to play the roles of redeemer or Levir, and most death-related practices are the obligation primarily of family members. Redemption is an expectation of close male kin on the father's side, as I have discussed. When brothers or uncles or first cousins are unavailable, other male relatives of the clan might be called upon to play the role of redeemer (Lev 25:48). The role of Levir is also a responsibility of male kin, specifically brothers who share the same domicile (Deut 25:5–10) or even the father of the dead man without an heir (Gen 38) or other agnatic kinsmen (Ruth 3:9, 12–13; 4:1–13).[81] As for death-related practices, most are normally the province of immediate family members, with some expected only of male kin on the father's side. Close male relatives such as sons and brothers are required to bury the dead, and husbands are expected to bury wives under normal circumstances (cf. Lev 21:2–4, regarding the priest, whose circumstances differ). Mourning the dead is undertaken by immediate family members of both genders, including spouses, and the one biblical narrative that describes protecting unburied corpses from mutilation casts a female family member as agent

(2 Sam 21:10–11). In contrast to these more inclusive practices that involve female relatives, evidence suggests that it is sons who observe ancestral rites for dead fathers (2 Sam 18:18), and it seems likely that the maintenance of the family tomb was the responsibility of close agnatic kin. Friends, for their part, might fill in for family members who are not present, as might treaty partners. They might bury the dead, as the Jabesh-Gileadites do for their lord Saul and his sons in 1 Sam 31:11–13, or play the role of primary mourner in the absence of relatives, as the old prophet of Bethel does in the story of the Judean man of God in 1 Kgs 13:29–30.[82] It may be that friends or treaty partners could also play a part in ancestral cult practices or tomb maintenance in the absence of family members, although the evidence for this is not very clear.[83] Finally, there is no evidence that friends were normally interred together, as relatives were, or that they expected to be reunited with dead friends in the afterlife, which may have been the case for family members, as I have discussed.[84]

Friends and allies do, however, have their own distinct responsibilities with respect to death-related rites. They are expected to be comforters (*mĕnaḥămîm*) in contexts of death, and their absence is noted by texts (Ps 69:21; Lam 1:2, 16). As the behavior of Job's three friends in the Job prologue illustrates, comforters embrace the mourner's rites and support the mourner in a variety of ways (Job 2:11–13). Jeremiah 16:7 suggests that a mourning context includes the presence of comforters who break bread with the mourner "to comfort him concerning the dead" and cause him to drink from "the cup of consolation on account of his father or his mother." It is likely that relatives who are not immediate family members are also assumed to play the comforter role along with friends, since mourners are typically close relations (Lev 21:2–4), though the evidence for this is not very clear.[85]

Friends also have the obligation to enact rites of comforting in non–death-related mourning contexts such as that of petition of the deity; as noted, it is very likely that such ritual action in contexts of petition is incumbent upon family members as well. The disloyal friends and relatives condemned in the psalms of individual complaint for keeping their distance from the petitioner or even acting in a hostile and aggressive manner toward him have in effect rejected the role of comforter. Ex-friends are even said to rejoice over the misfortunes of the petitioner as enemies do (Ps 35:26), in contrast to the petitioner's loyal supporters, who are said to "delight in" his "vindication" (Ps 35:27). The proper role of a friend in a context of illness and petition is brought into relief by Ps 35:13–14, in which the suffering petitioner speaks of what he did for his friends when they were in trouble:

> As for me, when they were sick my clothes were sackcloth,
> I afflicted myself with fasting ...[86]
> I walked around as would one mourning (his) mother,
> I was prostrated, (dressed as) a mourner.[87]

When his friends were ill, the petitioner embraced mourning rites as if he were mourning his own mother. He did this in order presumably to support the unmentioned petitions of the sick friends for a restoration of their health.[88] The text assumes not only that this kind of supportive comforting is an expectation of friends, but that normally it is reciprocal, not unlike other behaviors associated with friendship. The lack of reciprocation, as well as the hostile actions of these ex-friends, is at issue in the psalm.

Gradations of Friendship

Several texts bear witness to the idea that there can be gradations of friendship. Deuteronomy 13:7 speaks of a particularly intimate friend "who is as yourself," whom the text classifies with close relatives. Implicit in the characterization of this exceptional friend is comparison with other friends who are not so close. Proverbs 18:24 explicitly contrasts the exceptional friend "who clings more closely than a brother" with "friends for friendly exchanges," suggesting that the exceptional friend is in a class by himself, comparable to and even surpassing a brother when it comes to loyalty, intimacy, and, perhaps, maintaining close physical proximity.[89] Proverbs 18:24 may recognize other friends who fall between the two types mentioned explicitly, who might not be exceptional but might be good for more than "friendly exchanges," though the text is completely unclear about this, and about what constitutes "friendly exchanges." The focus of Prov 19:4, in contrast to 18:24, is the friend who is attracted by potential material gain or other status enhancements: "Wealth adds many friends, / But the poor man is separated from his friend." Such friends as these might well be ranked lowest among friends, though the verse says nothing about this. Just as Lev 21:2–4 speaks explicitly of a man's closest familial intimates such as parents, children, brothers, and unmarried sisters, drawing a contrast with other family members, so too do biblical texts know of gradations of friendship, contrasting the exceptional friend with other friends both implicitly and explicitly and recognizing the existence of friends motivated by possible personal profit (Prov 19:4) and friends "for friendly exchanges" (Prov 18:24). It may be that the gradations of friendship witnessed in these texts are modeled on gradations of familial intimacy, though here I can only speculate, given the meager evidence that survives. Nonetheless, texts reflect an awareness of differences among friends with respect to emotional intimacy, motivation for friendship, fulfillment of obligations (e.g., loyalty), and, possibly, physical presence.

Thus, the perspective of biblical texts with regard to the existence of gradations of friendship is not altogether different from that of Aristotle, who identifies and ranks several types of friendship, including friendship of the good, friendship motivated by utility, and friendship with pleasure as its goal (*Nicomachean Ethics* 8.3–4). Though these three friendship types differ from those suggested by biblical texts in a number of ways, there is some overlap. The "friends for friendly exchanges" of Prov 18:24 might be comparable to Aristotle's friend who seeks pleasure; the friend drawn by wealth in Prov 19:4 is apparently not dissimilar to Aristotle's friend motivated by utilitarian aims. The outstanding friend of Prov 18:24 is evidently superior to other friends primarily on account of his loyalty, intimacy, and, possibly, proximity (he "clings more closely than a brother") and that of Deut 13:7 probably on account of his intimacy (he is "as yourself"). In contrast, the primary quality that characterizes Aristotle's superior form of friendship is shared virtue or excellence (*aretē*), which will give rise to trust, pleasure, and even utility.

Conclusion

Friends and family members share a number of common characteristics and obligations, and these are expressed through both explicit comparisons and implicit common classifications, with the friend always compared to the relative, who the texts suggest is the paradigmatic intimate. Both relatives and friends have a duty to be loving (emotionally and behaviorally), loyal, and supportive, particularly in times of adversity; they are also expected to be trustworthy. Behavioral parity emerges as a central dimension of the relationship of friends to one another and that of family members among themselves. It is an expectation of both friends and relatives that manifestations of loyalty and support ("that which is good" or "good things") will be repaid to one who has behaved loyally, and those who fail to reciprocate appropriately are castigated by texts of various types (e.g., prophetic materials, psalms of individual complaint, wisdom texts).[90] Although some texts condemn equally friends and family members who fail to live up to these expectations (e.g., Ps 38:12), at least one passage casts the failure of friends as more to be expected than that of relatives, suggesting implicitly that in the writer's view, familial ties are typically stronger than the bond between friends (Prov 19:7). Yet the possibility of the exceptional friend who might exceed the family member in demonstrations of loyalty and support or in personal intimacy is recognized by several biblical texts (e.g., Deut 13:7; Prov 18:24).

Friends and family members also have separate obligations that set them apart as distinct social actors (e.g., the roles of redeemer and Levir are restricted to male kinsmen on the father's side; a number of death-related practices are normally expected only of family members, some specifically of agnates). In addition, it seems likely that friends are rarely if ever referred to using familial terminology (e.g., "brother"), another way in which friends are distinguished from relatives. Allies, for their part, are cast as distinct from both friends and family and are best described as both fictive friends and fictive kin. The ally is routinely referred to as "brother," in contrast to the friend, and as "friend," in contrast to the family member.[91] It also seems unlikely that an alliance is assumed to have a genuine emotional dimension, in contrast to the relations of family members with each other and those of at least some friends. A man's wife, too, is a distinct social actor, sharing expectations with both relatives and friends (e.g., loyalty and trustworthiness) but exempted from a number of familial duties, not unlike the friend (e.g., the role of redeemer), though the friend's intimacy, like that of kin, is generally understood to be nonsexual, in contrast to that of the wife.[92]

Perhaps the closest social analogue to a man's male friend in the world of the biblical text is the kinsman on a man's mother's side. Like the friend, he is evidently expected to be loyal and provide support, and in contrast to agnatic relatives, he is not required to play the roles of redeemer or Levir, nor is there any clear evidence that he is among those with a primary obligation to bury the dead, maintain the family tomb, or enact ancestral rites. Not unlike the friend or ally, he might be expected to fill in for agnatic kin when they are not present, though about this I can only speculate, given the absence of evidence.[93]

2 Failed Friendship

Failed friendship is a surprisingly common theme in biblical and other West Asian texts. Disloyal friends appear in psalms of individual complaint such as Psalms 28, 35, 38, and 88; in prophetic anthologies such as Jeremiah and Micah; and in Proverbs and Job, among other texts. Friendships that fail to fulfill expectations contribute to unstable social relations according to extant sources. For Mic 7:5 and Jer 9:3, untrustworthy friends are representative of a society's decline, as is the disintegration of marriage and family ties. The Marduk and Shulgi prophecies from Babylon represent friends in violent conflict as emblematic of social collapse, not unlike unburied corpses and aggression between brothers.[1] Psalm 15:3 speaks of the person who is fit to "dwell on Yhwh's holy mountain" as one who does not wrong a friend, suggesting that one who does such a thing is unworthy of divine favor, not unlike the person who commits slander according to this text. Thus, failed friendship and the conflict it engenders are presented as social evils, a blight in the eyes of Yhwh comparable to other symptoms of social distress such as the collapse of familial relationships and larger societal structures. In this chapter, I explore the theme of failed friendship and its ramifications by identifying the behaviors that transform a friend into an ex-friend or even an enemy and how such actions compare with those of treaty violators, disloyal relatives, and enemies who were never friends or allies and who are not relatives. I study the idioms of failed friendship, comparing them with idioms of treaty violation, idioms used of disloyal family members, and those employed to characterize the behavior of other enemies. I also examine the deity's role in the failure of friendships and consider why the loss of friendship is not typically mentioned among the curses that might afflict a treaty violator or another type of offender and why having loyal friends is not mentioned in extant petitionary prayers such as Solomon's prayer in 1 Kings 8 or in collections of blessings such as Deut 28:1–14. Finally, I examine the topos of the disloyal friend in the psalms of individual complaint, asking how it functions to promote the psalmist's purpose: persuading the deity to intervene on the sufferer's behalf. Like failed friendship, familial relationships that do not live up to expectations are strikingly commonplace in biblical narratives (e.g., the stories of Cain and Abel; Jacob and Esau; and Amnon, Tamar, and Absalom) and are also at issue in the psalms of individual complaint (e.g., Ps 38:12) and wisdom literature (e.g., Prov 19:7), with parallels in cuneiform and other West Asian sources.[2] In this chapter, I compare the representation of failed friendships to that of failed familial relationships.

Actions That Constitute Rejection of the Friend

What behaviors cause friendships to fail and what idioms are used to describe those behaviors? Aside from general, nonspecific actions such as doing wrong (*rāʿâ*) to the friend (Ps 15:3), biblical texts treating failed friendship speak of both specific actions and particular examples of inaction through which rejection of a friend is realized and communicated. Some manifestations of rejection might be characterized as active or even aggressive (e.g., deceiving the friend, spreading lies about the friend, or rejoicing over the friend's misfortune); others, in contrast, involve a lack of engagement or action where such is expected (e.g., standing at a distance or being far from a friend in need). I begin with several examples of inaction that constitute and convey rejection.

"To stand at a distance" or "be far from" a person, particularly at that person's time of need, are fairly prominent idioms of rejection by means of inaction, especially in the psalms of individual complaint, and not infrequently used of the friend. Sometimes, such rejection is represented as a matter of choice, as in Ps 38:12, where the complainant's "loving friends[3] stand at a distance from [*ʿāmad minneged*]" his "affliction," and in Prov 19:7, where the poor man's friends are said to be "far from him [*rḥq*]." In other texts using these idioms, Yhwh is said to be the cause of the rejection, as in Ps 88:9: "You made my friends [*měyuddāʿay*, lit., "those known to me"] be far from me."[4] Such idioms of rejection are also used of family members who refuse to play expected roles, as Ps 38:12 demonstrates: At the time of his suffering, says the psalmist, "my relatives [*qĕrôbay*] stand at a distance."⁵ Texts that speak of treaty violation use similar idioms. In Jer 2:5, Israel's ancestors are described as going far (*rḥq*) from Yhwh when they reject him and worship other gods:

> What wrong did your ancestors find in me,
> That they went far from me,
> Going after that which is empty and becoming empty?

Obadiah 1:11 castigates the Edomites, Judah's allies, for standing at a distance (*'āmad minneged*) when Jerusalem fell. Lamentations 1:2 states that personified Jerusalem, in the figure of a mourning widow, has no comforter since her allies have rejected her; in 1:16, she states that a comforter who would restore her spirit is "far from" her. The petitioner of the psalms of individual complaint commonly calls upon Yhwh not to be far off or stand at a distance, but to deliver him from his travails, implicitly suggesting that by not helping, Yhwh is behaving in a manner not unlike the psalmist's ex-friends and whatever other enemies might be in view: "God, do not be distant from me! / My God, hasten to help me!" (Ps 71:12).⁶ In fact, the author of Psalm 38 uses these idioms of both Yhwh and disloyal friends in the same composition: The sufferer complains that "loving friends" stand at a distance from his affliction in v. 12, while Yhwh is petitioned not to be far from him in v. 22. Thus, standing at a distance or being far from are idioms of rejection used not only of the friend, but of disloyal family members, of treaty partners, and, in the case of the psalms of individual complaint, of Yhwh by Yhwh's supplicant. In all cases it is assumed that the allegedly absent or distant person or entity—whether it be a friend, a relative, a treaty partner, or the deity—has violated an obligation by not demonstrating loyalty, for example, by helping at a time of need (e.g., Ps 38:12 or Obad 1:11).

Another idiom of rejection that might be characterized as an example of inactivity where activity is expected is "to forget about" (*škḥ*) the friend. In Job 19:14, Job's relatives (*qĕrôbay*) are criticized for having "failed" or "ceased" (evidently meaning "ceased/failed to be present"), while his friends (lit., "those known" to him) are said to have forgotten him: "My relatives have ceased to be present, / My friends have forgotten me."⁷ "To forget" in this context is associated with abandonment, both physical and emotional, as the whole of Job 19:13–14 suggests: Brothers are far away from Job; what are likely friends (*yōdĕ'ay*, "those who know me") are estranged from him; relatives have ceased to be present; friends (*mĕyuddā'ay*, "those known to me") have forgotten him. Just as a friend might be forgotten by a friend, so Yhwh frequently claims that Israel has forgotten him, that is to say, broken the covenant (e.g., Deut 32:18; Jer 2:32; Hos 8:14). Sometimes it is Yhwh himself who is accused of forgetting Israel, particularly after disaster: "Zion says, 'Yhwh has abandoned me, / My lord has forgotten me'" (Isa 49:14). In all of these cases, it is assumed that the party forgetting has failed to fulfill expectations, whether they be those of a friendship not explicitly cast in treaty terms, as in Job 19:14, or those of a formal treaty, as in texts such as Jer 2:32 or Isa 49:14. In the latter example, the accusation of abandonment through forgetting is followed by reassurance that Yhwh has not—could not—forget Israel:

> Does a woman forget her infant?
> A mother the child of her womb?[8]
> Though these might forget,
> I will not forget you!

Thus, the image of the forgotten friend evokes the idea of unjustified abandonment, not unlike the treaty partner who has been forgotten.[9]

In addition to several idioms of inactivity such as "to stand at a distance from," "to be far from," or "to forget," texts express rejection of the friend using a number of idioms suggesting action or even aggression. One such idiom is to treat the friend as an "abomination." Job 19:19 reads: "All the men of my council abominate [t'b] me, / They whom I loved have turned against me [Ni hpk bĕ-]." Similarly, Ps 88:9 speaks of the petitioner becoming an abomination to his friends because Yhwh has alienated them from him: "You made my friends ['those known to me'] be far from me, / You made me into an abomination [tô'ēbâ] to them." What, precisely, does it mean to treat someone as an abomination? Job 19:19 suggests that one component of such treatment is to turn against the abominated person; Ps 88:9 indicates that keeping one's distance is another. Deuteronomy 23:4–9, a text that speaks of certain aliens to be excluded from the Israelite community either permanently (Moabites and Ammonites) or temporarily (Edomites and Egyptians), suggests that abominating others in this context means excluding them permanently and not abominating them means allowing them to enter the community eventually: "You shall not abominate the Edomite for he is your brother. Nor shall you abominate the Egyptian, for you were a resident alien in his land. Children of the third generation who are born to them may enter the assembly of Yhwh" (vv. 8–9).[10] The unclean animal, which is excluded from the Israelite diet, is labeled an "abomination" in Deut 14:2, as are forbidden sexual unions according to Lev 18:22, 26, 27, 29, 30. Thus, abomination idioms are used consistently to speak of active exclusion and rejection—of particular aliens, unclean edible animals, and certain sexual acts—and even suggest abhorrence or hatred in some contexts (e.g., Deut 7:26; Ps 119:163).[11] Though less commonly than the idioms "to stand at a distance" or "be far from," "to abominate" occurs as an idiom of treaty violation in a few contexts (e.g., 1 Kgs 21:26; Ezek 16:52). It is also used of Yhwh rejecting Israel after it has transgressed, as in Ps 106:40 and Amos 6:8.[12]

"To pay back that which is evil instead of what is good" is a second idiom of active rejection and it particularly foregrounds the expectation of reciprocity between friends. It occurs in Ps 35:12 where it is used of disloyal friends who were described as "violent" or "false" witnesses (*ʿēdê ḥāmās*) in the previous verse: "They pay me back that which is evil instead of what is good, / Bereavement for my person (?)."[13] Verses 13–14 then speak of what the petitioner did for the friends when they were sick, underscoring the inappropriateness of their behavior now that the petitioner is the one in need. In Ps 7:5, the petitioner states rhetorically that if he has paid back (*gml*) that which is evil to his friend (*šōlĕmî*), he deserves to be pursued and overtaken by his foes.[14] A similar idiom occurs in Ps 38:21, although in this example it likely applies to disloyal family members as well as to unfaithful friends, both of whom are mentioned together in v. 12. Another version of the idiom occurs in Ps 109:5 and may apply either to friends or family members or to both at the same time.[15] The idiom "to pay back that which is evil instead of what is good" in all cases assumes a preexisting, positive, reciprocal relationship between two parties that has been violated by the one who acts malevolently. It is used not only of friends and possibly family members, but also of people who have benefited from fair and even generous treatment by others who (allegedly) do them wrong in return. In Gen 44:4, 6, Joseph's brothers, who are unaware that they are dealing with Joseph, are accused of paying back that which is evil instead of what is good when they allegedly steal from Joseph before their departure from his court. In Jer 18:20, Jeremiah accuses his adversaries of paying back that which is evil instead of what is good though he had petitioned Yhwh on their behalf in the past:

> Should that which is evil be paid back instead of what is good?
> But they have dug a pit for my life!
> Remember how I stood before you,

> Speaking favorably [*ṭôb*] of them,
> In order to turn back your rage from them.

Oddly, the idiom "to pay back that which is evil instead of what is good" is not used of treaty violators, in contrast to other idioms I have discussed (e.g., "to stand at a distance" or "to be far from"), even though its focus is reciprocity, a central tenet of covenant relationships of all types.[16] Finally, and perhaps obviously, I note that the idiom is never used of enemies who were never friends and are not relatives, given its assumption of preexisting positive relations that have now been violated.[17]

To pursue a friend, to devise or seek to do harm to him, or to attempt to kill him are—needless to say—acts that are understood to constitute the friend's rejection. In Job 19:21–22, Job confronts his three friends, accusing them of doing the opposite of what they are obligated to do at his time of trouble:

> Favor me, favor me, you are my friends,
> For the hand of God has struck me.
> Why do you pursue [*rdp*] me like God?
> With my flesh you are not satisfied![18]

In Ps 35:3–4, the petitioner's pursuers (*rōdĕpîm*), evidently ex-friends, are described as "those who seek my life" and "those who devise evil against me"; in Ps 38:13, the sufferer's opponents are described as "those who seek my undoing [*dōrĕšê rāʿātî*]" and "those who seek my life [*mĕbaqšê napšî*]," likely a reference to relatives as well as friends, who are said to stand at a distance in the previous colon. In Ps 71:13, the enemies of the petitioner, who might be ex-friends, disloyal relatives, or other foes, are described as "those who seek my undoing [*mĕbaqšê rāʿātî*]" and "adversaries of my life [*śōṭĕnê napšî*]."[19] Elsewhere, relatives are said to pursue (*rdp*) with hostile intent (Gen 31:23), and former allies might do the same (Amos 1:11), not unlike enemies who were never friends or treaty partners and are not relatives (Gen 35:5; Exod 14:8; Josh 24:6).

Speaking words of deceit or treachery to or against the friend is mentioned in a number of texts, including Jer 9:7; Ps 28:3; 35:20; and possibly Pss 38:13; 62:5. In Jer 9:7, the wicked person deceives his friend, outwardly displaying the good will expected of friendship, while inwardly plotting the friend's ruin:

> [His] tongue is a slaughtering arrow [*ḥēṣ šōḥēṭ*],
> Treachery he speaks with his mouth,

> He speaks positively [*dbr šālôm*, lit., "speaks good will"] to his friend,
> But privately he sets his trap.[20]

In Ps 28:3, doers of iniquity are characterized as "those who communicate their good will [*šālôm*] to their friends, / But (have) evil in their hearts." Similarly, Ps 62:5 speaks of associates—possibly disloyal friends—who "with their mouths bless, / But secretly they curse." In these examples, the wicked person is a hypocrite, acting as if he were loyal, saying the right thing (lit., speaking "good will") as expected, while secretly harboring hostility. Other texts speak of hostile friends devising "words of treachery" or "deceit" instead of communicating their "good will" (Ps 35:20), likely a reference to treacherous statements made about the friend to others rather than deceptive words said to the friend himself, given that the text suggests that the enemies should have spoken positively but did not.[21] In Ps 38:13, the psalmist's foes, who likely include ex-friends and who are said to pursue his life, "speak treacherously all the day," perhaps also a reference to the kind of deceiving of third parties about the friend that is evidently mentioned in Ps 35:20. The theme of the untrustworthiness of hypocritical friends is addressed in a number of other texts, including Jer 9:3–4 and Mic 7:5–6, which advise that friend and relative are not to be trusted; Jer 9:4, for its part, also condemns the man who deceives his friend and does not speak the truth to him.

Rejoicing over a friend's misfortune constitutes rejection of a friendship in a most public way, since it is mourning in response to a friend's calamity or illness that is expected as a demonstration of loyalty and affiliation, as the behavior of the psalmist in Ps 35:13–14 makes clear ("When they were sick, my clothes were sackcloth"). Yet in Psalm 35, the supplicant's enemies—ex-friends—rejoice at his "stumbling" (v. 15), gathering against him. In vv. 19 and 24, Yhwh is called upon not to allow these foes to rejoice over the psalmist's calamity, and in v. 26, the petitioner calls for the shaming of "those who rejoice in" his "misfortune." In contrast to these disloyal friends, friends who are loyal to the petitioner are referred to as "those who delight in my vindication," and they are called upon to rejoice and cry out joyfully when the vindication comes, thereby perpetuating and communicating their affiliation with the psalmist (v. 27). That it is the enemy who rejoices at the time of one's calamity is made clear by 2 Sam 1:20, where the poet calls for the news of Israel's defeat at Mt. Gilboa to be withheld from the Philistines, "lest the daughters of the Philistines rejoice, / Lest the daughters of the uncircumcised exult." That it is one's own affiliates—family members, friends, allies—who mourn at such a time is made clear by 2 Sam 1:24: "Daughters of Israel, weep for Saul!" Another text which illustrates the expectation that the enemy will rejoice at the time of one's calamity is Prov 24:17, though the text is critical of the norm. It states: "When your enemy falls, do not rejoice, / When he stumbles, let your heart not exult."[22]

In addition to feelings of joy, rejoicing in the biblical context has specific behavioral components, including festive eating and drinking, singing joyful songs, wearing special garments, and anointing with oil. These acts are the diametrical opposite of mourning rites such as fasting, wearing sackcloth, weeping, intoning dirges, and strewing ashes or dirt upon the head.[23] This relationship of rite and its opposite or antitype is well illustrated by Isa 22:12–14, as are the ramifications of not enacting the appropriate rites required by the context (in this particular case, impending calamity):

> The Lord Yhwh of hosts called on that day,
> For weeping and mourning,
> For tonsure and for wearing sackcloth.
> But instead there was joy and rejoicing,
> The slaying of cattle, the slaughter of sheep,
> The eating of flesh and the drinking of wine,
> "Let us eat and drink for tomorrow we die."
> Then Yhwh of hosts revealed himself in my hearing [as follows]:
> "This iniquity shall not be forgiven to you [= Israelites] until you die."[24]

Inappropriate rejoicing in Isa 22:12–14 is a transgression with serious ramifications: It offends Yhwh and will not be forgiven during the lifetime of the offenders. Similarly, to rejoice over the calamity of a friend is a transformative act: It makes one into an enemy and is very likely also an unforgivable offense.

"To hate" is an idiom evidently used of the complainant's ex-friends in Ps 35:19: "Let my enemies without cause [*šeqer*] not rejoice over me, / Let those who hate me [*śōnĕʾay*] without justification [*ḥinnām*] not wink maliciously."[25] The petitioner's enemies in Ps 38:20, who are likely friends as well as family members, are also said to hate him: "Those who despise me wrongfully [*šeqer*] are many." Psalm 109:4–5 contrasts the psalmist's "love" with his enemies' adversarial (*śṭn*) behavior: "They pay me back that which is evil instead of what is good, / Hatred in place of my love." "To hate" (*śānēʾ*)

is the opposite of "to love" (*'āhēb*), an idiom of loyalty with—at times—emotional resonances, used both of family members and of friends in biblical texts, as I discussed in the previous chapter.[26] The idioms "to hate" and "to love" are also used in treaty contexts, where hating the treaty partner represents treaty violation and loving the treaty partner means demonstrating loyalty to him, as in Exod 20:5–6 par. Deut 5:9–10. Here, Yhwh describes himself as a zealous god who punishes descendants for the iniquity of their ancestors to the third and even the fourth generation of "those who hate me," but "who practices loyalty [*ḥesed*] to the thousands, to those who love me, that is, those who keep my commandments."[27] Similarly, David is castigated for "loving those who hate you" and "hating those who love you" when he mistreats his loyal army by mourning for his rebel son Absalom after he has been killed (2 Sam 19:6–9). As these examples suggest, love in a treaty context is expected to be reciprocal. The same is true of love among friends. In Job 19:19, Job complains of friends who have turned against him (*hpk bĕ-*), though he had "loved" them, implying that the friends have done wrong. Thus, "those who hate" the sufferer "without justification" in Ps 35:19, and "wrongfully" in Ps 38:20, also described as his enemies in each text, are, like treaty breakers and Job's disloyal friends (Job 19:19), clearly people who have violated a previously established relationship premised on reciprocal acts of loyalty, not unlike those who "pay back that which is evil instead of what is good, / Hatred in place of my love" in Ps 109:5. (In the latter case, the offenders are also said not to have remembered "loyalty" [*ḥesed*] in v. 16.) That relationship is, in the context of Psalm 35, evidently a friendship while Ps 38:20 likely refers both to friends and to family members. In Psalm 109, the relationship in question is either a friendship, a familial tie, or both. The fact that the enemies of Ps 35:19 have hated "without justification" and those of Ps 38:20 despise "wrongfully" implies that the petitioner in these psalms is innocent, having done nothing untoward that might warrant the hatred of his foes.

A final idiom of rejection that might apply to friends is "to act as an adversary toward [*śṭn*]." Acting as an adversary (a *śāṭān*) toward another constitutes rejection according to Ps 38:21: "They who pay back that which is evil instead of what is good, / Acting as an adversary toward me . . ."[28] As I have discussed, disloyal friends and unfaithful relatives are mentioned together in Ps 38:12, and these are likely the people in question in v. 21 as well. Psalm 109:4 may refer to friends when it states that "in place of my love, they act as adversaries toward me," though it could just as easily refer to relatives or to both friends and relatives. Given that the friend might be accused in these texts of being an adversary, what might it mean to play such a role? Psalm 109:4–5 associates playing the adversary with malevolent treatment and hatred; in v. 20, the adversaries "speak that which is evil against" the complainant's "life," quite possibly in a legal setting. A legal context is also suggested by the sufferer's call for his enemy to be judged, with an adversary (*śāṭān*) standing to the foe's right, presumably to accuse him (Ps 109:6; cf. Zech 3:1).[29] In Ps 38:20, the enemies who "hate wrongfully" and "are many" may well be the adversaries of the following verse, likely acting in a judicial context.[30]

Biblical texts speak of both divine and human adversaries, locating them in judicial settings (e.g., Zech 3:1) and elsewhere (Num 22:22; 1 Sam 29:4; 1 Kgs 5:18). An adversary might challenge a decision, as Abishay does in 2 Sam 19:22 when he demands that David put Shimi to death for cursing David though David is reluctant to do so. In 1 Kgs 11:14, 23, and 25, Solomon's foreign enemies Hadad the Edomite and Rezon of Damascus are described as his adversaries. Divine adversaries such as "the Satan" accuse the innocent of crimes (Zech 3:1–2) or potential crimes (Job 1:11) in the context of the divine court, and Satan (without the definite article) incites humans to do wrong (1 Chr 21:1).[31] What seems clear from this evidence is that adversaries can be both human and divine and might level accusations in legal settings or challenge decisions or cause problems in extralegal contexts. To play the adversary in Psalms 38 and 109 seems to involve at least in part leveling hostile accusations—false according to the psalmists—likely in a legal setting that result in or follow a rupture of relations. Enemies—in this case, ex-friends—who accuse the petitioner in a legal setting are also mentioned in Ps 35:11–12, though they are not referred to by the term "adversary." Nonetheless, they are described as "violent" or "false" witnesses who stand up and "ask me about things I do not know," thereby paying back that which is evil instead of what is good according to the psalmist.[32]

In addition to rejection realized and communicated through both action and inaction, biblical texts speak of states of estrangement that might exist between parties, including friends, who formerly enjoyed good relations. According to some of these texts, such alienation is the result of offensive action taken by one party against the other or of inaction where supportive acts are expected. Job 19:13 speaks of the estrangement of what are likely friends ("those who know me"): "My friends are completely estranged from me [*'ak zārû mimmennî*]."[33] Here, the rupture in relations is likely the result of inaction rather than action, as suggested by the idioms used in the other cola of vv. 13–14: forgetting, standing at a distance, failing to be present. A comparable idiom is used of treaty violation in Isa 1:4, where a sinful Israel is said to have "become estranged" (*nāzōrû ʾāḥôr*) from Yhwh through the act of spurning him; similarly, "to be estranged from" (*nāzōrû min*) is used in Ezek 14:5 of Israel's alienation from Yhwh "because of their 'idols.'"[34] In Ps 69:9, the sufferer speaks of being estranged (*mûzār*) from his brothers, "an alien to the sons of my mother," evidently on account of bearing reproaches (shame) because of his "zeal" for Yhwh's "house."[35] In the case of Job 19:13, the estrangement of Job's friends as a result of their inaction is said to be caused directly by Yhwh; in the examples of sinful Israel in Isa 1:4 and Ezek 14:5, alienation from Yhwh is the Israelites' own fault, the result of their transgressions; in Ps 69:9, it would appear that the petitioner's separation from family members is the result of his own overzealousness for Yhwh. In each of these cases, a state of alienation is said to exist, the result of inaction where action is expected or of offending actions of some kind. As with many of the idioms of rejection discussed here, a state of estrangement might describe the relations of friends, those of family members, or those of treaty partners.

Disloyal Friends, Family Members, Treaty Partners, and Other Enemies: Similarities and Differences

A number of the offending actions ascribed to disloyal friends, family members, and treaty partners are shared in common with those attributed to enemies who were never friends or allies and who are not relatives. In contrast, other offensive acts or examples of inaction are unique to people who have previously enjoyed positive, and sometimes formal, relationships with one another (e.g., friendship, family ties, or treaty relations). One example of the former is the aggressive act of pursuit (*rdp*). In Ps 35:3, 4, the pursuers are evidently ex-friends, as they are in Job 19:21–22; in Ps 109:16, on the other hand, they might be friends, family members, or some combination of each, but whoever they are, they were bound to the sufferer they pursue by a relationship that required "loyalty" (*ḥesed*). Yet pursuit is also a characteristic behavior of enemies who were never friends or allies and are not relatives, as the examples of Exod 14:4, 8, and 9 and Josh 2:5, 7 demonstrate: In Exodus 14, Pharaoh pursues the fleeing Israelites to the Sea of Reeds; in Joshua 2, the king of Jericho orders his men to pursue the

Israelite spies who have been hidden away by Rahab. Other cases of aggressive action shared in common by disloyal friends, relatives, and treaty partners, on the one hand, and enemies who never enjoyed a positive previous relationship, on the other, include rejoicing over one's misfortune, abominating one, and acting as one's adversary. In contrast to these acts, a number of other offending behaviors are associated only with people who violate the expectations of a previously established relationship requiring loyalty such as a friendship, a family relationship, or an alliance. Examples of these include standing at a distance at a time of need instead of being present and helping out, paying back that which is evil instead of what is good, and hating instead of loving. In each of these cases, the loyal actions required by the preexisting relationship have not been manifested, and hostile action or inaction has been substituted for them, with damage or termination the result.

The issue of damage versus termination as the result of disloyalty is an interesting one, given the differences between voluntary associations (e.g., friendships and at least some treaty relationships) on the one hand and familial ties by blood on the other.[36] In the case of friendships and voluntary treaty relationships such as alliances of equals, offensive actions or inaction is often portrayed as sufficient cause to terminate the preexisting relationship, with the offender recast and treated as an enemy. The ex-friends of the psalms of individual complaint are not only referred to as "enemies without cause" and "those who hate me without justification" (e.g., Ps 35:19), but the sufferer calls for their shaming (Ps 35:4, 26) and curses them in a number of other ways, including calling for their military defeat, exile, and pursuit by the angel of Yhwh (Ps 35:4–8).[37] Such cursing is an act typical of an enemy, not a friend. Once done, it cannot easily be undone, and therefore any chance of reconciliation is likely eliminated.[38] Second Samuel 10:1–19 illustrates the transformation of a treaty partner into an enemy. The Ammonites, David's allies, intentionally shame David's emissaries when they come to the Ammonite court to offer comfort after the king of Ammon's death, thereby humiliating David himself. By doing so, the Ammonites have "made themselves odious [*b'š*] to David" (v. 6), and war follows, with David defeating the Ammonites and their allies, presumably recovering his honor by so doing. Once they have become "odious," it seems likely that there can be no reconciliation with the Ammonites, as the previous relationship between Israel and Ammon has evidently ceased to exist and has been replaced by one of mutual hostility and aggression. It is an interesting fact that biblical texts which speak of failed friendship or terminated alliances seldom if ever raise the issue of reconciliation between parties. The few military narratives that mention peace usually refer to a peace imposed by a victor on the vanquished, and these are generally not ex-treaty partners in any case. An example of this is 2 Sam 10:19. Here, the Aramean allies of the Ammonites are said to "make peace with Israel and serve them."[39] Proverbs 16:7 might be an example of reconciliation between ex-friends that is initiated by Yhwh, if indeed the man's enemies are his former friends, but unfortunately, the identity of the foes in this context is wholly unclear: "When Yhwh finds favor with a man's actions, / Even his enemies he causes to be at peace with him." Even if the foes who make peace are former friends, the mechanics of their reconciliation with the favored man are obscure. Do they apologize for their disloyal acts and ask for forgiveness, as a transgressing worshiper of a deity might?[40] In short, reconciliation between estranged friends is a subject about which we would like to know much more.[41]

What of disloyal blood relations? In contrast to evidence pertaining to voluntary associations such as friendships and alliances, there is little biblical data to suggest that such familial ties are subject to termination. A brother does not typically cease to be a brother, even if he has behaved dreadfully. A recalcitrant son who offends constantly is to be executed by the community, according to Deut 21:18–21, but he is not said to be disowned by his parents.[42] Close family members such as the brother, son, or daughter who incite one to worship gods other than Yhwh are to be killed, but nothing is said about ending their familial ties with one (Deut 13:7–12). Untrustworthy and disrespectful nuclear family members are said to be a man's enemies in Mic 7:5–6, but nothing in the text suggests that they cease to be family members. Nonetheless, several texts seem to conceive of the possibility of disowning blood relatives and bear witness to the existence of a rhetoric of termination. Among these texts is Deut 33:9, which speaks of Levi as

> One who says regarding his father and his mother,
> "I do not see them,"
> His brothers he does not recognize [Hi *nkr*],
> His sons he does not know [*yd'*].

This statement in Deut 33:9 is intended to emphasize the extreme zeal of the Levites, who, according to Exod 32:27–29, executed even immediate family members who had worshiped the golden calf, thereby earning their priestly status. Assuming that Deut 33:9 alludes to something analogous to the events narrated in Exod 32:27–29, as most scholars believe, the meaning of Deut 33:9 seems to be that the Levites ignored blood relationships—in effect, they disowned their kin—killing offenders irrespective of their status, as one is also commanded to do in Deut 13:7–12.[43] That this is understood to be a painful and exceptional act is underscored by the words of Exod 32:29, which states that each Levite won his commission "at the cost of his son and his brother." Thus, in contrast to texts such as Deut 13:7–12 and 21:18–21, which say nothing about the possibility of terminating blood relatives who are serious offenders, Deut 33:9 appears to take the opposite position and bear witness to a rhetoric of familial termination that seems also to be reflected in Isa 63:16. Here, Abraham is said not to "know us" (*yd‘*), and Israel is said not to "recognize us" (Hi *nkr*); in contrast, Yhwh is "our father" and "our redeemer." Though much about the passage remains obscure, the rhetoric of familial termination is not unlike that found in Deut 33:9.[44] In short, it would seem that according to a few sources, familial ties might be subject to termination under certain circumstances, in contrast to many other texts, which do not suggest this possibility. Whether relatives who are said to be enemies in the psalms of individual complaint have been disowned or not remains unclear.

Causes of Failed Friendships

Failed friendship, as mentioned, might be caused either by choices made by friends or by divine intervention and influence on the behavior of friends. A divine role in the failure of friendships is acknowledged explicitly in texts such as Ps 88:9, 19 and Job 19:13–14.[45] According to Ps 88:9, Yhwh has made the psalmist's friends be far from him, transforming him into an abomination in their eyes. In Job 19:13–14, it is both friends and family members whom Yhwh has alienated from Job. At the same time, other texts suggest that human agency brings about the decline and termination of friendships. Psalm 15:3 states that one who is worthy to dwell on Yhwh's holy mountain does not wrong a friend, among other behaviors to be avoided. This statement suggests implicitly that doing wrong to a friend is a choice, not unlike slandering with the tongue (v. 3) or, in contrast, doing that which is right (v. 2). If one chooses not to do wrong but to do what is right, one is deemed most worthy according to the psalmist, who seems not to consider the possibility that Yhwh could cause the offender to act maliciously for his own purposes. Psalm 35:12–13 also assumes that friends choose to act loyally or disloyally. Here, the petitioner insists that he behaved in a manner befitting a loyal friend when his friends were sick; in contrast, his friends have paid back that which is evil instead of what is good (v. 12), choosing, the text implies, to be disloyal. Nothing is said about Yhwh causing their hostile, disloyal acts; it would appear rather that they are the result of their own volition. In Ps 38:12, friends, like relatives, stand at a distance, evidently by their own choice, in contrast to the friends of Ps 88:9, 19 and the friends and family members of Job 19:13–14, who are kept away by Yhwh's intervention. Yhwh's acting to alienate friends and family members in Psalm 88 and Job 19 is one way in which he has increased the sufferer's misery. In Ps 88:15, it is said to be a manifestation of his rejection of the petitioner: "Why, Yhwh, do you spurn my life, / Hide your face from me?" Elsewhere in Psalm 88, Yhwh is said to have put the sufferer in a deep, dark pit; his wrath "lies" upon him; he afflicts him with his breakers (vv. 7–8); he is enraged at him (v. 17). Thus, the alienation of friends in a text such as Psalm 88 is one among a number of punishments meted out to the suffering petitioner by Yhwh, apparently as a penalty for unnamed offenses. According to Job 19:13–22, the loss of friends is one of several social deprivations suffered by Job, who is also bereft of family members (*qĕrôbay*), servants, nonfamilial household residents (*gērîm*), his wife, and his children, all because of Yhwh's intervention. In the case of Job, the reader is aware that the primary character is innocent, and his suffering, at least according to the book's prologue, is a test (see Job 1–2). Psalm 88, in contrast, suggests that the sufferer has committed offenses, though these are not mentioned explicitly, as they are in Ps 38:5–6 or Ps 69:6.

Cursing Disloyal Friends, Disloyal Friends as a Curse

The call for the shaming of unfaithful friends and relatives is a common motif, witnessed frequently in the psalms of individual complaint (e.g., Pss 35:4, 26; 40:15, 16; 69:7; 70:3, 4; 71:13, 24).[46] The humiliation of disloyal treaty partners is also a widespread theme in biblical texts (e.g., Deut 28:25, 48).[47] Shaming is but one of a number of curses that might be pronounced against foes, including ex-friends, treaty violators, disloyal relatives, or other enemies. In Ps 109:6–20, people who may be friends, family members, or some combination of relatives and friends are cursed by the sufferer for having spread "words of hatred" about him (v. 3) and for acting as an adversary instead of reciprocating "love" (v. 4), among various offenses:

> Let his days be few in number,
> Let another take his office (?).[48]
> Let his children become fatherless,
> His wife become a widow . . .
> Let his lender take everything he has,
> Let outsiders dispossess him of his property.
> Let him not have one who is loyal,[49]
> Let there not be one who shows favor to his orphans . . .
> Because he did not remember to act loyally ['śh ḥesed],
> But pursued a poor, afflicted man. (vv. 8–9, 11–12, 16)

Psalm 35 is similar in its denunciation of friends who pursue the petitioner and seek his life:

> Let them be driven back and be shamed,
> those who plan to harm me.
> Let them be like chaff before the wind,
> (with) the Angel of Yhwh thrusting (them) down.
> Let their way be darkness and slipperiness,
> (with) the Angel of Yhwh their pursuer.
> For without reason, they hid their net for me (in a) pit (?).[50] (vv. 4–7)

The curses enumerated by these two psalms are not unlike those found in suzerain-vassal treaties and include a short life, loss of position, surviving widow and children bereft and abandoned, loss of property and possessions to lenders, military defeat by enemies, exile, and shame.[51] Disloyal allies are also cursed in this manner, as Obad 1:15, 18 and Lam 4:21–22 demonstrate, as are enemies who share no previous positive relationship with the imprecating party. Obadiah 1:15 states that Edom's "recompense" will turn back upon its own head; 1:18 envisions the House of Jacob and the House of Joseph consuming the House of Esau (= Edom). In 1 Sam 17:43, Goliath curses (Pi *qll*) David before their individual combat. Jeremiah 50:2–3 envisions curses coming to fruition against the Babylonians who had destroyed Jerusalem, conquered Judah, and exiled its elite:

> Tell among the nations and report,
> Lift up a standard and make known,
> Do not conceal, but say:
> "Babylon is taken,

> Bel is put to shame,
> Marduk is dismayed.
> Her idols are humiliated,
> Her dung balls dismayed.
> For a people from the north has ascended against her,
> It will make her land into a devastation.
> There shall be no dweller in her,
> Human and animal shall depart."

Divine agents enforce imprecations, as any number of texts illustrate. In Ps 35:5–6, the sufferer calls for Yhwh's angel, acting as Yhwh's agent, to put curses into effect, harassing the sufferer's enemies. According to 1 Sam 17:43, Goliath curses David by his gods, indicating their expected role in the enforcement of the imprecation. And in Deut 28:20–24, Yhwh himself will unleash punishments against the Israelites if they violate the covenant with him. Gods serving as enforcers of treaty stipulations is in fact a common motif in treaties themselves, as the Sefire inscriptions and Esarhaddon's Vassal Treaty well illustrate.[52]

Even though disloyal friends and family members are cursed for their offenses in texts such as Psalms 35 and 109, not unlike unfaithful treaty partners or other enemies in other texts, a call for enmity between friends or between family members is exceedingly rare in curse formulae themselves. The many covenant imprecations enumerated in Leviticus 26 and Deuteronomy 28, as well as curses evidenced in other biblical and nonbiblical texts, do not usually include strife between friends or between relatives, or the loss of friends and the alienation of family members, in contrast to such typical curses as loss or lack of progeny,[53] ill health,[54] famine and crop failure,[55] military defeat,[56] exile,[57] disability,[58] lack of burial,[59] loss of name,[60] and lack of rest in the afterlife.[61] An exception to this pattern is Psalm 109, whose litany of curses includes the following: "Let him not have one who is loyal, / Let there not be one who shows favor to his orphans" (v. 12). "One who is loyal" is someone obligated to practice loyalty (ḥesed), most likely a friend or a relative in the context of Psalm 109.[62] The second colon of the verse suggests that at least part of what constitutes loyalty is care for the dead man's surviving children.[63] That the enemy who is being cursed should not have one who is "loyal" therefore means that he should lack friends and relatives who are willing to fulfill their obligations to him after he has died. Aside from taking care of his children, such obligations might also include burial, mourning, and—for family members specifically—ancestral rites, among other possibilities.⁶⁴ The curse of lacking "one who is loyal" is particularly apt in the context of Psalm 109, given the disloyalty of the sufferer's foe ("He did not remember to act loyally"; v. 16).

Although conflict between friends or relatives is not typically mentioned in biblical or other curse formulae, it is sometimes presented in texts as emblematic of social decline and even collapse. Examples of this include Mic 7:5–6 and the Marduk and Shulgi prophecies from Babylon. In Mic 7:5–6, social decline is exemplified by friends, spouse, son, daughter, and daughter-in-law who act not as intimates should, but as enemies do: Friends are not to be trusted; a man must watch what he says to his spouse; a son treats his father as if he were a fool; and a daughter defies her mother, a daughter-in-law her mother-in-law. In short, intimates behave in ways that are opposed to societal norms. The Marduk Prophecy and the Shulgi Prophecy both speak of the collapse of society, in the first case as a result of Marduk's departure to Elam, in the second because of factors now unclear due to the text's state of preservation. The Marduk Prophecy uses the following image of strife to evoke social disintegration: "Brother consumes his brother, friend strikes down his friend with a weapon."⁶⁵ The Shulgi Prophecy is similar: "Companion fells his companion with a weapon, friend kills his friend with a sword."⁶⁶ Violence between friends and between family members is paired with other symptoms of social degeneration, including piling up unburied bodies, illness, injustice, and disrupted travel in the Marduk Prophecy and the selling of children and abandonment of spouses in the Shulgi Prophecy. Some of these acts or conditions are typical of curses (e.g., lack of burial, illness); some, such as loss of loyal friends, are not.

Just as strife between friends or between family members is rarely encountered as a curse, so gaining and retaining friends and having loyal relatives are not typical of the content of blessings, in contrast to successful procreation,⁶⁷ abundant food and livestock,⁶⁸ prayers received,⁶⁹ a long life,⁷⁰ and victory over enemies.⁷¹ When Solomon petitions Yhwh, he asks that his prayers be heeded, that his progeny reign forever, that the people's sin be pardoned if they repent, that there be no famine or drought or plague or exile for the people if they return to Yhwh, that the legitimate supplications of individuals be answered, and that Yhwh bring military victory to his people (1 Kgs 8:23–53). But he says nothing about securing loyal friends and allies and having faithful relatives. When Tiglath-Pileser III petitions the gods in exchange for the monumental basalt bulls that he erects for them at Hadattu, he asks for the preservation of his life and prolonging of his reign, the well-being of his progeny, successful harvest, and avoidance of illness, but not for loyal friends, allies, or family members.[72] The blessings of Deut 28:1–14, for their part, are similar, promising obedient Israelites military victory over enemies, prosperity, and other goods, but these do not include loyal friends, allies, and relatives.

Why is it that having loyal friends and relatives generally goes unmentioned in blessing formulae, and the loss of friends and the alienation of family members is rarely formulated as a curse? This question is especially apt, given texts, both biblical and cuneiform, that speak of conflict between friends and between family members as emblematic of social decline and even collapse, along with developments frequently associated with the content of curses (e.g., lack of burial, illness). It is impossible to answer this question with any confidence, though it may be that the loss of loyal friends and family members was simply thought to be a less profound punishment than lack of progeny, famine, illness, exile, and other characteristic curses. Similarly, it is possible that retaining loyal friends and family members was thought to contribute less to a blessed state than would having abundant food, securing an heir, experiencing good health, and living a long life, which are typical blessings. But here I speculate.

Unfaithful Friend and Disloyal Relative in the Psalms of Individual Complaint

The disloyal friend makes his appearance in more than a few biblical texts. As mentioned, he is found in the psalms of individual complaint, in prophetic texts such as Jeremiah and Micah, and in wisdom materials such as the book of Job and Proverbs.[73] He is not unlike the unfaithful family member, a surprisingly common presence throughout the biblical anthology. The disloyal friend and his counterpart, the treacherous relative, are recurring characters in the psalms of individual complaint, and so we might refer to them as constituting topoi in these texts. We might also ask how their presence functions to promote the psalmist's purpose: persuading the deity to intervene on his behalf.[74] Complainants accuse friends and family members of a variety of offenses that constitute disloyalty: they tell lies about or to the sufferer (Pss 28:3; 35:20; 38:13, 20; 62:5), stand at a distance from him in his time of need (Pss 38:12; 88:9), hate him (Pss 35:19; 38:20; 109:5), pay back that which is evil instead of what is good (Pss 35:12; 38:21; 109:5), bear false witness against him (Ps 35:11), rejoice over his misfortune

(Pss 35:15, 19, 24, 26; 38:17), and pursue him and even seek his life (Pss 35:3–4; 38:13; 109:16), among other unacceptable actions and manifestations of inaction. They become, in effect, the sufferer's foes and are called "enemies" on any number of occasions, as I have discussed. In a fascinating twist, Yhwh is sometimes accused implicitly of abandoning the supplicant in his time of need, as Ps 35:17 suggests: "My Lord, how long will you see? / Save my life . . . !"[75] Though Yhwh is said to be unresponsive to and disengaged from the sufferer, not unlike the alienated friends and relatives in a text such as Ps 38:12, in the psalms of individual complaint there is always hope that Yhwh will change his stance and intervene when petitioned to do so, in contrast to disloyal friends and family members, who are presented as incorrigible.

How does the disloyalty of friends and relatives function to help secure Yhwh's saving intervention? That friends and family members are said to treat the complainant in a hostile or indifferent manner adds to his suffering and brings his isolation and vulnerability into relief, as do other images underscoring the petitioner's defenselessness and solitude: "As for me, I was like a deaf person, unable to hear, / Like a mute person, who could not open his mouth" (Ps 38:14).[76] In Ps 109:16, the sufferer refers to himself as "afflicted and poor"; in Ps 88:5, he is "like a man without strength"; in Ps 35:10, he describes himself as "afflicted" and "poor," vulnerable to "his plunderer"; in Ps 70:6 he is "afflicted and poor." In some of the psalms of individual complaint, petitioners refer indirectly to their embrace of petitionary mourning rites, likely intended to attract the attention of the deity to their plight and to communicate repentance in cases where the sufferer acknowledges transgressions (e.g., Pss 38:5–6, 19; 69:6). Psalm 109:24 speaks of the supplicant's fasting: "My knees stumble from fasting, / My flesh is lean, without fat"; in Ps 71:21, the petitioner expresses confidence that Yhwh will comfort him, suggesting that he is in a state of mourning; Ps 69:21 is similar, mentioning expected comforters whom the psalmist does not find. Like the embrace of petitionary mourning rites, the supplicant's isolation, vulnerability, and suffering, which are to a large degree the result of his abandonment and even oppression by family members and friends in a number of these psalms, should function—at least in the mind of the petitioner—to attract Yhwh's attention and interest and thereby secure his deliverance of the complainant. According to Ps 35:22, Yhwh should intervene precisely because he has witnessed the hostile acts of the sufferer's ex-friends: "You have seen, Yhwh, do not be silent, / My Lord, do not be far from me!" Psalm 109:21–22 is similar, stating that Yhwh should deliver the petitioner "for [*kî*] afflicted and poor am I, / My heart within is wounded."

Yet the supplicant of the psalms of individual complaint is not always alone in his suffering. In Ps 35:27, loyal friends are mentioned, and they are called upon to praise Yhwh and rejoice at the petitioner's acquittal:

> Let them cry out joyfully and rejoice,
> Those who delight in my vindication,
> Let them say always,
> "Yhwh who delights in the well-being of his servant is great."

These loyal friends serve as a counterpoint to the faithless friends, who are mentioned in v. 26:

> Let them be ashamed and humiliated,
> Those who rejoice in my adversity,
> Let them be dressed in shame and disgrace.

If anything, the mention of steadfast friends brings the disloyalty of the faithless friends into greater relief, suggesting implicitly that their faithlessness is without a basis, as the psalmist asserts directly elsewhere (e.g., in v. 19, where enemies are referred to as "those who hate me without justification" and "enemies without cause"). Nonetheless, the presence of loyal friends in Psalm 35 also functions to lessen the isolation of the petitioner, which is obviously more profound if he has no supporters, as appears to be the case in other psalms of individual complaint.

Conclusion

In this chapter, I have spoken at some length about the hostile behaviors of friends toward friends—both their specific actions and examples of their inaction in contexts where action is expected—that constitute and communicate rejection. I have also examined the idioms used by our texts to describe these antagonistic behaviors. Examples of inaction when active intervention is expected include standing at a distance or being far from a friend in need, or forgetting about that friend; examples of active, even aggressive behaviors toward a friend that realize and signal rejection include deceiving the friend, spreading lies about him, abominating him, pursuing him with an intent to harm him, paying back that which is evil instead of what is good, and rejoicing over his misfortune and hating him. Several other idioms, such as acting as an adversary and not practicing loyalty (*ḥesed*), may also be used of friends who reject friends, though the contexts in which these idioms occur as easily suggest that the actions are those of family members or a mixed body of relatives and friends. All of these hostile behaviors, whether examples of inaction or action, result in estrangement between friends.

Many of the behaviors understood by our texts to constitute rejection of the friend are the same as those said to characterize disloyal relatives, treaty partners, or both. Such people might be described as standing at a distance, being far from, forgetting about (treaty partners), or paying back that which is evil instead of what is good (family members). All of these acts, and others I have discussed, such as hating instead of loving and not practicing loyalty, assume a preexisting set of obligations that have not been fulfilled, and this is why these particular behaviors are not associated with enemies who were never friends or treaty partners and are not family members.[77] Other acts, in contrast, might characterize such enemies as well as disloyal family members, treaty partners, and friends. These include rejoicing over someone's misfortune, pursuing with an intent to do harm, abominating, and acting as an adversary. These acts do not necessarily presume previous ties between the parties, in contrast to behaviors that assume a bond such as friendship, family status, or a treaty relationship.

Although many of the behaviors that constitute rejection are ascribed not only to disloyal friends, but also to unfaithful treaty partners and family members, the results of hostile actions and examples of inaction that manifest disloyalty may differ, depending on the status of the disloyal person in question. If the relationship is one of voluntary association (e.g., friendship or alliance), texts frequently portray the bond as broken, with the offender recast as an enemy and evidently no possibility of reconciliation. But if the tie is familial, the evidence is more ambiguous: some texts seem to suggest that such a relationship very likely survives—at least technically—even the worst offenses, while a few others suggest the possibility of the termination of family members.

Texts suggest that failed friendship might be caused by the choices made by friends themselves or by Yhwh's decision to intervene in order to bring about suffering. Some texts describe friends who choose to keep their distance at a time of trouble (e.g., Ps 35:12–13), while other passages are clear that friends are kept away by Yhwh (e.g., Ps 88:9, 19). Some passages speak of friends who forget their friends or have become estranged from them because Yhwh has caused them to do so (Job 19:13, 14), while other texts speak of friends who choose to bear false witness (Ps 35:11) or rejoice over a friend's misfortune (Ps 35:15). Hostile acts of friends due to Yhwh's intervention may be intended to punish people who are understood to be offenders (e.g., Ps 88) or innocent people who must be made to suffer for reasons other than transgressions (e.g., Job). In Psalm 88, the supplicant believes himself to be rejected by Yhwh and the target of his wrath (vv. 15, 17). Job, for his part, suffers many losses, including the loss of his friends, though he is innocent, a fact emphasized by the book's prologue.

Like other enemies, disloyal friends and family members might be cursed (e.g., Pss 35:4–7; 109:6–20), yet to have a faithless friend or relative is itself rarely mentioned as a curse, although conflict between friends and relatives is sometimes presented as emblematic of social decline or collapse. Psalm 109:12 is the exception. Here, the psalmist who curses his enemy asks that he should have no one who fulfills obligations of loyalty (*mōšēk ḥesed*, lit. "one who maintains loyalty").[78] This is most likely a friend or relative in the context of Psalm 109, which does not seem to concern itself with treaty partners. One manifestation of loyalty, according to this verse, is care for a dead man's orphans. Just as having disloyal friends and relatives is rarely attested as a curse, to have a faithful friend or family member generally goes unmentioned in blessing formulae. The reasons that friends and relatives are rarely invoked in curses or blessings are unclear, though it may be that having disloyal friends and family members was thought to be less of a privation than famine, childlessness, or exile and that having loyal friends and relatives less of a boon than fertility, abundant food, and long life.

Disloyal friends or family members, recurring characters of the psalms of individual complaint, likely function to help secure Yhwh's saving intervention on behalf of the suffering complainant. Their hostility increases his suffering and underscores his isolation and vulnerability; like the psalmist's embrace of petitionary mourning rites, the presence of disloyal friends and relatives should help, at least according to the psalmist, to attract Yhwh's interest and secure his intervention. Yhwh has witnessed the supplicant's suffering, including how the psalmist's ex-friends and hostile family members have treated him. Psalm 35 also mentions loyal friends, who serve as a counterpoint to disloyal friends, bringing the faithlessness of the latter into greater relief and suggesting implicitly that their disloyalty is groundless, as the petitioner himself claims (e.g., Ps 35:19). Nevertheless, the mention of loyal friends diminishes the isolation and vulnerability of the petitioner of Psalm 35.

3 Friendship in Narrative

Friendship as it is represented in prose narrative has received more attention from specialists than other aspects of biblical friendship, most likely because the characters of narrative are often more fully realized than the anonymous friends mentioned in the psalms of individual complaint, Proverbs and Job, and prophetic texts.[1] The friends who appear in narratives are usually named, unlike those in other texts. Their decisions and actions—good and bad—when they are portrayed, contribute to plot development. Their motivations might not always be clear and might sometimes be complex; they might express a range of emotions; they might ask questions; they might offer and ask for commitment; they might fulfill obligations; they might betray trust. Certain friendships represented in prose narrative might have some basis in the relationships of historical personages (e.g., David and Jonathan); others are more likely literary creations in their entirety, without any such foundation (e.g., Ruth and Naomi, Job and his three friends).[2] In either case, the biblical text provides us with narrative portraits of friends and their friendships, which lend themselves readily to literary analysis. Though Jonathan and David and Ruth and Naomi have attracted by far the most interest from commentators, and will be of central concern to me as well, I will also discuss in this chapter other friendships represented in biblical narrative. These include Job and his three comforters, Jephthah's daughter and her companions, and Amnon and Jonadab (2 Sam 13). I begin with Ruth and Naomi.

Ruth and Naomi

I understand the book of Ruth as a narrative about a friendship between two widows of different generations and different national backgrounds who share a connection to the family of their dead husbands and, through that connection, help one another to survive, prosper, and remain together in the same community.[3] Why characterize their bond as a friendship? Although the technical vocabulary of friendship is mainly lacking in the narrative and Ruth and Naomi are identified as mother-in-law and daughter-in-law throughout the text, the voluntary nature of their association after the deaths of their respective husbands is brought into relief in the novella's first chapter and continues to move the plot forward as the story develops.[4] In the later chapters, one can speak of mutual affection and elements of behavioral parity characterizing their new, voluntary relationship (e.g., mutual trust, love, loyalty, and good will, features of friendship that I have discussed). Though ultimately their link by marriage to Elimelek's clan will provide the two of them with security and prosperity through the person of Boaz and the child Ruth bears him, their enduring choice of one another, their mutual affection, and their acts of reciprocity are what allow them to achieve this end.

Naomi, who left Judah with her husband and two sons on account of a famine, settles in Moab, a neighboring kingdom. After her husband Elimelek dies, her sons Mahlon and Kilyon marry Moabite women, Ruth and Orpa. Then Mahlon and Kilyon die without issue, leaving the three women on their own, as widows.[5] When the famine in Judah ends, Naomi begins the trek back to Bethlehem, with her two daughters-in-law accompanying her. After Naomi urges them both to return to their natal houses in Moab, Orpa agrees to go, but Ruth refuses, "clinging" (*dbq*) to Naomi (1:14). That Ruth's "clinging" is a choice rather than the fulfillment of an expectation is made clear by Naomi's speech in 1:8–9: "'Go, return each woman to her mother's house! May Yhwh be loyal to you [*'āsâ ḥesed*] as you have been with the dead and with me! May Yhwh grant to you that you may find a place of repose, each in the house of her husband.'[6] Then she kissed them and they lifted up their voices and wept." That the two daughters-in-law have fulfilled every familial expectation with respect both to their husbands and to Naomi and are therefore free to go their own way with Naomi's approbation is made clear by Naomi's statement that Ruth and Orpa have been loyal both to Mahlon and Kilyon and to her. Had they failed to be loyal in any way, had they not done all that might be expected of them, the author would not have had Naomi make such a statement. In short, leaving Naomi to find new husbands is presented as a sensible choice that would bring no disrepute upon either Ruth or Orpa.[7] When the women still refuse to leave her and insist on returning to Judah with her (1:10), Naomi presses them in 1:11: "Why should you go with me? Do I still have sons in my body that they might become your husbands?" Naomi's statement seems to suggest the possibility that other sons could play the Levir role that living brothers might potentially play for their dead brothers without issue, thereby providing each of the dead with an heir. Yet, as a number of scholars have noted, such living brothers, even if they existed, would not be fathered by the same man and therefore would not be obligated to play the Levir as it is understood in other biblical texts. Therefore, the presuppositions about the Levir role reflected in Naomi's statement must be different from those of texts such as Deut 25:5–10, Genesis 38, and even Ruth 4:5, 10. At all events, Naomi's statement underscores Ruth's and Orpa's lack of further obligation to their dead husbands and to Naomi.[8] Thus, whatever association Ruth continues to maintain with Naomi and the family of her dead husband Mahlon is completely voluntary in nature, fulfilling no familial expectations. In a word, the relationship of Ruth and Naomi begins anew as a bond of choice. Ruth insists on accompanying Naomi back to Bethlehem, and Naomi chooses to accept Ruth's decision to do so: "When she saw that she was determined to go with her, she stopped speaking to her, and the two of them went until they came to Bethlehem" (1:18–19). Given that the new bond between Ruth and Naomi is both voluntary and reciprocal in nature and that familial obligations do not constitute it, I analyze it as a friendship.

Ruth refuses to leave Naomi, even after Orpa has done so and even when urged by Naomi once again to do so (1:15). Replying to Naomi's urgings, Ruth says: "Don't press me to leave you ... for wherever you go, I will go, and wherever you spend the night, I will spend the night; your people shall be my people, and your god my god. Where you die, I will die and there I will be buried.[9] May Yhwh do thus to me, and more also, if (even) death separates me from you" (1:16–18).[10] This remarkable declaration is rich with meaning. It consists of a series of separate statements that commit Ruth to remain with Naomi for life and even beyond, one of which is a declaration formulated in the style of an adoption that embraces Naomi's people and her god, and another an oath of loyalty to Naomi sworn by Yhwh.

64   Friendship in Narrative

Ruth is clearly determined to remain with Naomi for the rest of her life and uses declarations of intent, including an adoption-like declaration as well as oath-taking, to commit herself unalterably to this course of action.

Adoption formulae state that which will be once the adoption is realized.[11] In Gen 48:5, Jacob adopts his grandsons Ephraim and Manasseh by saying to Joseph: "As for your two sons . . . they shall be mine [*lî hēm*]."[12] In 2 Sam 7:14, Yhwh says the following of David: "I shall become his father and he shall become my son." In Jer 31:33, Yhwh states regarding Israel: "I shall become their god and they shall become my people."[13] Hosea 2:25 has Yhwh say, "You are my people [*'ammî 'attâ*]," and Israel say, "(You are/Yhwh is) my god."[14] Such formulae function to make real new relationships just as termination formulae end existing relationships.[15] Ruth's statement that Naomi's people shall be her people and Naomi's god her god is adoption-like in its structure and the fact that it is cast as a formal declaration.[16] For Ruth to commit herself to Naomi's god while apparently still in Moabite territory is striking, though her commitment is not ultimately surprising given that the two of them are going to settle in Bethlehem, where Yhwh is worshiped as the national god of Judah.[17] Ruth's embrace of Naomi's people is also noteworthy, given that the text seems to assume that Ruth and Orpa have already left their natal people by marrying Israelite resident aliens in Moab.[18] It may be that the formal embrace of Naomi's people is intended to underscore the voluntary nature of Ruth's and Naomi's continuing association because Ruth's husband Mahlon is dead and Ruth owes nothing further to her family by marriage, including her mother-in-law. Like Orpa, she is free to go back to her natal people with no disapprobation whatsoever, but she chooses not to do so.[19]

Ruth's oath by Yhwh is the third prominent feature of her speech in 1:16–18.[20] In her oath, Ruth states that even death will not separate her from Naomi. This pledge is directly related to that which precedes it: Ruth's statement that wherever Naomi dies, she will die and be interred. Both the oath and Ruth's preceding statement suggest that she intends to be buried with Naomi, presumably in the same tomb. Would this be possible for two widows related only by marriage? Though interment of married women who predecease their husbands is represented as occurring in the tomb of the husband's family (e.g., Gen 49:31), there is little or no data pertaining directly to the burial of widows. There is, however, indirect evidence that suggests the possibility either of burial in the tomb of the husband's family or of interment with the widow's natal family, depending on circumstances.[21] Ruth can speak of death and burial as she does because she seems to assume the possibility of burial in her husband's and father-in-law's family tomb. Naomi and Ruth will both be buried in the tomb of the family of their husbands, as wives normally would be, and that is how they can remain together even after death. It would not be possible otherwise, as the locus of burial is determined by familial ties, and their natal families—and nations of origin—differ.[22]

That ties with a dead husband's family are assumed to continue for the widow if she desires it is what allows Ruth to make her dramatic promise and the plot of the novella to develop as it does.[23] Naomi and Ruth go to Bethlehem and receive support from Boaz, a kinsman of their husbands. The continuing nature of the women's ties to the clan of Elimelek, Naomi's dead husband, is best illustrated by 2:20, where Boaz is described by Naomi as "*our* relative" (*qārôb lānû*) and "one of *our* redeemers" (*miggō'ălēnû*). This rhetoric suggests not only the absorption of the women into the clan of their husbands, just as one would expect, but also its continuing validity for them as widows.[24] Their husbands' agnate is their relative; their husbands' kinsmen on the father's side who may serve as redeemers are theirs as much as their husbands'.[25] That the narrative subtly brings into relief this dimension of the women's relationship is not insignificant: It is their tie to the family of their dead husbands that will allow them not only to remain together in the same community, but also to help one another and ultimately to prosper through Ruth's marriage to Boaz. When Ruth speaks of even death not separating her from Naomi, it is more than simply a declaration about the degree of her commitment to Naomi; it is a statement that alludes subtly to their shared family by marriage, and what it can do for them once they return to Bethlehem.

As mentioned, Ruth and Naomi are both widows, women without a male decision-maker, protector, or provider. Their husbands are deceased; Naomi has no living children and Ruth none living or dead; Ruth's father-in-law Elimelek is dead and so, presumably, is Elimelek's father, Naomi's father-in-law. Although the word "widow" does not occur anywhere in the novella, it is their status as widows that allows them to choose to stay together and to support one another both materially and otherwise as they seek to move forward in their lives. In short, it allows for their friendship. That they are not under the authority of a male relative means that they make their own decisions, including the choice to remain together when this is neither required nor expected; that they have no male provider means that they must provide for themselves, something they attempt to do through reciprocal acts of initiative; that they have no male protector underscores their vulnerability and leads initially to Boaz's emergence in the role of protector and ultimately husband to Ruth. Though still formally mother-in-law and daughter-in-law, the two women nonetheless share the status of widow, and the new, voluntary association that they have both embraced features manifestations of mutual affection and behavioral parity, characteristics of friendship in other biblical texts. Ruth helps Naomi, Naomi helps Ruth: Ruth takes the initiative to get food for the two of them (2:2) and succeeds (2:17–19; 3:17); Naomi acts to get Ruth a husband (3:1–4), something that would make her happy (3:1), benefit both of them materially, and provide them both with security (4:14–15). Naomi advises Ruth regarding her work in the fields (2:22) and her developing relationship with Boaz (3:18); Ruth follows her advice (2:23; 3:6) and goes beyond it, seeking success in her dealings with Boaz (3:9). Though the text does not say so in as many words, Ruth and Naomi share a bond of mutual affection; they seek one another's welfare consistently, and each pays back that which is good in exchange for the good done by the other. In short, they behave toward one another as ideal male friends ought to behave according to texts such as Pss 35:12–14; 88:19; Job 19:19; and Prov 17:17.[26]

The verb "to cling to" (*dābaq bĕ-*) occurs in 1:14, where it is said that Ruth "clung to" Naomi when Orpa left Naomi to return to her people and her god(s). The same verb occurs three more times in the book with reference to Ruth's gleaning in Boaz's field. In 2:8, Boaz instructs Ruth to "cling to" (*dābaq 'im*) his girls who are harvesting grain, meaning to glean closely behind them as they work; in 2:21, Ruth relates Boaz's directions to Naomi; and in 2:23, she is said to follow them (*dābaq bĕ-*). Ruth's "clinging" to Boaz's female reapers provides her with security out in the field, as Boaz intends (2:9) and as Naomi notes with approbation (2:22); it also provides her with sustenance (2:9). Yet why, through the repeated use of the verb "to cling to," does the author so obviously establish a link between Ruth's ongoing and permanent voluntary affiliation with Naomi, an affiliation characterized by emotional engagement and loyalty, and her temporary association with Boaz's harvesters, which serves utilitarian purposes?[27] Perhaps the use of the verb "to cling to" in both 1:14 on the one hand and 2:8, 21, and 23 on the other is intended to bring into relief the common physical locus implicit in the verb as well as the concrete benefits such a shared location might bestow. Just as Ruth "clings" by choice to Naomi—which means that she will not be separated from her physically, and, by implication, that the two women will support one another and profit from so doing—so Ruth "clings" physically to Boaz's harvesters for her protection and sustenance.

But Ruth's loyal clinging to Naomi also brings to mind the clinging of the exceptional male friend to his friend in Prov 18:24. In that verse, this friend distinguishes himself from other friends. While there are friends "for friendly exchanges," he "clings more closely than a brother." Clinging is clearly an activity of both intimate friends and close relatives (e.g., brothers) according to Prov 18:24, and in that context, it may suggest a combination of loyalty, close emotional bonding, and physical proximity. The verb "to cling to" in Ruth 1:14 may be similarly intended to evoke the fidelity, proximity, and emotional engagement of both the ideal relative and the ideal friend, roles that Ruth combines in herself at this turning point in the story. Furthermore, the verb "to cling to" may be intended to function as a bridge between an in-law relationship that has been characterized by Ruth's exceptional loyalty, something Naomi points out (1:8), and a new, voluntary bond, realized by an exceptional declaration of commitment on Ruth's part. In short, "to cling to" in 1:14 may suggest continuity of commitment as the relationship between Ruth and Naomi evolves from one in which familial obligation was the primary component to one in which choice is front and center, given that clinging is characteristic of both the idealized family member and the exceptional friend according to Prov 18:24.[28]

If Naomi and Ruth have a new, voluntary, and reciprocal relationship not shaped by familial expectations, why does the author continue to use familial language in the narrative? Posed differently, what purpose does it serve the author to refer frequently to Naomi as Ruth's mother-in-law and Ruth as Naomi's daughter-in-law and to have characters in the story refer to them in this manner? Other terms of identification are also used along with these identifiers. At several points, Naomi refers to Ruth as "my daughter," as does Boaz (2:2, 8, 22; 3:1, 10, 11, 16, 18), and Ruth is frequently called "the Moabite woman" by the narrator and by characters in the story (e.g., 1:22; 2:2, 21; 4:5, 10). It is best to consider all such terms at once as we strive to make sense of them in context. I begin with "my daughter." Besides functioning as a term of endearment for both Naomi and Boaz, the use of "my daughter" by both Naomi and Boaz suggests that Ruth is younger, a member of the generation that follows theirs.[29] That Boaz is older than Ruth is made clear by his statement in 3:10 commending her for "not going after young men, either poor or rich"; that Naomi belongs to the generation preceding Ruth's is obvious. The use of "mother-in-law" and "daughter-in-law" in the narrative may also be understood as an indicator of age difference, though I believe there is more intended by the author's employment of this pair of terms. Though Ruth and Naomi have a new relationship characterized by choice, mutual affection, and behavioral parity, their common tie to the family of Elimelek is key to the development of the novella's plot and their ultimate survival and prospering in the same community. Thus, the author's perpetuation of the in-law terminology may be intended to underscore the continuing importance of the two women's tie to the family of their dead husbands and to foreshadow future positive developments for them both in the context of that family. It seems to me less likely that terms such as "daughter-in-law," "mother-in-law," and "daughter" are intended to highlight status differences between Ruth and Naomi as some have argued. Whatever status differences remain after the commencement of their new bond are muted to a large degree by the narrative's emphasis on volition and reciprocity.[30] Finally, the emphasis on Ruth's Moabite origin may bring into relief the degree to which she has sacrificed in order to "cling" to Naomi and accompany her to Bethlehem. As Boaz states with approbation, she has "abandoned" (*'āzab*) her father, her mother, and her birthplace to "go to" (*hālak 'el*) a people she had not known previously (2:11).[31] Ruth's voluntary presence in Judah as an alien also brings her lower status than she would have at home, as her response to Boaz's generosity in 2:10 suggests: "Why have I found favor in your sight that you recognize me, even though I am a foreigner?" Finally, Ruth's Moabite origin might also serve anti-xenophobic purposes, as many scholars have argued, though our ignorance regarding the date and context for the novella's composition cautions against putting too much weight on such a speculation.[32]

Ruth's flawlessness as a friend and a person deserves comment, as does Naomi's more multifaceted and complex character. Although Ruth is more fully drawn than the unnamed loyal friends of a text such as Psalm 35 who delight in the psalmist's vindication, her perfect loyalty as wife, daughter-in-law, and friend; her enthusiastic commitment to Naomi; her generosity to Naomi and Boaz; and her willingness to sacrifice for Naomi's sake reveal a character without complexity, one completely lacking in ambivalence, selfish motivations, bad moods, jealousy, self-pity, self-doubt, and actions and words that are in any way incongruent. According to Boaz, everyone in the community knows that Ruth is an ideal woman ("a woman of strength," 3:11).[33] More complex and interesting as a character is Naomi, who accedes to Ruth's decision to accompany her to Judah, though without enthusiasm. Upon arriving in Bethlehem, Naomi complains to the women of the town about how Yhwh has made her suffer, claiming that "Yhwh has brought me back empty," even though she has with her a most loyal and caring friend in Ruth. Although Naomi comes across as worn down and unappreciative of what is good in her life at the end of chapter 1, she is enlivened beginning in chapter 2, expressing enthusiasm for Ruth's accomplishments in the field (2:18–19, 20), offering advice to Ruth regarding her safety (2:22), and finally taking the initiative in 3:1–4, coming up with a plan to secure Boaz as Ruth's husband.[34] In so doing, she reciprocates Ruth's efforts on her behalf and emerges as a genuine friend to Ruth. Even here, however, Naomi stands to benefit from Ruth's marriage, eventually gaining a grandson who will lift her spirits and provide for her in old age (4:15), though her stated motivation in 3:1 is Ruth's happiness alone.[35] In a word, while growing as a character, Naomi retains her complexity; in contrast, Ruth remains fairly consistent and predictable.[36] Boaz, too, is a more complex character than is Ruth, given the self-doubt he expresses when he thanks Ruth for choosing him rather than a younger man (3:10).[37]

Jonathan and David

Several narratives embedded in the larger text of 1 Samuel concern the relationship of Jonathan and David.[38] Most prominent among these are 1 Sam 18:1–4; 19:1–7; 20:1–21:1; and 23:14–18.[39] In three of the four texts, the relationship is clearly cast as a covenant, though the nature of the treaty differs from text to text, with David in the subordinate role in 20:1–10, 18–22, 24–41, and 21:1; Jonathan the vassal in 20:11–17, 23, 42, and 23:14–18; and a treaty of unclear nature assumed in 18:1–4.[40] The fourth text, 19:1–7, may also suggest a treaty relationship of some kind between David and Jonathan, though this is not entirely clear. In addition to the presence of treaty language, the relationship is also one of brothers-in-law according to the narrative in 18:27: David marries Saul's daughter Michal at Saul's invitation.[41] Although the word *rēaʿ* with the meaning "friend" and other terms for "friend" are not used of Jonathan and/or David in the Jonathan-David narratives, the relationship of David and Jonathan is almost universally described as a friendship.[42] Given the prominence of treaty idioms in the narrative, it is fair to ask whether such a designation is justified. Are David and Jonathan friends who have formalized their relationship through the idiom of treaty-making? Or are they simply bound by a formal, political covenant and nothing more? I argue that Jonathan and David are justifiably characterized as friends in at least some of the narratives that describe their relationship. Though it might be possible to explain acts of loyalty such as Jonathan's defense of David before Saul (19:4–5) as the fulfillment of treaty obligations, passages that speak of or represent an emotional bond between David and Jonathan suggest that there is more to their relationship than simply a covenant tie. And the fact that their bond is represented as superseding Jonathan's relationship with his father in several of the narratives is also reason to think that for the authors of these texts, a strong, personal commitment is in view rather than simply a treaty relationship.[43]

The text of 1 Sam 18:1–4 states that the "self" or "life" (*nepeš*) of Jonathan was "bound" to the "self" or "life" of David; that Jonathan "loved him as himself"; that Jonathan and David cut a covenant "when" or "because he loved him as himself"; and that Jonathan removed his garment and gave it to David, along with his weapons and other personal items.[44] Like other narratives that tell of the relationship between David and Jonathan, this passage is imbued with the idiom of covenant, mentioning both that Jonathan and David cut a covenant (*kārat bĕrît*) and that Jonathan loved David as himself, the latter an idiom used in treaty settings to communicate loyalty to the treaty partner. As is often pointed out, Esarhaddon requires his vassals to swear as follows: "[You swear] that you will love Ashurbanipal, the crown-prince, son of Esarhaddon, king of Assyria, your lord as [you do] yourselves."[45] In other words, the vassals bind themselves by oath to be loyal to their overlord's son when he comes to the throne, and the idiom used is to love the treaty partner as one would oneself. Whether Jonathan's loving of David in this manner suggests David's subordination to him, his subordination to David, or a treaty of equals remains unclear, though it is worth noting that Jonathan is the initiator of the formalization of their relationship according to this text: He loved David as himself, and they cut a covenant when/because he did so according to v. 3.[46] In addition, Jonathan gives David his clothes, weapons, and other personal items according to 18:4, not unlike Saul's gift of weapons and armor to David according to 17:38–39, actions thought by some to be tied to treaty-making.[47]

Besides the covenant idioms used of the relationship of Jonathan to David in 1 Sam 18:1–4, there is the text's initial statement that the "self" or "life" (*nepeš*) of Jonathan was "bound" to the "self" or "life" of David. This idiom occurs only one other time in the Hebrew Bible. In Gen 44:30–31, it describes the relationship of Jacob to his youngest son Benjamin, whom he is elsewhere said to love (44:20): The "self" or "life" of Jacob is said to be "bound" to that of Benjamin, and were Benjamin to die, Jacob would die of grief (*yāgôn*).[48] In contrast to the idiom to love someone else as oneself, the binding of selves/lives is not otherwise used in treaty settings and appears to be highly charged emotionally. In Gen 44:30–31, the binding of selves/lives conveys the love of a father for a favorite son, a love so intense that the death of the son would put the father in his grave. A comparably intense emotional resonance is therefore possible for the idiom when it occurs in 1 Sam 18:1; at minimum, the idiom suggests that an emotional bond has been established between Jonathan and David. The possibility of emotional bonds between men in the biblical text, even strong ones, is also supported by texts such as Deut 13:7–12, Exod 32:27, and Prov 18:24, which speak of or suggest the existence of the exceptional friend. I would not want to argue that the bond imagined in 1 Sam 18:1 is necessarily analogous in its details to that of a parent and beloved child; only that it is represented as emotionally resonant, possibly intense, at the very least for Jonathan.[49] Jonathan establishes the emotional bond (his "self" or "life" is bound to that of David) as well as the formalization of the relationship through treaty-making (they cut a covenant "when" or "because" Jonathan "loved" David "as himself"). In fact, according to 18:1–4, David is an agent only in his participation in making the covenant ("Jonathan and David cut a covenant"); otherwise, Jonathan is the initiator and David is portrayed following his lead.

First Samuel 19:1–7 is a second text that portrays the relationship of Jonathan and David. Though Saul has ordered David's death, Jonathan "delighted exceedingly in David" (v. 1) and therefore tells David of Saul's plan to have him executed, demonstrating loyalty to David rather than to his own father the king.[50] Jonathan even constructs a plan to persuade Saul to change his mind about David, speaking well of him to Saul. According to Jonathan, David has been loyal to his master Saul; he is innocent of any crime; and his actions have profited Saul. Furthermore, Saul should not risk committing a serious transgression against his loyal servant David (vv. 4–5). As a result, Saul swears an oath by Yhwh not to have David killed, and Jonathan, after informing David of developments, brings him back into Saul's presence and service.

Though lacking in treaty idioms such as "to cut a covenant" or "to love *x* as oneself," 1 Sam 19:1–7 may hint at the existence of a treaty between Jonathan and David in its use of the idiom "to delight in" (*ḥāpēṣ bĕ-*). This expression, when used elsewhere, can suggest the favor of a suzerain: In 1 Sam 18:22, David is told that Saul, his lord, "delights in" him and that "all his servants love" him.[51] Or it can suggest the loyalty of vassals, as in 2 Sam 20:11, where those who are loyal to David's nephew and commander Joab and to David are told to pursue the rebel Sheba: "Whoever delights in Joab and whoever belongs to David, after Sheba!"[52] Thus, the idiom's use in 1 Sam 19:1 may suggest that a treaty is in the background, though the assumptions underlying it remain unclear.[53] At the same time, a case can be made that the idiom may also have an emotional resonance in the context of 1 Sam 19:1, given several texts in which $ḥāpēṣ$ means "to take pleasure in," with friend or family member as the subject. An example is Ps 35:27, in which friends loyal to the psalmist are described as "those who delight in my vindication [$ḥăpēṣê ṣidqî$]"; another example is Ps 109:17, where it is said of a disloyal friend or relative that "he did not delight in blessing," with the implication that a loyal friend or family member would so delight.[54] In both examples, it may be that an emotional component is implied for delighting, given the personal, emotional connection that may exist between friends or family members.[55] Thus, the idiom's use in 1 Sam 19:1 could suggest an emotional bond between Jonathan and David, while at the same time it may also hint at a formalized relationship between the two men.[56] At all events, it is Jonathan's great delight in David—whatever its exact meaning—that clearly motivates his actions on David's behalf in the narrative, including his choice to allow his fidelity to David to trump his loyalty to his father and king, Saul.

First Samuel 20:1–21:1 is certainly the most complex narrative treating the relationship of Jonathan and David. Aside from its various text-critical challenges, it appears to contain a later interpolation in vv. 11–17, 23, and 42 that reverses the treaty statuses of Jonathan and David assumed in vv. 1–10, 18–22, 24–41, and 21:1 and seems to share a common ideology with 23:14–18.[57] I treat the core narrative first and then the interpolation. After fleeing from Saul, David meets Jonathan and protests Saul's attempts to have him killed (v. 1). In this narrative, Jonathan seems unaware of Saul's intentions—contrast 19:1–7—insisting that he would know if Saul wanted to do David harm. In v. 3, David suggests that Saul knows that Jonathan favors him and that Jonathan would "be grieved" (MT) or would "take counsel" with David (LXX^B) were he to find out about Saul's desire to harm David, and that is why Saul has kept his intentions a secret.[58] David thereupon suggests a plan to discover whether Saul will act decisively against him (vv. 5–7) and demands that Jonathan act loyally (*'āśâ ḥesed*) with him, "for you brought your servant with you into the covenant of Yhwh" (v. 8). Jonathan then promises to tell David if he finds out that Saul intends to kill him (v. 9). Throughout the narrative of vv. 1–10, 18–22, 24–41, and 21:1, David uses idioms of subordination to describe his relationship with Jonathan (e.g., he refers to himself as "your servant" in vv. 7, 8) and he acts in a subordinate manner in Jonathan's presence (v. 41, where he bows three times). Although the supplement of vv. 11–17, 23, and 42 also casts the relationship of Jonathan and David as a treaty and has Jonathan promise to report any malicious intentions of Saul to David (v. 13), it, like 23:14–18, imagines that treaty to be one in which Jonathan is subordinate to David. It is David whom Yhwh will cause to prosper, and in a reversal of 20:8, in which David demands that Jonathan be loyal to him, it is Jonathan who insists that David should never cut off his loyalty (*kārat ḥesed*) to Jonathan's house (v. 15).[59]

Though replete with treaty language, 1 Sam 20:1–10, 18–22, 24–41, and 21:1, like 18:1, contain material that suggests an emotional bond between Jonathan and David. Verse 41 is of interest in this regard. After David comes out of hiding, he bows three times to Jonathan, an act indicative of his subordination; then "each kissed the other and they wept together."[60] These reciprocal ritual acts of affection suggest the existence of an emotional bond between the two men.[61] Kissing and weeping as ritual acts can have strong emotional resonances, as Gen 33:4 and Ruth 1:9, 14 indicate. These texts pair kissing with weeping in a context of strong emotion: the reunion of brothers in the case of Gen 33:4 and the parting of in-laws in Ruth 1:9, 14.[62] Like Gen 33:4, 1 Sam 20:41 concerns a reunion, and like Ruth 1:9, 14, the actors are related by marriage. In Gen 33:4, as in 1 Sam 20:41, the subordinate party's multiple acts of prostration before the dominant party precede an emotionally charged reunion. Yet in Gen 33:4, reciprocal, emotionally resonant ritual action (weeping) is preceded by a series of highly emotive acts undertaken by the dominant party alone: "Esau ran to meet him, embraced him, fell upon his neck, kissed him and they wept." Although 1 Sam 20:41 assumes that Jonathan and David are bound by a treaty in which David is subordinate, the reciprocal ritual acts of kissing and weeping narrated in this verse strongly suggest a personal, emotional bond between the two men, a bond best described as a friendship.[63] As I have argued previously, behavioral parity is a norm of biblical representations of friendship and biblical friendship vocabulary, even if equality of the parties in all respects is not. I observed elements of such behavioral parity in the Ruth-Naomi narrative, and it is assumed by the various texts that validate the reciprocation of that which is good to those who have acted appropriately (e.g., Ps 35:12–14). In 1 Sam 20:41, the behavioral parity is expressed through a series of reciprocal ritual acts (kissing and weeping), not unlike the reciprocal acts of comforting expected of the friend in Ps 35:12–14. The difference is in the timing: In 1 Sam 20:41, behavioral parity is enacted by both parties simultaneously (they kiss one another and weep together); in Ps 35:12–14, each party to the friendship is expected to play the role of comforter when his friend is in need, and the psalmist's disloyal friends are castigated for failing to do so when he was in trouble.

First Samuel 23:14–18 is the shortest of the four Jonathan-David narratives under consideration. David, a fugitive from Saul's court, receives Jonathan in Horesh. Jonathan assures David that there is nothing to worry about: "'Fear not, for the hand of Saul my father will not find you! As for you, you will be king over Israel. I, myself, will become your second-in-command [*mišneh*] and Saul my father knows it.' The two of them then cut a covenant before Yhwh." The covenant they cut is obviously one in which Jonathan is cast as vassal and David as suzerain, given that David will be king and Jonathan will serve him as a royal official.[64] It is not unlike the treaty between them in 20:11–17, where Jonathan is the subordinate party, though Jonathan's role as David's "number two" here is unique. As with 19:2 and 20:9, 12, 13, Jonathan is portrayed choosing to be loyal to David instead of his father Saul, but here Jonathan explicitly relinquishes his claim to the throne, imagining himself as David's supporter rather than as successor to his father as king. This narrative clearly serves the purposes of apologists who wish to cast David as the legitimate successor to Saul, as many have pointed out.[65] The heir to Saul's throne, Jonathan, not only recognizes what is inevitable, but declares his enthusiastic support for it. In contrast to 1 Sam 18:1 and 20:41, this narrative contains nothing that necessarily suggests a strong emotional bond between David and Jonathan, nothing, in other words, that suggests the existence of a friendship, though as in 18:1 and 20:41, a treaty relationship between the men is assumed. It seems unlikely that Jonathan's surrender of the throne to David and his support for David as a court officer are intended to be understood as anything other than demonstrations of political loyalty. In fact, they are acts that constitute the suzerainty treaty established between David and Jonathan according to v. 18.

It is likely that most if not all of the narratives of Jonathan and David presume a treaty relationship of some kind between the two men. In 1 Sam 20:1–10, 18–22, 24–41, and 21:1, David is subordinate to Jonathan; in 20:11–17, 23, 42, and 23:14–18, it is Jonathan who plays the role of vassal; in 18:1–4, the nature of the treaty is unclear, as it is in 19:1–7, assuming there is indeed a covenant presupposed in the latter text. In contrast, only a few passages unambiguously evidence a personal relationship that we might describe as a friendship: 1 Sam 18:1, on account of the binding of lives/selves, a nontreaty idiom of emotion as evidenced by its use in Gen 44:30–31; and 1 Sam 20:41, which speaks of reciprocal ritual acts of affection best understood as motivated by strong emotions.[66] Thus, if we are to speak of a friendship in the narratives of Jonathan and David, we ought to focus our attention on 18:1–4 and 20:1–10, 18–22, 24–41, and 21:1, the larger narratives in which the evidence for a friendship occurs.[67] Given that the relationship of David and Jonathan is unambiguously conceived as a covenant in these two passages, it seems best to conclude that the men are portrayed as having a friendship that has been formalized through covenanting, not unlike the friendship described in Ps 55:21, in which a disloyal friend is apparently accused of breaking a covenant with the psalmist: "He sent forth his hand against one with whom he enjoyed good relations [*šōlēm], / breaking his treaty [bĕrît]."[68] That the treaty breaker is a friend is suggested by vv. 14–15, in which he is addressed directly as "a man like myself" (ʾĕnôš kĕʿerkî) and "my gentle intimate" (ʾallûpî ûmĕyuddāʿî), one with whom the complainant made "sweet fellowship" (namtîq sôd).[69] Furthermore, the disloyal friend is contrasted with "enemies" and "haters" whom the psalmist could resist and from whom he could hide himself, presumably because they are not trusted, in contrast to the disloyal friend. In Psalm 55, the treaty that formalizes the friendship appears to be one of equals, in contrast to that which is assumed by 1 Sam 20:41; as mentioned, 1 Sam 18:1–4, for its part, is unclear about the nature of the covenant. The formal inequality assumed by 20:41 may be due to Jonathan's position as prince and royal heir. In any case, 20:41 suggests that a friendship need not be formalized with a parity treaty if it is to be formalized; it can be formally unequal and nevertheless be characterized by emotional engagement, behavioral parity, and even volition.

Thus, the two instances of the Jonathan-David friendship formalized through the treaty idiom are not unique in biblical texts. In Psalm 55, we have another example of a friendship formalized through the making of a treaty, as indicated by the reference to a violated covenant. Though formalization of friendship through treaty-making is clearly evidenced, there is no way to know how many examples of biblical friendship are to be understood as formalized in this way.[70] It may be that such formalization is assumed by our authors to be commonplace or even universal, or conversely, quite rare and unusual. Without the presence of distinct treaty rhetoric (e.g., *kārat* or *ḥillēl běrît*), we cannot judge just how many of the friendships portrayed or referred to in biblical texts were thought to have been formalized as covenants. Why formalize a friendship through treaty-making? Perhaps such formalization, whether rare or commonplace, would have been thought to reassure both parties to a friendship that their mutual expectations would indeed be met, given the typical sanctions for covenant violation.[71] An informal friendship, in contrast, would presumably not be understood to presuppose the same severe penalties.[72]

Appendix: 2 Sam 1:26

In addition to 1 Sam 18:1–4 and 20:41, the two narratives that clearly suggest a friendship between David and Jonathan that has been formalized by a treaty, there is 2 Sam 1:26, a verse of David's Lament over Saul and Jonathan in which David states with respect to Jonathan: "Your love for me was wondrous, surpassing the love of women." This comparison of Jonathan's love to the love of women (*'ahăbat nāšîm*) does not suggest a treaty relationship, given that love comparisons in treaty contexts are constructed differently. Typically, the love of treaty partners is compared—"My father loved you, and you in turn loved my father"—or covenant love itself is likened to another kind of love that requires fidelity, for example, Israel's loyalty to Yhwh in its "youth" was like that of a young bride to her husband (Jer 2:2).[73] In contrast, the love of women is best understood as a type of sexual-emotional love, since women are not evidenced as partners in treaties and their love is typically associated with emotions and with actual or potential sexual activity, as in 1 Sam 18:20, 28; Hos 3:1; and Prov 5:19.[74] Because of the comparison of Jonathan's love to the love of women in this verse, I have argued elsewhere that it is the only text among those concerned with Jonathan and David that might plausibly be construed to suggest a homoerotic relationship between the men.[75] Yet, the reference in 1:26 to Jonathan as "my brother" likely suggests a treaty of equals or may refer to the in-law relationship of Jonathan and David presumed by prose narratives such as

1 Sam 18:27.⁷⁶ If the text assumes a parity treaty as I suspect it does, we have in 2 Sam 1:26 another instance of the David-Jonathan relationship represented as a friendship—this time likely with homoerotic overtones—that has been formalized as a treaty relationship.⁷⁷ Furthermore, in 2 Sam 1:26, David's words evoke a strong emotional bond with Jonathan and acknowledge Jonathan's love for him, in contrast to 1 Sam 18:1, where Jonathan's "self" or "life" is said to be bound to the "self" or "life" of David but nothing is said of David's feelings for Jonathan. Thus, 2 Sam 1:26 is not unlike 1 Sam 20:41, where the men enact reciprocal ritual acts of kissing and weeping that suggest a shared emotional engagement and commitment.

Three Brief Narratives of Friends

Though the stories of Ruth and Naomi and Jonathan and David have attracted more attention from commentators, several shorter narratives of friends are to be found in the Hebrew Bible, and these are also worthy of our attention for what we might learn from them about the narrative representation of friendship in the biblical text. In contrast to the more developed tales, these stories are brief, sometimes only a few verses in length. I discuss three such narratives: the stories of Job and his three comforters, Jephthah's daughter and her companions, and Amnon and Jonadab.⁷⁸

Job and His Comforters

In Job 2:11–13, Job's friends Eliphaz the Temanite, Bildad the Shuhite, and Zophar the Naamatite learn of Job's travails, consult with one another, and travel from their homes to be with Job:

> When the three friends of Job [*rēʿê ʾiyyôb*] heard about all this misfortune [*rāʿâ*] which had befallen him, they came, each from his place: Eliphaz the Temanite, Bildad the Shuhite, and Zophar the Naamatite. They took counsel together to come to move back and forth for him and to comfort him.⁷⁹ When they raised their eyes from afar, they did not recognize him, and lifted up their voices and wept. Each tore his garment and they threw dirt heavenward upon their heads. They sat with him on the ground seven days and seven nights and none spoke a word to him for they saw that (his) pain was exceedingly great.

Job's three friends do precisely what friends are expected to do at the time of a calamity, a death, or an illness: They join the sufferer and like the sufferer, they embrace mourning rites such as moving the body back and forth, strewing dirt or ashes on the head, weeping, tearing garments, and sitting on the ground. Friends, allies, and others who participate in mourning rites with mourners are often referred to by the biblical text as "comforters" (*měnaḥămîm*).[80] According to Jer 16:7, comforters of one who is mourning the dead break bread with him "to comfort him concerning the dead" and cause him to drink from "the cup of consolation on account of his father or his mother."[81] One who comforts a sick friend embraces mourning rites, presumably in order to petition the deity to intervene on behalf of the sufferer and end his suffering (e.g., Ps 35:13–14). And those who have endured calamity also expect friends or allies to play the role of comforter (e.g., Lam 1:2).[82] Job is mourning the deaths of his children and a variety of non–death-related calamities, including the loss of many of his possessions and his own affliction with disease (1:13–19; 2:7–8). These are referred to collectively as "all this misfortune" (*kol hārāʿâ hazzōʾt*) in 2:11 and prompt Job's three friends to join him, fulfilling all expectations.

Yet Job's three friends of 2:11–13 are represented quite differently both in the poetic dialogues that follow the prose prologue of chapters 1 and 2 and in the prose epilogue in 42:7–9. In the poetic core of the book, the three friends challenge Job regarding his innocence and elicit from him accusations of wrongdoing. They are referred to as "troubling" or "mischievous" comforters (*měnaḥămê ʿāmāl*, 16:2), indicating that they are not playing the comforter role appropriately.[83] They are also called "worthless healers" (*rōpěʾê ʾĕlîl*, 13:4), suggesting, like "troubling comforters," that the friends do not offer the consolation comforters are expected to provide.[84] In 19:21–22, the three are said to pursue Job instead of acting favorably toward him. Job even accuses them of causing him to suffer, "crushing" him with words and humiliating him, all acts associated with enemies rather than friends (19:2–3).[85] In short, the three comforters of the poetic dialogues are, at least in Job's eyes, only marginally better than the disloyal friends mentioned in 19:13–14, who are estranged from Job and have forgotten him, and the "men of his council" in 19:19, who abominate him, having turned against him. Like these other friends, the three fail to fulfill expectations according to Job, even if they superficially embrace their appropriate role as comforter; voluble and critical in the extreme, their representation in the poetic dialogues contrasts with their portrait in the prose narrative of 2:11–13, where they do not say a word to Job on account of the degree of his suffering. Thus, the sensitive and loyal friends of the prologue are portrayed differently from the nonconsoling and even hypocritical friends of the poetic core.

In the prose epilogue, the three friends are rebuked directly by Yhwh for not speaking the truth concerning him, in contrast to Job; they are then ordered by Yhwh to make sacrifices to him for their own benefit. In addition, Job is to pray on their behalf in order to protect them from Yhwh's wrath (42:7–9).[86] Presumably, their misrepresentation of Yhwh consists of assuming that Job must be guilty of transgressions in order to have been afflicted in such a manner. The words of Eliphaz in 4:7 are an example of their perspective on suffering as represented in the poetic core of the book:

> Remember, who is the innocent one who has perished,
> And where are the upright destroyed?
> As I have seen [it], those who plow wickedness,
> And sow trouble, harvest them.

This is a conventional and commonplace viewpoint in wisdom texts, as scholars have often noted, and may well reflect the same set of ideas attributed to the three friends of Job by the writer of the epilogue.[87] Yet interestingly, in the epilogue, the friends are not reproved by Yhwh for being poor comforters to Job or even for being his oppressors, as they are by Job himself in the poetic dialogues. Nothing at all is said in the epilogue about their behavior toward Job. This suggests that the author of the epilogue does not share the perspective of Job of the poetic core—and likely that of the poet who composed it—on the behavior of Job's friends, but sees their faults differently. In a word, the three friends of the combined prologue and epilogue come across as loyal to Job, though misguided in their understanding of Yhwh's ways, while the three friends of the poetic dialogues are represented in a less flattering way, embracing the comforter role only superficially, failing to provide consolation as comforters should, and instead assuming an accusatory stance toward Job that is unjustified.

How ought we to explain this contrast between the representation of the three friends of the prose prologue and epilogue on the one hand, and that of the three friends of the poetic dialogues that lie between them, on the other? The narrative prologue and epilogue are often viewed as a separate composition from the poetic core of Job, with either the poetic dialogues or the prose narrative deemed older.[88] If the prose narrative is indeed later than the poetic core, as some scholars argue, the portrait of the three friends in 2:11–13 and 42:7–9 might represent an attempt by the author of the prologue and epilogue to ameliorate their representation, just as he evidently seeks to temper the severity of Job's losses by having his family and possessions restored to him (42:11–13) and the obscurity of the deity's decisions and actions by providing the Satan's challenge as the context for Job's tribulations (1:6–12; 2:1–6).[89] Why would the narrator seek to portray the three friends in a better light? The prose writer may have found Job's strident responses to the friends in the dialogues too severe, given the conventional nature of their words, and therefore he sought to cast the friends more positively by underscoring their acts of loyalty and sensitivity as comforters in chapter 2. As many have noted, the author also portrays Job as the epitome of patience in suffering in the prologue, much in contrast to the angry, accusatory Job of much of the poetic core.[90] It may be that the prose narrator seeks to present a more idealized portrait of both Job and his three friends, having found their portrayal in the poetic dialogues somehow not to his liking, perhaps because of their greater complexity and believability as characters.[91] Since we read the prologue first, our views of both Job and his friends are already under formation when we encounter them in the dialogues, effectively tempering their portrayal there; the epilogue, for its part, has the last word, with the friends rebuked by Yhwh for their lack of understanding with respect to him, but not for any failure of loyalty or sensitivity to Job.

Jephthah's Daughter and Her Companions

Female friendship is once again in view in the story of Jephthah's daughter and her companions, an episode of the larger Jephthah narrative. Jephthah, one of the judges, makes a rash vow: He will sacrifice the first thing to greet him when he returns home should Yhwh keep him safe and give him victory in battle against the Ammonites (Judg 11:30–31). When Jephthah arrives home after his triumph, his daughter, an only child, comes out to meet him, dancing and playing the hand drum (v. 34). Upon seeing her, Jephthah tears his garment, a mourning gesture that is sometimes used to acknowledge an anticipated calamity or death, for once a vow is made, it must be paid, as Jephthah acknowledges (v. 35). Jephthah's daughter, whose name is never provided by the narrator, is portrayed as a noble fatalist, accepting the inevitable, though she asks for a modest reprieve: "Let this thing be done for me: Give me leave for two months that I might descend the mountains (?) and weep over my virginity [ʿal bětûlay], I and my friends [*rēʿōtay/raʿyōtay*]" (v. 37).⁹² She does precisely this, returns, and is sacrificed in fulfillment of her father's vow. The pericope ends with a notation that it became a regular observance in Israel for women to commemorate Jephthah's daughter four days in the year.⁹³

How Jephthah's daughter intends to spend her final two months of life is not without interest. The purpose of her traveling is to weep over her virginity (v. 37), which presumably means to bewail the fact that she will die without experiencing sexual intercourse with a man, as the narrator makes explicit in v. 39: "And as for her, she did not know a man." To die without knowing a man sexually means to die without bearing children, and this fact likely constitutes at least part of what Jephthah's daughter mourns when she bewails her virginity. Her mourning, however, is in company, as all mourning ideally ought to be, for she is accompanied by her female friends in her travels. In v. 37, Jephthah's daughter's friends are mentioned in such a way that the text implies that they, too, will weep over their friend's virginity. In the following verse, Jephthah's daughter is said to weep, though nothing is said about the ritual behavior of her friends.⁹⁴ At all events, the text seems to be suggesting that the friends play the role of comforter for Jephthah's daughter as she experiences her calamity. Although the word "comforter" is not used by the text to describe them, they behave as comforters do: They are present with Jephthah's daughter, separating themselves from quotidian life with her; they embrace her mourning rites—they weep with her according to v. 37—not unlike comforters in any number of other texts.⁹⁵ Yet these comforters are women comforting a woman who is experiencing a calamity, and this sets them apart from the male comforters of men mentioned elsewhere in the biblical text (e.g., 2 Sam 10:1–5; Job 2:11–13). If this understanding of the narrative is correct, the story enriches our perspective on the biblical representation of female friendship, as Ruth contains nothing comparable.⁹⁶ It also enhances our understanding of the gendered dynamics of biblical mourning, particularly in the context of personal calamity. It may be that the text's authors and audience assume that a woman mourning a personal calamity expects the company and consolation of friends as much as any man does.

Amnon and Jonadab

The first chapter of the Absalom story in 2 Samuel 13 is a component of the larger narrative of Absalom's rise and fall (2 Sam 13–19). The chapter begins by noting that Absalom, son of David, had a beautiful sister named Tamar, who was loved by her half brother Amnon (v. 1). Though Amnon deems Tamar completely out of reach, his friend (*rēaʿ*) and first cousin Jonadab, described by the text as "an exceedingly worldly man," thinks otherwise. In response to Amnon's distraught state, Jonadab concocts an elaborate ruse to get Amnon and Tamar together: "Lie down on your bed and pretend to be sick. When your father comes to see you, say to him, 'Let Tamar, my sister, come and feed me food and prepare the food in my sight in order that I might see and eat from her hand'" (v. 5).[97] Amnon follows his friend's advice and receives a visit from his father David, who orders Tamar to wait on her half brother. After she serves him food, Amnon rapes her and expels (*šlḥ* Pi) her from his house. Tamar, described as a "devastated woman" (*šōmēmâ*), embraces mourning rites on account of her calamity and goes to her brother Absalom's house and remains there, her marriage prospects likely diminished.[98] Absalom, for his part, hates Amnon for what he did and plots to have him put to death. Two years later, at a shearing festival hosted by Absalom, Amnon is murdered by Absalom's order, and David's other sons who were also invited flee (vv. 28–29). When a false report reaches David that all of the princes have been killed by Absalom, Jonadab steps forward and reassures David that that is not the case; he then tells David of Absalom's intent to kill Amnon from the day Amnon raped Tamar (v. 32). The sons of David arrive safely, just as Jonadab had promised.

Jonadab plays a significant yet not easily understood role in this narrative. It is he who comes up with the plan to give Amnon access to Tamar and it is he who reveals to David—after the fact—Absalom's longstanding intent to avenge the rape of his sister by having Amnon killed (vv. 32–33). Why is it that Amnon's friend Jonadab is privy to Absalom's machinations? The narrative suggests that Absalom's plan is a secret, not common knowledge, and the fact that Amnon allows himself—and is allowed by David—to attend the feast indicates both Amnon's and David's ignorance of the plan according to the storyteller.[99] Is the narrator suggesting that Jonadab was also a confidant of Absalom? Or has he become one, after falling out with Amnon for whatever reason? Jonadab does not seem to embrace mourning rites when the court learns that Amnon has been killed, in contrast to David, his courtiers, and his sons. He also demonstrates no feeling upon hearing of Amnon's death, reassuring David twice that "Amnon alone is dead" (vv. 32, 33). Though not a son of David, Jonadab is a close paternal relative, and it is likely that the story's author and audience would have assumed that playing the role of comforter was incumbent upon him, as much as it is upon David's courtiers, who are said to tear their garments and weep on learning the news (13:31, 36). Thus, it is possible to see in the text's words and its silences a Jonadab who not only encourages his friend Amnon to pursue his baser impulses, but also does not remain loyal to him, withholding knowledge of Absalom's plan to kill Amnon and not playing the role of comforter to David once Amnon has died, possibly because he is now Absalom's friend and confidant rather than Amnon's.[100] That Jonadab would conceal Absalom's plans from David is an act of striking disloyalty, particularly because Amnon is David's heir.[101] Given all that remains unsaid in the text, this scenario is at best only a possibility, but if my reading has merit, it reveals a friend (Jonadab) who gets his friend (Amnon) into serious trouble and is not ultimately loyal to him or to his uncle and lord, David. If Jonadab really does eschew comforting David on account of Amnon's death, by doing so he is publicizing his loyalty to Absalom, his dissociation from Amnon, and his distance from David, whose courtiers and relatives are expected to embrace his ritual stance.[102] On the one hand, it is difficult to believe that Jonadab would dare to openly defy David in this way, but on the other, the text is silent about his embrace of mourning rites, leaving open the possibility. Furthermore, other relatives of David defy him openly in the narratives of his reign, including his sons Amnon and Absalom and his nephew Joab. Jonadab's defiance may simply be part of a larger topos.

Conclusion

Narrative portraits contribute significantly to our understanding of friendship as it is represented in biblical texts. Prose representations of friendship frequently offer the reader named characters who are more fully realized than the anonymous friends mentioned in wisdom texts such as Proverbs and the Job dialogues, prophetic texts, or the psalms of individual complaint, friends who are often little more than one-dimensional types.[103] In addition to richer characterizations, narrative renderings of friendship often provide us with data regarding the biblical representation of friendship that we would not otherwise have. For example, they tell us about some of the ways in which women's friendships were conceived by biblical authors, something about which we know next to nothing from poetic sources. And from prose texts, in contrast to nonnarrative materials, we learn much about how biblical authors might imagine both friendships of people sharing most or all personal characteristics and friendships between those who differ with respect to wealth, social status, life stage, or some combination of these. Thus, narrative enriches our understanding of the dynamics of behavioral parity, an expectation of friendship in nonnarrative contexts (e.g., the psalms of individual complaint and wisdom texts) as well as in narrative, through detailed character development in particular narrative settings.

The contrast between the anonymous friends of many nonnarrative contexts and the more developed and often named friends of prose writing is quite striking. To bring this difference into relief, one might compare the unnamed betrayers of the supplicant in the psalms of individual complaint both to Jonadab of 2 Samuel 13 and to Ruth. Those who betray the complainant in Psalm 35 are said to seek his life, plan his undoing, pay back that which is evil instead of what is good, and rejoice at the psalmist's misfortune. In Psalm 38 disloyal friends stand at a distance from the suffering petitioner and appear to seek his life and pursue his undoing. In Ps 55:21 the ex-friend threatens the psalmist physically (he "sent forth his hand against one with whom he enjoyed good relations [*šōlēm]").[104] Not only are these disloyal friends unnamed, but their behaviors are stereotypical and they are not portrayed as having any kind of complexity: They display no ambivalence about or hesitation in their hostile behavior and no inconsistency in their treatment of the complainant. In a word, they are all bad, all of the time, with no redeeming or complicating features.[105] To these flat, one-dimensional betrayers of trust we might first compare Amnon's friend Jonadab in 2 Samuel 13. Although sensitive to Amnon's emotional state and responsible for encouraging and facilitating Amnon's pursuit of Tamar, Jonadab appears to feel no regret at the news of Amnon's murder and expresses none ritually, though such is expected, perhaps because he has changed sides and now identifies publicly with his other first cousin, Amnon's half brother and the facilitator of his murder, Absalom. If this is the case, Jonadab's loyalty to Absalom even seems to trump his obligations to David, his lord and king. Thus Jonadab comes across as a complex, unpredictable figure who manifests both extremes of fidelity and treachery at once in his person. Ruth, like Jonadab, is named, in contrast to the anonymous betrayers of the sufferer in the psalms of individual complaint. We learn something of her personal history and much about her character from the narrative. But in contrast to Jonadab, Ruth is not a particularly complex character. Her behavior is consistently flawless, and she comes across as wholly predictable, without inner conflicts—even idealized. In short, she is more developed as an individual than are the ex-friends of texts such as Psalms 35 and 38, but less so than a complex character such as Jonadab.

Women's friendship, rarely mentioned outside of prose sources, is the focus of both the narrative of Ruth and Naomi and the story of Jephthah's daughter and her companions, and from these narratives we learn much we would not otherwise know about the ways in which female friends might be represented. Women are portrayed as friends by biblical authors, just as men are, and as in narratives about male friends such as Jonathan and David, technical friendship terminology is not always present in stories of women's friendship. Nonetheless, both the story of Ruth and Naomi and the narrative of Jephthah's daughter and her friends bring into relief features of biblical friendship seen elsewhere. The friendship bond between Ruth and Naomi, which develops after Ruth has fulfilled all familial obligations, is both voluntary and reciprocal, and manifestations of behavioral parity characterize it, along with other features common to the representation of biblical friendship (e.g., emotional bonding, loyalty, trust, and good will). Though not stated explicitly by the text, Naomi and Ruth express mutual affection, they seek one another's welfare, and each of them reciprocates that which is good to the other, as male friends ought to do according to a text such as Ps 35:12. Jephthah's daughter's companions, unnamed by the narrator though identified as "friends," respond loyally to her calamity; they accompany her on her two-month journey and seem to play the part of comforters, just as male friends are obligated to do for a man experiencing calamity or illness or when responding to a loved one's death according to texts such as Job 2:11–13 or Ps 35:12–14. Thus, both of these narratives of women's friendship suggest implicitly a set of friendship norms for women that are not unlike those evidenced for men in other texts.

Behavioral parity, in contrast to formal equality of social status, wealth, life stage, or other personal characteristics, is a broadly attested expectation of friendship across biblical texts, mentioned most frequently in the breach. Various passages suggest either explicitly or implicitly that the friend is expected to seek a friend's welfare (e.g., Ps 35:27), act favorably toward the friend (e.g., Job 19:21), be trustworthy (e.g., Mic 7:5), and reciprocate that which is good for the good received from the friend (e.g., Ps 35:12–14). Yet friendship vocabulary and nonnarrative representations of friendship, for all that they might tell us about the expectation of behavioral parity, say little about the differences in personal characteristics that might exist between friends.[106] They also do not tell us much about the possibilities of friendship between social, material, or life-stage peers.[107] In contrast, narrative enriches our understanding of the dynamics of behavioral parity by introducing friendships that are unequal in one or more ways as well as those in which no hierarchical dimension is suggested at all. Naomi and Ruth remain mother-in-law and daughter-in-law, even after their friendship commences, even if the narrative's emphasis is other than their formal status difference. Jonadab and Amnon are formally unequal, given Amnon's status as the king's son and heir. Although David is a rising military figure, Jonathan is heir to the throne; thus, they are not formally peers. The text also suggests differences in relative wealth between David and the royal court of Saul (e.g., 1 Sam 18:23). In addition, Jonathan and David are portrayed in a number of the narratives as unequal treaty partners, with Jonathan in the subordinate role in some texts (e.g., 1 Sam 20:11–17, 23, 42) and David the vassal in others (e.g., 1 Sam 20:1–10, 18–22, 24–41; 21:1). In contrast, other Jonathan-David narratives and 2 Sam 1:26 may cast David and Jonathan as equals in their covenant. For their part, Job and his three comforters are evidently peers in terms of social status, likely also in terms of wealth and life stage. Finally, Jephthah's daughter and her companions are presented without a hint of inequality among them.[108]

Thus, in terms of personal characteristics, narrative representations of friendship suggest several possible combinations: friends who are unequal in most or all respects, friends who are unequal in some respects (e.g., in terms of social status or wealth) but equal in others (e.g., with respect to treaty status or life stage), and friends who are peers in most or all respects.[109] Yet whatever the combination of personal characteristics, the same set of presuppositions about behavioral parity as evidenced in nonnarrative sources is suggested—mainly implicitly—by narrative representations of friendship: friends are expected to seek each other's welfare, support one another when times are bad, be loyal, and reciprocate appropriate behavior. Thus, even a friendship between people who are not peers in every respect requires behavioral parity. Just as the suzerain of a suzerain-vassal treaty has obligations to the vassal, so a friend who has greater social status or wealth owes his friend loyalty and other goods of friendship.

4 Friendship in Ben Sira

The focus of my final chapter is the representation of friendship in the second-century BCE Hebrew wisdom text Ben Sira, known by the title the Wisdom of Jesus, Son of Sirach, or Ecclesiasticus in many Christian Bibles.[1] Ben Sira is of particular interest to me for a number of reasons: The work was composed in Hebrew, and a lot of the Hebrew survives; the author has much to say about friendship; he stands in the biblical wisdom tradition, like the authors of Proverbs and Job; and he writes from a Hellenistic context, thereby allowing us to assess the degree of the influence of Greek thought on his ideas about friendship. Furthermore, the work is a part of the Catholic and Eastern Orthodox Old Testament and therefore properly biblical in the view of several major Christian communities, although its status among Jews and Protestants is noncanonical.[2] Thus, Ben Sira is an appropriate place to bring to an end our inquiry into the representation of friendship in the Hebrew Bible. I begin with an assessment of Ben Sira's vocabulary and idioms of friendship, noting both continuities and discontinuities with earlier biblical sources. Then I consider Ben Sira's ideas about friendship in comparison with the ideas of earlier biblical texts, including those in the wisdom tradition (both traditional and skeptical). Finally, I evaluate the evidence that may suggest the impact of Greek ideas about friendship on Ben Sira.

Ben Sira's Vocabulary and Idioms of Friendship

Working mainly from the surviving Hebrew text and, secondarily, what can be reconstructed with confidence from the versions, I now turn to

Ben Sira's vocabulary of friendship and the distinct idioms of friendship he employs.[3] Not surprisingly, a number of the terms for a friend and the distinct idioms of friendship familiar to us from earlier biblical texts are also to be found in Ben Sira. Words for "friend" in Ben Sira include *ʾōhēb*, *rēaʿ*, and *mērēaʿ*, with *ʾōhēb* the most common—in contrast to earlier sources that tend to privilege *rēaʿ* over *ʾōhēb*—and with *mērēaʿ* occurring rarely, as in earlier biblical texts.[4] An ex-friend or false friend is called an enemy (*śōnēʾ*), not unlike in earlier materials.[5] The expression *ʾanšê šĕlômĕkā*, "those with whom you enjoy good relations," occurs once in Ben Sira (6:6 [A; Beentjes 6:5]): "Let those with whom you enjoy good relations be many, / But let your trusted intimate [*baʿal sôd*] be one in a thousand." It is more commonly used of friends in earlier texts (e.g., Jer 20:10; Ps 41:10), which also speak of friends communicating their good will to one another (*dbr šālôm*; Jer 9:7; Pss 28:3; 35:20).[6] Ben Sira uses the verb *bāṭaḥ* ("to trust") in regard to friendship (6:7 [A; Beentjes 6:6]) as well as the idiom "stand at a distance" (*minneged ʿāmad*) for the disloyal friend (37:4 [B]; similarly 6:8 [A; Beentjes 6:7], with *ʿāmad* alone), as do earlier biblical texts.[7] He utilizes the expression "to turn against" (*hpk bĕ-*) in 6:12 (A; Beentjes 6:11) with reference to the disloyal friend, as does Job 19:19: "If you suffer misfortune, he will turn against you [*yahăpōk bĕkā*]."[8] He insists that a friend should neither forget (*šākaḥ*) nor abandon (*ʿāzab*) his friend (37:6 [B, D]), rare though attested idioms of friendship in earlier biblical texts.[9] As in earlier materials, the particularly intimate friend may be described as a "friend who is as yourself" (*rēaʿ kĕnapšĕkā*; 37:2 [B]).[10]

In addition to vocabulary and idioms of friendship shared with earlier biblical texts, Ben Sira associates a variety of expressions and words with friendship that are either not tied to friendship or not attested at all in extant earlier materials. Some of these usages are likely his innovations; others may simply be current in his environment. Perhaps most prominent among these is his use of the word *ḥābēr*, "companion," to refer to the friend. The word *ḥābēr* occurs occasionally in earlier biblical texts but not with reference to friends.[11] In Ben Sira, by contrast, *ḥābēr* can be used to refer to the friend, as 6:10 (A; Beentjes 6:9) demonstrates clearly, through apposition: "There is a friend [*ʾôhēb*], a companion of the table [*ḥābēr šulḥān*], / But he will not be found on a day of trouble."[12] After Sir 37:5 (B, D) states that the "good friend" (*ʾôhēb ṭôb*) fights against the "outsider" (*zār*), the following verse (B, D) urges that the "companion" (*ḥābēr*) not be forgotten or abandoned in wartime, suggesting through parallelism that the *ḥābēr* and *ʾôhēb ṭôb* are closely related, if not identical individuals. Furthermore, on several occasions, Ben Sira's grandson, who translated the Hebrew text into Greek, appears to render *ḥābēr* as *philos*, "friend" (6:10; 37:6; perhaps 7:12 [A]).[13] Nonetheless, on occasion Ben Sira seems to distinguish between the *ḥābēr* and the *rēaʿ*, as in 7:12 (A): "Do not plan wrongdoing against a brother, / Or likewise against a friend or companion [*rēaʿ wĕḥābēr*]."[14] Though some interpreters have understood this to suggest a nonfriendship meaning for *ḥābēr*—for example, an "associate" or "companion" who is not a friend—this may be reading more in the text than is warranted. Rather than "a descending order of intimacy: brother, friend, companion (or associate)," as Skehan and Di Lella put it, it seems more likely that Sir 7:12 suggests that all three categories of person share the same implicit classification: intimates not to be wronged.[15] Thus, the *ḥābēr* in a text such as Sir 7:12 may not be the equivalent of the *rēaʿ*, but he is still classified as an intimate, and therefore, presumably, a friend. How exactly he might be distinct from the *rēaʿ* unfortunately remains unclear. The idea of gradations in friendship is attested elsewhere in Ben Sira—as in earlier biblical texts—and may be suggested here as well if both *rēaʿ* and *ḥābēr* refer to types of friends, as I suspect they do.[16] Understanding *ḥābēr* in Sir 7:12 to refer to a friend is consistent with its use in texts such as 6:10 and 37:5. What remains unclear are the differences in nuance among the terms *ʾōhēb*, *rēaʿ*, and *ḥābēr* as Ben Sira uses them.

Aside from *ḥābēr*, a number of other friendship-related words and idioms occurring in Ben Sira either are not attested or have no clear friendship associations in earlier biblical texts. These include the expression *baʿal sôd*, "trusted intimate" (6:6 [A; Beentjes 6:5]), which is not unlike *mĕtê sôdî*, "intimates," used of friends in Job 19:19;[17] the verbs Hit *ndḥ*, "to remove oneself," and Ni *str*, "to hide oneself" (6:11, *yitnaddeḥ*; 12, *yissātēr* [A; Beentjes 6:10, 11]), where earlier biblical texts most often have "stand at a distance" (*ʿāmad minneged*) or "be far from" (*rāḥaq*) (e.g., Pss 38:12; 88:9; Prov 19:7); the idiom "to turn into (an enemy)" (Ni *hpk lĕ-*; 6:9 [A; Beentjes 6:8]; 37:2 [B, D]), used of friends in Ben Sira but not in earlier sources;[18] the terms *ʾōhēb ṭôb* ("good friend"; 37:5 [B, D]), *ʾōhēb ʾĕmûnâ* ("true friend"; 6:14–16 [A; Beentjes 6:13–15]), and *ʾōhēb yāšān*/*ʾōhēb ḥādāš* ("old friend"/"new friend"; 9:10 [A]); and the expression "like him/you" (*kāmôhû/kā*), used of the friend in 6:11, 17 (A; Beentjes 6:10, 16): "When times are good for you, he is like you"; "for like him, so is his friend." Other terminology used of friends in Ben Sira but not in earlier biblical sources includes the friend as a "helper" (*ʿōzēr*) in Sir 13:22 (A; Beentjes 13:21), a text that Corley argues "echoes" Prov 19:14, which has *rēaʿ*;[19] the friend who supports (*smk*) his friend according to Sir

12:17 (A) and 13:21 (A);[20] several terms for friends who share commensality (*baʿălê laḥmĕkā* [9:16 (A)]; *ḥābēr šulḥān* [6:10 (A; Beentjes 6:9)]; *ʼôhēb mabbîṭ ʼel-šulḥān* [37:4 (B)]);[21] and the verb *nāṭaš*, "to abandon," as in Sir 9:10 (A): "Do not abandon an old friend."

Finally, some important words and idioms used of friendship in earlier biblical sources are not found in the extant Hebrew text of Ben Sira. Though the word *mĕyuddāʿ*, "one who is known (to me)," is used of friends in texts such as 2 Kgs 10:11 and Ps 55:14, it is not attested in the Hebrew manuscripts of Ben Sira.[22] Similarly, Ben Sira does not bear witness to the use of the word *ʼallûp*, possibly "gentle (one)," with regard to the friend (Jer 11:19; Mic 7:5; Ps 55:14). Reflexes of the verbal root *dbq*, "to cling to," are lacking in Ben Sira's friendship discourses (contrast Prov 18:24; Ruth 1:14), and the verb "to abominate" (*tʿb*) and its derivatives, including the noun "abomination," are not used to describe the behavior of unfaithful friends (contrast Ps 88:9; Job 19:19).[23] Disloyal friends in Ben Sira are not said to "pay back that which is evil instead of what is good" or "pay back that which is evil" (*šlm* [Pi]/*śym*/*gml rāʿâ*/*raʿ* [*taḥat ṭôbâ*]) as they are in Pss 7:5 and 35:12 (and likely in Ps 38:21 and possibly in Ps 109:5), even though disloyalty in friendship is a preoccupation of Ben Sira.[24] Friends are not said to communicate their good will to one another (*dbr šālôm*), as they are in texts such as Jer 9:7; Pss 28:3; 35:20; disloyal friends are not said to be "far from" (*rāḥaq*) a suffering friend, as they are in Ps 88:9 and Prov 19:7. Words for the female friend are not attested (*rēʿâ*, *raʿyâ*; cf. Judg 11:37, 38), nor are friends described as "those who delight in my vindication" (*ḥăpēṣê ṣidqî*), an expression used of friends in Ps 35:27, nor are they said to "pursue that which is good" (*rādap ṭôbâ*), as is likely the case in Ps 38:21. The idiom the "self" or "life" of *x* was bound to the "self" or "life" of *y* (*qšr nepeš*) is lacking in Ben Sira's rhetoric of friendship, in contrast to 1 Sam 18:1, where it is used of Jonathan and David. Finally, hendiadys constructions such as "my loving friends" (*ʼōhăbay wĕrēʿay*, Ps 38:12) or "my gentle intimate" (*ʼallûpî ûmĕyuddāʿî*, Ps 55:14) are not attested in Ben Sira. As with vocabulary and idioms found in Ben Sira but not in earlier biblical texts, words and expressions attested in earlier biblical materials that are absent from Ben Sira may reflect innovation on Ben Sira's part or simply current practice in his time and place.

Ben Sira's Ideas About Friendship

Along with continuities of vocabulary and idioms, Ben Sira shares ideas about friendship with earlier biblical sources. According to earlier materials and Ben Sira, love is a norm between friends and has both emotional and behavioral resonances.[25] To be loyal and trustworthy are manifestations of such love and are an expectation of friendship, as texts such as Jer 9:3; Mic 7:5; Ps 41:10; and Sir 6:7 (A; Beentjes 6:6), 22:23, and 27:17 make clear. Offering active support in times of need rather than making oneself inaccessible or forgetting the friend is a specific way in which friends are thought to be loyal in both Ben Sira and earlier biblical texts.[26] Ben Sira elaborates upon the loyalty theme found in older texts through his particular emphasis on helping and supporting the friend in time of need and his use of the rhetoric of help (*'zr*) and support (*smk*).[27] He may well have borrowed this rhetoric directly from earlier texts such as Pss 3:6; 37:17, 24; 54:6; 119:116; and 145:14, which speak frequently of Yhwh as "supporter" and "helper" of the suffering petitioner, if the association of this rhetoric with friendship was not already established in his environment. If Ben Sira did innovate in this manner, he may have done so in order to enrich his treatment of loyalty in the context of friendship.[28] As in earlier biblical texts, behavioral parity is a norm of friendship, with loyalty and trust ideally expressed reciprocally. Just as one should be loyal to a friend in difficult times, so should the friend be constant when one suffers misfortune. The norm of behavioral parity is, as in earlier texts, most often suggested implicitly, frequently in contexts in which disloyalty is the focus (e.g., 6:8–13 [A; Beentjes 6:7–12]; 37:1–4 [D, partially B]; 13:21–23 [A]), though also in passages in which Ben Sira urges appropriate behavior (e.g., 22:23; 37:5–6 [B, D]). As in earlier texts such as Deut 13:7, Prov 17:17, and Prov 18:24, friends and family members share an implicit common classification in Sir 7:18 (A), in this instance suggested by parallelism: "Do not trade a friend for money, / Nor a [] brother for the gold of Ophir."[29] Here, brother and friend belong to a single class of people whom one should value more than material wealth.[30] In 7:19, Ben Sira adds the wife to the class of people to be embraced and not rejected, just as Deut 13:7 classifies the wife and intimate friend with other close family members: "Do not spurn a skillful wife, / For the value of her favor exceeds that of pearls."[31] Other ideas shared by Ben Sira and earlier biblical texts include the notion that friends are "like" their friends, as in Ps 55:14, where the friend is described as an equal, literally, "a man like me" (*'ĕnôš kĕ'erkî*), and in Sir 6:11, 17 (A; Beentjes 6:10, 16) and, by implication, in 13:15–16 (A; Beentjes 13:14–15).[32] Finally, commensality as a component of friendship is witnessed in both Ps 41:10 and Sir 6:10 (A; Beentjes 6:9), 9:16 (A), and 37:4 (B), including the idea that the friend benefits from one's hospitality. In Ps 41:10, the friend eats the psalmist's food; Sir 9:16 speaks of one's dining guests (*baʿălê laḥmĕkā*), who should be righteous people.

More interesting perhaps are ideas Ben Sira expresses about friendship that are not attested, or at least are uncommon, in earlier biblical texts. One such notion is that friends provide well-timed guidance to their friends: In the words of Sir 40:23, "Friend and companion lead [*nhg*] in a timely manner."[33] Presumably, this statement refers to the sage advice a sensible friend might provide, a topic about which earlier texts are mainly silent.[34] The completion of this verse offers yet another idea, one that is unattested in earlier material: that a capable wife is superior to the helpful friend and companion: "But better than both is a skillful wife." Although the wife is occasionally classified implicitly with the intimate friend and close family members in earlier biblical texts (e.g., Deut 13:7) and elsewhere in Ben Sira (7:19 [A]), she is never said to be their superior.[35] If direct comparisons are made in earlier materials, they are between friend and male relative (e.g., the brother), as in Prov 18:24 or 19:7, and in some instances, the friend is deemed the superior intimate, as in Prov 18:24: "There is a friend who clings more closely than a brother." It is remarkable that Ben Sira, who has many positive things to say about loyal friends, ultimately ranks even the most helpful of them below the skillful wife.[36]

Another idea witnessed in Ben Sira that is apparently absent from earlier materials is the notion that reconciliation between estranged friends is sometimes possible. Although earlier texts speak frequently of disloyal friends and the damage they might cause, nowhere is the possibility of reconciling with them discussed in any clear way, as I noted in Chapter 2.[37] In contrast, Ben Sira speaks of the possibility of reconciliation several times. According to 22:21–22, he who draws the sword or speaks against a friend (literally, "opens the mouth") can still achieve reconciliation, but he who reveals a secret dooms a friendship.[38] Ben Sira 27:21 is similar, stating that "there is reconciliation [*diallagē*] for contention [*loidorias*]"—meaning that after a falling out there is the possibility of making up—as long as the split was not occasioned by the revelation of confidences (*mustēria*).[39] Clearly, for Ben Sira, the exposure of confidential information is an unforgivable failing in a friend, something he speaks about frequently, as others have noted.[40]

Yet another theme absent from earlier texts but explored by Ben Sira is material generosity to friends who are evidently not in need. In 14:13 (A), Ben Sira urges his readers to practice such liberality: "Before you die, do good [*hêṭēb*] for a friend, / Give him that which you possess."[41] Preceding this statement, Ben Sira declares that one ought to be generous with oneself as well: "If you have it, be good to yourself" (14:11 [A]). Earlier biblical texts suggest that nonmaterial support of friends is expected, as I have discussed, even if the expectation is communicated implicitly (see, e.g., Pss 35:27; 38:12; 88:19). In addition, some earlier texts imply that a poor man is entitled to expect material support from his friends (Prov 14:20; 19:7),[42] but this is different from the belief that one ought to be materially generous to friends who are not poor. In 22:23, Ben Sira encourages his audience to be loyal to a friend in need, presumably meaning provide him with material support when he is short on resources.[43] Here, he may be developing what is implicit in Prov 14:20 and 19:7. In any case, the generosity envisaged by Ben Sira is evidently material in 14:11, 13 and 22:23, although 22:23 speaks of particular circumstances (poverty), while the statements in 14:11 and 13 are noncircumstantial and therefore rather different from what is found in earlier biblical texts.

Another difference between Ben Sira and earlier materials is Ben Sira's explicit emphasis on assigning appropriate value to the friend. As I have mentioned previously, Ben Sira urges readers not to undervalue the friend or brother in 7:18 (A), as they are advised not to reject a skillful wife in 7:19, for these are worth far more than money or other valuable possessions. Friend, brother, and wife form an implicit class in this passage: intimates who ought to be valued above material wealth. The sentiments of Sir 6:15 (A; Beentjes 6:14) are similar, though the formulation is different; here, the "faithful friend" is said to be "beyond price" and the good he provides immeasurable.

Finally, for Ben Sira, a "good friend" is a fighting friend (37:5–6 [B, D]), an understanding absent from earlier biblical materials dealing with friendship:

A good friend ['ôhēb ṭôb] makes war with an outsider [zār],
Before enemies he will grasp a shield.
Do not forget a companion [ḥābēr] in battle,
And do not forsake him through (the division of?) your spoil.[44]

Scholars debate whether the passage is meant to be understood literally or metaphorically. My own preference is to understand it literally, as advice to the soldier.[45] In any case, it seems likely that Ps 35:1–2 has influenced the formulation of Sir 37:5, as others have noticed.[46] In Ps 35:1–2, it is Yhwh who is called upon to fight for the sufferer; in Sir 37:5, the "good friend" is characterized as one who fights for his friend. Thus, older material concerning Yhwh is apparently drawn upon to formulate the novel image of the fighting friend, just as earlier texts portraying Yhwh as a support and help to sufferers are likely a source used to enrich the image of the friend who helps and supports his friend in time of need (e.g., 13:22 [A; Beentjes 13:21]). The same pattern seems likely for the image of the friend as helpful leader or guide in Sir 40:23, as I have discussed (see n. 34). In contrast, the idea of Sir 37:6 that the friend should not abandon or forget his friend is not novel but shared with earlier biblical texts such as Prov 27:10 and Job 19:14, as I have noted previously. In fact, the assertion that the friend should not forsake his friend is expressed in a style not unlike that of Prov 27:10.[47] Thus, Sir 37:5–6 perpetuates certain earlier ideas and vocabulary relating to friendship and, at the same time, likely modifies—or reflects modification of—other earlier ideas not originally related to friendship in order to apply them to the friend. In addition to the impact of earlier biblical texts such as Ps 35:1–2 on the formulation of Sir 37:5–6, the text likely also betrays Greek influence, as I suggest in the next section.

Not unlike some vocabulary and idioms extant in earlier materials, a number of ideas associated with friendship in biblical sources antedating Ben Sira are missing or mainly absent from Ben Sira. In contrast to texts such as the narrative of Jephthah's daughter and her companions (Judg 11:34–40) and the book of Ruth, Ben Sira has nothing to say about female friendship. In this the book is close to earlier wisdom materials, which tend to present friendship as a bond between men.[48] Friendship formalized by a treaty, a phenomenon evidenced in texts such as 1 Sam 18:1–4; 20:41; and Ps 55:14–15, 21, is neither mentioned nor hinted at in Ben Sira. Nor is the role of the friend as "comforter" in contexts of mourning, calamity, or petition, so central to texts such as Judg 11:37, 38; Ps 35:13–14; Job 2:11–13; 13:4; 16:2, as discussed.[49] As with vocabulary and idioms of friendship, it is difficult to know when Ben Sira is innovating with respect to ideas about friendship and when his presentations more likely reflect shared or even common usage in his social setting.

Evidence of the Influence of Greek Ideas on Ben Sira's Friendship Ideology

Given that Ben Sira lived and wrote in a Hellenistic context, it should come as no surprise that he was very likely influenced to at least some degree by Greek notions of friendship.[50] Our challenge is to identify where such influence might be confidently discerned and its possible sources (literary or oral), questions about which there has been much debate and little agreement.[51] In order to address these questions, I begin by identifying apparent borrowings that are as easily or more easily explained as ideas shared in common with earlier biblical materials. Thus, if an idea about friendship is attested in both Greek literature and earlier biblical texts, I shall not assume that its presence in Ben Sira is the result of borrowing. Greek materials may have exercised an influence on Ben Sira, but if earlier biblical parallels are extant for a particular idea, Greek influence cannot be established with any confidence.[52] In contrast, in cases in which the influence of earlier biblical materials cannot be ascertained but parallels in Greek thought are evidenced, we can be more confident of the possibility of Greek influence of some kind.[53] Nonetheless, we must keep in mind that Ben Sira himself may or may not be directly responsible for one or another apparent borrowing. I begin my assessment with four examples of ideas shared in common by Ben Sira, earlier biblical texts, and Greek materials.

A number of ideas about friendship expressed by Ben Sira are found both in earlier biblical materials and in Greek literature. That wealth multiplies friendships and poverty erodes them is noted in Prov 19:4: "Wealth adds many friends, / But as for the poor man, he is separated from his friend." Ben Sira 13:21 (A), likely elaborating on Prov 19:4, adds a specific circumstance—misfortune—and contrasts the experience of rich and poor: "A rich man who totters finds support in a friend, / But a poor man who totters is driven from friend to friend," suggesting rejection of the poor man by his friends.[54] The following verse, Sir 13:22, speaks of the rich man's numerous "helpers," likely building upon the reference to the rich man's "many friends" in Prov 19:4, as Corley argues.[55] Going beyond Prov 19:4, Sir 13:22 adds the idea that the rich man is popular even when his words are despicable and the poor man is rejected even when his speech is sensible.[56] The statement in Sir 13:22 that "there is no place" for the poor man, even if he is wise, may build on the claim in Prov 19:4 that the poor man "is separated from his friend." Theognis, for his part, states that the rich will have many friends and the poor few, not unlike Prov 19:4 (lines 929–30).[57] Might Theognis have also influenced Ben Sira either directly or indirectly? Although such influence is possible, it cannot be established with any confidence, given the likely impact of Prov 19:4.

Another example of an idea common to Ben Sira, earlier biblical sources, and Greek materials is the notion that behavioral parity or reciprocity is a central building block of friendship. Aristotle expresses this in no uncertain terms: In an ideal friendship, "in every respect each friend gets from the other things that are the same as, or similar to, the things that the other gets from him—which is in fact what ought to belong to friends" (*Nicomachean Ethics* 8.4 1156b 34–35).[58] He goes on to state that in the two other, inferior types of friendship—that of utility and that of pleasure in his theorization—the same kind of reciprocity should apply. In Ben Sira and earlier biblical texts, behavioral parity is also assumed to be a norm of friendship generally, though it is usually communicated implicitly rather than explicitly, in contrast to Aristotle, and is often spoken of in the breach.[59] An example of this is the complaint in Ps 35:12 that ex-friends have paid back the psalmist that which is evil instead of what is good, a claim that implies that good treatment in exchange for manifestations of beneficence is the norm. In Sir 37:5–6 (B, D), the "good friend" who fights for his friend against the "outsider" stands in parallel with the "companion" (*ḥābēr*) who should not be forgotten in battle, suggesting implicitly a reciprocal understanding of friendship's obligations. As in earlier biblical texts, and in contrast to Aristotle, the norm of behavioral parity is conveyed implicitly in Ben Sira. That behavioral parity is so central to friendship in earlier biblical materials suggests that we not be overly hasty to assume Greek influence on Ben Sira's notion of reciprocity in friendship.

A third example of an idea attested in Ben Sira, earlier biblical texts, and Greek literature is the notion that some friends will prove to be unreliable or actively disloyal at a time of crisis when loyalty is expected. Psalm 35:15 speaks of disloyal friends who rejoice when the psalmist stumbles; Ps 38:12 mentions friends who stand at a distance from the suffering petitioner; Ps 41:10 recalls the once trusted friend who "eats my food" but has acted in a hostile manner; and Job 19:14 states that Job's friends—literally, "my intimates," *měyuddāʿay*—have forgotten him in his time of need. For its part, Sir 6:8–13 (A; Beentjes 6:7–12) speaks of the friend with whom one eats "who will not be found on the day of trouble," the friend "who will turn himself into an enemy," and the friend who "will hide himself from you" when things go awry. Warnings about such friends are paralleled in Theognis (e.g., lines 643–44, 697–98) as scholars such as Middendorp, Sanders, and Corley note.[60] In fact, that false friends remove themselves at times of misfortune is a common theme throughout Greco-Roman literature.[61] Cicero speaks of those who abandon their friends in their distress; Seneca, for his part, refers to people who run when confronted by their friend's adversity.⁶² Given the prominence of the topos of the disloyal friend in earlier biblical materials, its presence in a text such as Sir 6:8–13 comes as no surprise and militates against the assumption that the idea was derived from Greek thought, where the theme is also well attested. Sanders argues that Ben Sira nonetheless drew upon Theognis to elaborate upon the inherited theme of the disloyal friend, pointing to close parallels in language between Theognis and Ben Sira, for example, as regards table fellowship.⁶³ Yet Ps 41:10, a text that Sanders does not mention, also speaks of an unfaithful friend who ate the psalmist's food, as I have noted; it may in fact be the source for Ben Sira's statement about the disloyal friend who shares meals with his friend. In short, although Sanders is critical of Middendorp for overstating his case, Sanders, too, may have been too quick to assume Greek influence, at least with respect to the table fellow as disloyal friend.

A fourth case of overlap between Ben Sira, earlier biblical texts, and Greek materials is the conception of the friend as somehow related to, or an extension of, the self. Deuteronomy 13:7 mentions the intimate friend "who is as yourself" (*rēʿăkā ʾăšer kĕnapšĕkā*), and Ps 55:14 speaks of the friend who is "a man like me" (*kĕʿerkî*). Ben Sira, likely building on Deut 13:7, mentions a "friend who is as yourself" (*rēaʿ kĕnapšĕkā*) in 37:2 (B), deploring his transformation into an enemy.⁶⁴ He also speaks of the friend who is "like you" (*kāmôkā*) when times are good but who removes himself when misfortune strikes (A; 6:11 [Beentjes 6:10]) as well as the "loyal friend" (*ʾôhēb ʾĕmûnâ*) whose own friend is "like him" (*kāmôhû*) (A; 6:16–17 [Beentjes 6:15–16]). The idea that the friend is a "second self" or "another self" is common to Greco-Roman discourse on friendship, beginning with Aristotle. Is this idea the same as the biblical notion that the intimate friend is "as yourself" or "like you"? Though similar, the ideas are not exactly the same, and, like the close biblical parallels, the difference cautions against assuming Greek influence in this instance.⁶⁵

In contrast to ideas attested in Ben Sira, earlier biblical texts, and Greek sources, there are other notions about friends in Ben Sira that are not found in earlier biblical materials but are paralleled in Greek texts, some of which antedate the second century BCE. In addition, some of these ideas find parallels in Egyptian wisdom, as several scholars have noted.⁶⁶ I focus on four such ideas: that friends ought to be tested, that flatterers are not truly friends, that there is a type of friend who fights for his friend, and that the number of one's friends ought to be limited. It is among these examples that the possibility of Greek influence is most seriously to be considered, particularly if Egyptian parallels are lacking.

Although testing the friend to determine whether he is trustworthy is not mentioned in earlier biblical materials, testing in other biblical contexts is a relatively common theme. God tests Israel, and Israel, for its part, tests God (Exod 15:25; 16:4; 17:2, 7; 20:20; Deut 33:8). Yhwh tests individuals (Gen 22:1; Ps 26:2), and individuals might also put Yhwh to the test (Isa 7:12). In addition, people might test other people (1 Kgs 10:1).[67] Yet in Sir 6:7 (A; [Beentjes 6:6]), care and a healthy skepticism are urged when making friends, and friends must prove themselves through a process of testing: "If you acquire a friend, through testing [*běnissāyōn*] acquire him, / And do not be quick to trust him."[68] As is often pointed out, testing of friends and being slow to trust them are prominent themes in Greco-Roman discourses on friendship.[69] Aristotle speaks of testing friends (*Nicomachean Ethics* 8.4 1157a 21–22), as do Xenophon, Isocrates, Theognis, and Menander.[70] Such testing is a prominent theme explored by Roman authors such as Cicero (*On Friendship* 17, 20) and Seneca (*Epistles* 3.2, 9.9) as well. Some passages advise testing when a new friend is to be embraced, not unlike Sir 6:7 (e.g., Xenophon, *Memorabilia* 2.6.1; Seneca, *Epistles* 3.2); other texts speak of ongoing testing after a friendship is established (e.g., *Nicomachean Ethics* 8.4 1157a 21–22); and still others speak of testing in both contexts (e.g., Cicero, *On Friendship* 17, 20). Ben Sira's focus on testing at the point of a friendship's genesis is a commonplace in classical sources and may well reflect the influence of Greek thought, although Egyptian influence is also a distinct possibility, as Sanders and others have pointed out.[71]

Earlier biblical treatments of friendship have nothing to say about flatterers, in contrast to Ben Sira, who describes the many helpers who rally to and praise a rich man, even if his words are unworthy: "A rich man speaks and his helpers are many, / His repellent words are called beautiful." Furthermore, Ben Sira states that when a rich man speaks, "all are silent, his understanding [*śiklô*] they exalt to the clouds" (A; 13:22, 23). Ben Sira's evocation of the flatterers of the wealthy is striking and parallels treatments of flattery in Greco-Roman sources in a number of respects. These often distinguish flatterers from genuine friends and value frankness (*parrēsia*) in a friendship rather than disingenuous praise.[72] In fact, Cicero states that nothing is more inimical to genuine friendship than flattery (*On Friendship* 25).[73] Aristotle, for his part, identifies the flatterer as a man who tries to be agreeable to gain a financial or material advantage (*Nicomachean Ethics* 4.6

1127a 7–10).⁷⁴ Because most men love honor, says Aristotle, most love flattery: "for a flatterer is a friend who, if he is not inferior, pretends to be so and to love more than he is loved" (*Nicomachean Ethics* 8.8 1159a 15–17).⁷⁵ Although Ben Sira's image of the flatterer emphasizes his disingenuousness, it also suggests implicitly the flatterer's embrace of inferiority, an act motivated perhaps by an eye to the rich man's potential material largesse. The distinction between flatterer and friend, often stated explicitly in classical sources, is at best implicit in Ben Sira.⁷⁶ Given that flatterers do not appear in earlier biblical texts concerning friendship and that Ben Sira's evocation of them shares characteristics in common with their representation in classical sources, it is quite possible that Ben Sira's treatment has been influenced by Greek ideas.⁷⁷

The image of the fighting friend developed in Sir 37:5–6 (B, D) is unlike anything in earlier biblical materials dealing with friendship and very likely reflects the influence of both Greek thought and earlier biblical ideas and rhetoric in combination.⁷⁸ Corley may be correct that in the "good friend" who fights the "outsider" in Sir 37:5, "there seems to be a reference ... to the Greek idea" of the *symmachos,* rendered "ally," "comrade-in-arms," or "helper" by Corley. In order to support this claim, Corley cites parallels from Demosthenes and Xenophon.⁷⁹ But what of the *hetairos,* "companion," who is not infrequently described as a *philos* in Greek sources?⁸⁰ The *hetairos* is often mentioned in martial contexts, and, as Konstan points out, Patroclus is said to be Achilles' "dearest companion by far."⁸¹ Interestingly, LXX uses *hetairos* in Sir 37:5 along with *philos* in a combination where the Hebrew (B, D) has *'ōhēb ṭôb* ("good friend"). It is certainly possible that Ben Sira had the *hetairos* in mind when he spoke of the "good friend" who fights the "outsider." In any case the translator seems to have thought so, assuming that his Hebrew *Vorlage* was not unlike that which survives in extant manuscripts. As I discussed earlier, I believe the image is meant to be taken literally rather than metaphorically, in contrast to many other interpreters. I also suspect that a combination of Ps 35:1–2, a text that describes Yhwh fighting for the suffering psalmist, and earlier ideas and rhetoric of nonabandonment of the friend contributed to Ben Sira's portrayal of the fighting friend, along with the Greek idea of the *hetairos* or, alternatively, the *symmachos.*

Earlier biblical texts have nothing explicit or implicit to say about the ideal number of friends one should have, and even a text such as Prov 18:24, which recognizes different kinds of friends (both "friends for friendly exchanges" and the intimate friend), does not address their number in any specific way. In contrast, Ben Sira states that although one's friends (*'anšê šālôm*) should be many, one's "trusted intimate" (*baʿal sôd*) should be one in a thousand (A; 6:6 [Beentjes 6:5]).[82] Like Ben Sira, there are Greek texts that consider the ideal number of friends, and these often distinguish between different types of friends. Aristotle argues that one's friends ought to be limited to the maximum number of those who can live together and are friends with one another; he further notes that it is not possible to be an "ardent friend" (*philon sphodra*) to many at the same time and that even friends for pleasure and utility should be limited in number (*Nicomachean Ethics* 9.10 1170b 29–1171a 20).[83] Thus, Aristotle balances several practical considerations in his treatment. Theognis (lines 73–75) and Xenophon (*Memorabilia* 2.6.27) urge few friends, as Corley notes.[84] If *'anšê šālôm* in Sir 6:6 refers to friends, as I believe it does, Ben Sira's teaching is not that one should have few friends; it is that one should have only a few intimate friends. Whether my understanding of this passage, or that of Corley and others, is correct, Ben Sira's interest in the appropriate number of friends one should have may reflect concerns with the ideal number of friends common in Greek sources. In any case, this is a topic that earlier biblical sources leave unexplored, and Ben Sira's treatment may reflect Greek influence.

Conclusion

Ben Sira's vocabulary and idioms of friendship as well as his ideas about friendship are both continuous and discontinuous with the vocabulary, idioms, and ideas of friendship evidenced in earlier biblical texts. Perhaps surprisingly, there is no evident privileging of wisdom sources—either traditional or skeptical—over other earlier texts when Ben Sira draws upon inherited materials. As in older biblical texts, Ben Sira makes use of nouns, verbs, and idioms of friendship such as *rēaʿ* ("friend"), *'ōhēb* ("friend," "lover") *'îš/'ĕnôš šālôm* ("one with whom I enjoy good relations"), *bāṭaḥ* ("to trust"), *minneged ʿāmad* ("to stand at a distance"), *rēaʿ kĕnapšĕkā* ("a friend who is as yourself"), *šākaḥ* ("to forget"), and *ʿāzab* ("to abandon"), favoring some (e.g., *'ōhēb*) over others. Terminology that is rarely if ever associated with friendship in earlier biblical discourse is extended to the realm of friendship (e.g., derivatives of *ʿāzar* ["to help"] and *sāmak* ["to support"]; the term *ḥābēr* ["companion"]; expressions such as *baʿal sôd* for the intimate friend). Ben Sira makes use of modified versions of earlier terms (e.g., *ʼôhēb ṭôb,* "good friend"; *ʼôhēb yāšān/ḥādāš,* "old/new friend"; *ʼôhēb ʼĕmûnâ,* "true friend"). At the same time, he eschews some words and idioms that are relatively commonplace in earlier sources or occur in important friendship discourses. The friend is not referred to as *ʼallûp* (possibly "gentle one") or *mĕyuddāʻ* ("one who is known [to me]"). Ben Sira never speaks of friends "clinging" (*dbq*) to their friends, in contrast to Prov 18:24; nowhere are derivatives of the root *tʻb,* "to abominate," used with respect to the behavior of disloyal friends, in contrast to texts such as Job 19:19; the idiom "to pay back that which is evil (instead of what is good)" (*šlm* [Pi], *śym* or *gml raʻâ/raʻ* [*taḥat ṭôbâ*]) is not to be found in Ben Sira's discourses on friends; nor does Ben Sira use hendiadys constructions such as "my loving friends" (*ʼōhăbay wĕrēʻay,* Ps 38:12) in his discussions of friendship. No particular pattern of continuity or discontinuity with earlier biblical sources may be discerned in Ben Sira's use of the nouns, verbs, and idioms of friendship; he might draw upon or ignore the vocabulary and expressions of earlier wisdom texts (both traditional and skeptical), prophetic materials, the psalms of individual complaint, legal materials, or narrative texts. Two examples will serve to illustrate this lack of a pattern, specifically with regard to inherited wisdom texts: Although Ben Sira urges his audience not to abandon or forget friends (37:6 [B, D]), as does Prov 27:10 ("Do not abandon your friend or the friend of your father"), and—implicitly—Job 19:14 ("My intimates have forgotten me"), he disregards or rejects idioms derived from the verbs "to cling to" (e.g., Prov 18:24) and "to abominate" (e.g., Job 19:19) in his friendship discourses, even though these occur in important passages dealing with friendship in earlier wisdom materials. As noted, it is often not clear whether one or another of his usages suggests innovation on his part or simply reflects what is current in his environment.

Similar patterns apply to Ben Sira's ideas about friendship. Earlier notions are reproduced in Ben Sira with little or no change. Love between friends is an expectation, has both emotional and behavioral resonances, and is made manifest through acts of loyalty and demonstrations of trustworthiness, as in Jer 9:3; Ps 41:10; and Sir 6:7 (A). Behavioral parity is assumed to be the norm of friendship and is often suggested implicitly in contexts in which failed friendship is at issue (Ps 35:12–14; Sir 22:23; 37:1–4 [D, partially B]). As in earlier materials such as Deut 13:7; Prov 17:17; and 18:24, friends share an implicit common classification with family members in texts such as Sir 7:18 (A). Ideas manifest in earlier biblical sources are also elaborated and extended in Ben Sira. The book's particular emphasis on helping and supporting friends in time of need in its discourses on loyalty in friendship is an example of this, with the rhetoric of help (*'zr*) and support (*smk*) possibly borrowed directly from earlier texts that speak of Yhwh's help and support of sufferers (e.g., Pss 37:17, 24; 54:6). Gradations in friendship also appear to be more developed than in earlier texts such as Prov 18:24 and 19:4, although the differences in nuance in Ben Sira's use of terms such as *'ôhēb*, *rēa'*, and *ḥābēr* remain unclear. Ben Sira expresses a number of ideas that are not attested or are rare in earlier biblical materials. These include the friend or companion as leader (Sir 40:23), the capable wife as superior to the sensible friend or companion (Sir 40:23), and the possibility of reconciliation between estranged friends (e.g., Sir 22:21–22; 27:21). Although earlier texts such as Prov 14:20 and 19:7 speak of material support for poor friends and Ben Sira mentions this (Sir 22:23), he also urges his audience to extend such material largesse to friends in general (Sir 14:13 [A]), an idea absent from earlier texts concerned with friendship. Finally, several important ideas attested in earlier biblical sources regarding friendship are absent from Ben Sira. The possibility of female friendship is not acknowledged, the idea that a friendship might be structured as a treaty is not attested, and the role of friendship in settings of mourning, calamity, and petition is not mentioned. As with Ben Sira's vocabulary and idioms of friendship, his ideas concerning friendship display both continuities and discontinuities with those of earlier biblical materials, and no particular configuration of continuity or discontinuity may be discerned. Ideas from the psalms of individual complaint, prophetic texts, prose narrative, and poetic wisdom materials are adopted by Ben Sira (e.g., material support for poor friends [Sir 22:23], as in Prov 14:20; 19:7), while other earlier notions of friendship are not embraced, including ideas manifest in wisdom texts (e.g., comforting the friend at the time of calamity and death [Job 2:11–13; 13:4; 16:2]). Whether Ben Sira's choices represent innovation on his part or mirror usages common in his time and place is often difficult to determine.

The possibility of Greek influence on Ben Sira's thinking about friendship is much debated, and no broad consensus exists regarding either the extent of Greek influence or the mechanisms by which Greek ideas might have been communicated. Unlike some scholars, I believe the best that one can do is to estimate the likelihood of Greek influence on a case-by-case basis. Nonetheless, I have identified several potential examples of the influence of Greek thought. None of these has a parallel in earlier biblical texts, and only one has a close analogue in Egyptian wisdom. It may well be that Greek influence is to be discerned in Ben Sira's discourse on testing the new friend and being slow to trust him, in his portrayal of flatterers, in his image of the fighting friend, and in his notion that one should have few intimate friends, although the testing theme and its rhetoric are also evidenced in Egyptian wisdom, as Sanders and others have noted. Even in the few cases in which Greek influence of some sort is plausible, it is not easy to determine the manner in which it might have been exercised or whether Ben Sira himself is responsible for one or another apparent borrowing.

Conclusion

I begin my concluding remarks with a comparison of the representation of friendship in a number of distinct biblical literary types. Friendship is portrayed in the Psalms, particularly those of individual complaint; in legal materials such as Deut 13:7; in non-psalmic poetic texts such as "David's Lament over Saul and Jonathan" (2 Sam 1:26); in prophetic passages such as Jer 9:3 and Mic 7:5–6; in prose narratives such as the stories of David and Jonathan, Ruth and Naomi, Job and his three comforters, Amnon, Absalom, and Jonadab, and Jephthah's daughter and her companions; in pre-Hellenistic wisdom collections—both traditional and skeptical—such as Proverbs and the poetic sections of the book of Job; and in the Hellenistic wisdom collection Ben Sira. Friendship is represented both in biblical poetry and in prose narrative. Some of the texts of interest to us may be dated with confidence (e.g., Ben Sira, to the second century BCE), but most are difficult if not impossible to date. Ben Sira is not infrequently dependent on earlier biblical texts (both wisdom—traditional and skeptical—and nonwisdom); other texts in our purview display little or no evidence of dependence on earlier materials. Our texts sometimes share vocabulary, idioms, and ideas; sometimes they do not. The friends portrayed range from flat, one-dimensional types without any individuality to complex, strikingly singular people who may be conflicted and whose behavior is not necessarily consistent or predictable. We can chart the characteristics of friendship shared in common across literary types and bring the differences among those types into relief. In order to get a sense of the configurations of vocabulary, idioms, ideas, and portrayals pertaining to friendship across our sources, I focus my discussion on several important ideas about friends, with reference to vocabulary and idioms of friendship where relevant. I then consider the range of ways in which friends are portrayed in various biblical texts.

The classification of friends with family members is a broadly attested idea in biblical materials. It is evidenced across a number of literary types, including prose narrative (Exod 32:27), legal materials (Deut 13:7), prophetic poetry (Jer 9:3; Mic 7:5–6), psalms of individual complaint (Ps 38:12) and other psalms (Pss 15:2; 122:8), traditional wisdom (Prov 17:17; 18:24; 19:7), skeptical wisdom (Job 19:13–14), and Ben Sira (Sir 7:12, 18 [A]), which shares characteristics with traditional wisdom but is distinct in a number of ways, as I have discussed. Such classification is accomplished by means of explicit comparison, as in texts such as Prov 18:24 and 19:7, or, more commonly, implicit common classification. Implicit common classification of friends with family members may be achieved by means of the employment of a single list of intimates that includes friends, as in Deut 13:7, or, more frequently, through the use of parallelism either in poetic texts such as Jer 9:3, Psalm 15, Job 19:13–14, or Sir 7:12, 18 (A) or in prose narratives such as Exod 32:27. Such shared classification of friends and family members is rare in narrative because narrative seldom employs parallelism in the manner of Exod 32:27. In contrast to most prose, this narrative text has a parallelistic structure, suggesting a common class of intimates that includes both family members and friends: "Pass and return through the camp, from end to end, slaying each his brother, each his friend, each his relative." Explicit comparison and implicit common classification of friends and family members often privilege relatives as paradigmatic intimates to whom friends might be likened, and this tendency is evidenced in a number of different literary types. Examples include Prov 18:24, "there is a friend who clings more closely than a brother," and Deut 13:7, a text that includes the intimate friend in a list of familial intimates, suggesting implicitly that the close family members are paradigmatic intimates and the intimate friend is comparable to them. In contrast, comparison of family members to friends, a commonplace among some groups in contemporary Western societies, is unknown in biblical materials.

The assumption of behavioral parity as a requirement of friends, like family members, is also a widely attested idea, expressed both explicitly and implicitly, sometimes through the use of distinct idioms. We find the expectation of behavioral parity expressed in texts such as Ps 35:12–14 and 38:21 (seemingly with reference to both friends and family); Job 19:19; and Sir 6:8–13 (A), 22:23, and 37:1–4 (D, some B). It is expected even if friends are formally unequal, as in 1 Sam 20:41, where David bows three times to Jonathan before they embrace, or in the book of Ruth, whose central character Ruth is Naomi's daughter-in-law and a generation younger than Naomi. In some texts, the behavior in question is ritual in nature, as in Ps 35:12–14 (comforting at the time of personal calamity or illness) or 1 Sam 20:41 (reciprocal acts of affection [kissing and weeping]); in others, the behavior does not clearly have a ritual dimension (e.g., Ps 38:21, paying back that which is evil instead of what is good; Job 19:19, abominating in return for love). Most texts do not seem to distinguish between the expectations of family members and friends, requiring behavioral parity from both equally (e.g., Ps 38:21). Proverbs 19:7, however, seems to have higher expectations for family members, whose failure to be loyal is less easily explained than the same deficiency in friends, perhaps because relatives are thought by the author to be the paradigmatic intimates. The expectation of behavioral parity is sometimes communicated through the use of distinct idioms such as the expression *šlm* (Pi), *śym* or *gml rāʿâ/raʿ* [*taḥat ṭôbâ*], "to pay back that which is evil [instead of what is good]," as in Pss 7:5, 35:12, 38:21, and 109:5, although such idioms are not broadly attested across biblical literary types, in contrast to the idea of behavioral parity itself. The assumption of behavioral parity in friendship is not in the least surprising, given the importance of reciprocity in the larger context of social and even cultic relations according to biblical texts. Not only are friends, family members, and treaty partners expected to reciprocate good treatment; Yhwh himself states that his modus operandi is characterized by reciprocity: "Those who honor me I will honor and those who despise me will be diminished."[1]

The idea of the exceptional friend is known across several literary types. He appears among close family members in Deut 13:7; he is explicitly compared to the brother and found to be his superior in Prov 18:24; she is evoked in great detail in the book of Ruth; and in Sir 37:2 (B, D), his transformation into an enemy is the cause of grief (or, is a judgment) "approaching death."[2] The exceptional friend may be described as one who is "as yourself" (Deut 13:7; Sir 37:2 [B]); he may be said to "cling [*dābēq*] more closely than a brother" (Prov 18:24); alternatively, he may be called a "good friend," a "true friend," or a "trusted intimate" (*baʿal sôd*) (Sir 6:6, 14–16 [A]; 37:5 [B, D]). The idea of the exceptional friend suggests implicitly an assumption of gradations of friendship, for the exceptional friend can be exceptional only if other friends are not. Gradations of friendship are evidenced explicitly in the comparison of the exceptional friend to "friends for friendly exchanges" in Prov 18:24. Proverbs 19:4 suggests the idea of friends attracted by wealth, who might be ranked lower than other friends (e.g., the "friends for friendly exchanges" of 18:24) by the writer, although nothing is said explicitly about this. Ben Sira uses a variety of terms for friends, including several terms for the exceptional friend as I have mentioned, though unhappily, it is difficult to get a sense of how exactly Ben Sira might rank each type of friend (e.g., how the *rēaʿ* might compare to the *ḥābēr* in Sir 7:12 [A]). Thus, although the notion of the exceptional friend is strongly articulated in a variety of biblical texts, gradations of friendship, where they are evidenced, are less clear in their details.

Nonetheless, the gradations of friendship evidenced in a number of biblical sources might be profitably compared to Aristotle's classification of friends, for both similarities and differences are apparent. Aristotle provides a detailed theory of friendship, identifying and ranking three distinct types: friendship of the good, friendship motivated by utility, and friendship with the goal of pleasure (*Nicomachean Ethics* 8.3–4). Although Aristotle's three types of friendship differ from those suggested by biblical texts in a number of ways, there are characteristics in common. The "friends for friendly exchanges" of Prov 18:24 might be similar to Aristotle's friends who seek out pleasure; the friends who flock to the rich man in Prov 19:4 are evidently not unlike Aristotle's friends who have utilitarian aims. The exceptional friend of Prov 18:24 is apparently preeminent among friends primarily because of his loyalty, intimacy, and, possibly, proximity (he "clings more closely than a brother"); the exceptional friend of Deut 13:7 and Sir 37:2 (B) is outstanding most likely on account of his intimacy (he is "as yourself"). The quality that distinguishes Ben Sira's "good friend" of 37:5 (B, D) is clearly his loyalty, and the same can be said of Ruth. In contrast to exceptional friendship as understood in these biblical texts, where loyalty or intimacy seems of most concern, the primary quality that distinguishes Aristotle's preeminent form of friendship is shared virtue or excellence (*aretē*), which will give rise to trust, pleasure, and even utility.

Failed friendship is a topos across much of biblical literature, with disloyal friends present most prominently in the psalms of individual complaint, but also in the Job poetic dialogues (e.g., 19:13–14, 19); Proverbs (e.g., 19:4, 7); prophetic texts such as Mic 7:5 and Jer 9:3–4, 7; and Sir 6:9–11 (A) and 37:2 (D, B). Various idioms are used to describe the behavior of unfaithful friends (e.g., they "stand at a distance," "abominate," or "pay back that which is evil instead of what is good"), and they might be accused directly of failing to fulfill obligations (e.g., as comforters in Job 13:4 and 16:2). Failure in friendship might be attributed to the friends themselves, as in

Ps 35:12–14, or to Yhwh, who is said to use unfaithful friends as a tool to punish the sufferer in some psalms of individual complaint (e.g., Ps 89:9).[3] Disloyal friends are not infrequently mentioned with unfaithful relatives (e.g., Jer 9:3; Mic 7:5–6; Ps 38:12; Job 19:13–14), just as the exceptional friend might be classified with close familial intimates in other texts. Some passages contrast disloyal friends with faithful friends (Ps 35:26–27, implicitly). The theme of failed friendship, prominent in certain types of biblical literature, is infrequently attested in biblical prose narratives, which often portray idealized friendships, for example, Job and his three comforters in the Job prologue or Jephthah's daughter and her companions. An apparent exception to this pattern is the story of Jonadab and Amnon in 2 Samuel 13. Jonadab's behavior in this narrative manifests extremes of both loyalty and disloyalty toward his friend and cousin Amnon, and he appears eventually to abandon Amnon, attaching himself instead to Absalom, Amnon's half brother who orchestrates his murder. If my interpretation of Jonadab's behavior is correct, we are certainly justified in describing the Amnon-Jonadab friendship as a failure, characterized ultimately by Jonadab's disloyalty, even if no idioms of failed friendship are present in the text (e.g., "pay back that which is evil instead of what is good").

Friends are evoked in a variety of ways in biblical materials. The friends of the psalms of individual complaint and a number of wisdom and prophetic texts might be described as one-dimensional and completely lacking in individuality and complexity. They are unnamed and are usually characterized as disloyal in every respect, displaying stereotypical behaviors. They threaten the sufferer's life, plan to wrong him, fail to reciprocate that which is good, and rejoice at his stumbling (Ps 35). They are untrustworthy and speak lies (Jer 9:3–4; Mic 7:5). They forget the friend and even abominate him (Job 19:14, 19). Loyal friends, though rarely mentioned in these texts, are also relatively flat, lacking in individuality. In Ps 35:27, they are described as those who delight in the psalmist's vindication. In contrast to these friends, some texts portray friends who possess somewhat more individuality, although they, too, lack genuine complexity. These friends, who appear mainly in narrative contexts, often have names, indicating a degree of individuation. Sometimes we know details of their histories. But their behavior is predictable, and we would not be wrong to describe them as idealized. Here I am thinking of characters such as Ruth and Job's comforters in the Job prologue. Ruth is a good example of this second type of friend. She is as much the flawless friend as she is a perfect wife and daughter-in-law.

Her behavior is consistent, she displays no inner conflicts, she is generous to a fault, and she's never self-pitying or hostile to anyone. In a word, she may have a name and a history, suggesting individuation to some extent, but she is completely predictable and lacks complexity. In contrast to characters such as the friends of Psalm 35 and Ruth, several texts portray complex, highly individuated friends who are not predictable in their conduct, who display personal growth, who are, in a word, interesting characters. Naomi is one example, Jonadab another, David a third. I shall speak of Naomi here. Where Ruth is consistently flawless in her conduct, Naomi's behavior is difficult to predict as the story develops. She displays growth over time, transforming herself from a rather self-pitying complainer who takes Ruth for granted into an energetic agent of change whose advice and actions secure a future for both Ruth and herself. She is, in short, a foil for Ruth. In the biblical evocation of friends, narrative is the primary vehicle for constructing well-developed, complex, and interesting friends, friends who are otherwise lacking in biblical representations of friendship. We find examples of somewhat individuated friends in prose as well.

The relationship of the emotions to friendship is a challenge to assess, and simplistic, maximalist readings of our texts are to be avoided, given that verbs such as "to love" and "to cling to" are used not only of the relations of friends to one another and family members among themselves, but of treaty partners as well. This suggests the possibility of a range of nuances for these idioms, including political overtones in covenant contexts. Use of such idioms in a treaty setting may or may not tell us anything about the personal feelings of treaty partners, who may well feel no affection and harbor no genuine concern for one another, as I have discussed. Given the overlap of vocabulary and idioms of friendship and those of covenanting, how might we identify examples of the representation of friendship in which emotional bonding is clearly suggested? This is a critical question, given that the presence of evidence of genuine feelings of affection in a voluntary association is the most cogent way to establish the existence of a friendship as opposed to another kind of relationship that might, like a friendship, draw upon friendship vocabulary and idioms or suggest the assumption of behavioral parity (e.g., a treaty relationship between allies). In my view, the best way to argue convincingly that the portrayal of a friendship suggests an emotional dimension is to identify idioms or behavior in the description of the characters that cannot be explained in any other way.

A case in point is 1 Sam 18:1–4. The text states that the "self" or "life" (*nepeš*) of Jonathan was "bound" to the "self" or "life" of David; that Jonathan "loved" David "as himself"; that Jonathan and David cut a covenant "when" or "because he loved him as himself"; and that Jonathan removed his garment and gave it to David, along with his weapons and other personal items. The word *rēaʿ* with the meaning "friend"—as well as other terms for "friend"—are not used of Jonathan and/or David here or elsewhere in the David-Jonathan narratives, nor are they to be found in 2 Sam 1:19–27, David's Lament over Saul and Jonathan. Nonetheless, there is reason to describe 1 Sam 18:1–4 as a text narrating the beginning of a friendship, albeit one that is formalized through the idiom of treaty-making. Although it might seem at first blush that loving someone else as oneself conveys emotional content, this cannot be assumed, given that the idiom is used in treaty settings to communicate loyalty and 1 Sam 18:1–4 is manifestly a treaty setting, as indicated by the mention of Jonathan and David cutting a covenant. As I have mentioned, Esarhaddon, king of Assyria, requires his vassals to swear that they will love Ashurbanipal, his son and heir, as they do themselves. In other words, the vassals bind themselves by oath to be loyal to their overlord's son when he comes to the throne.

Given such parallels, it would be difficult to argue convincingly that the idiom "to love *x* as oneself" is necessarily intended to communicate anything about anyone's emotional state. But such is not the case with the statement that the "self" or "life" (*nepeš*) of Jonathan was "bound" to the "self" or "life" of David. As I have pointed out, this idiom occurs only one other time in the Hebrew Bible and not in the setting of a treaty. In Gen 44:30–31, it is used to describe the relationship of Jacob to his youngest son Benjamin, whom he is said to love in Gen 44:20. In contrast to the idiom to love someone as oneself, the binding of selves or lives appears to have unambiguous emotional resonance. In Gen 44:30–31, it conveys the love of a father for a favorite son, a love so intense that the son's demise would result in the death of the father. A similarly intense emotional resonance is therefore possible for the idiom when it occurs in 1 Sam 18:1, suggesting the potential for a profound emotional bond between male friends, a phenomenon that is also evidenced by 1 Sam 20:41, with its reciprocal ritual acts of affection between David and Jonathan. An emotional resonance is also evident in texts such as Deut 13:7–12, Prov 18:24, and Sir 37:2 (B), which suggest the intimacy of the exceptional friend, who is described as a friend who is "as yourself" or a friend "who clings more closely than a brother." Furthermore, Sir 37:2 (B) characterizes the transformation of the friend "who is as yourself" into an enemy as a cause of grief or as a judgment "approaching death," suggesting a significant emotional component to the relationship.[4]

Evidence suggests that at least some biblical friendships have been formalized by a treaty. Such formalization is indicated by the presence of distinct treaty language (e.g., idioms such as "to cut" or "to violate a covenant" [*kārat/ḥillēl běrît*], or "to love *x* as oneself") in combination with clear evidence of a friendship (e.g., a voluntary association characterized by some degree of emotional engagement). Friendships formalized by a treaty include the friendship of the psalmist and his friend who is described as "a man like me" and "my gentle intimate" (*'allûpî ûměyuddā'î*), with whom the complainant made "sweet fellowship," but who is also said to have "violated his covenant" (Ps 55:14, 21). Here, distinct friendship terminology and an idiom suggesting personal intimacy are employed in combination with an unambiguous treaty idiom.[5] A second example of friendship formalized by treaty is Jonathan and David's friendship as narrated in 1 Sam 18:1–4, with demonstrable emotional engagement indicated by the binding of selves or lives and the treaty indicated by the use of the idiom "to love *x* as oneself" and the mention of Jonathan and David cutting a covenant. Yet another example from the David story is 1 Sam 20:41, the narrative in which David bows three times to Jonathan before "each kissed the other and they wept together." Here, David's bowing indicates the subordination of a vassal, while reciprocal ritual acts of kissing and weeping suggest both emotional engagement and behavioral parity enacted ritually. Second Samuel 1:26 also likely bears witness to a friendship formalized through a covenant, in this case a treaty of equals, as suggested by David's use of the term "brother" for Jonathan. I believe this text suggests a strong emotional bond between the men, likely with homoerotic overtones, as indicated by the comparison of Jonathan's love to the love of women.

How common are friendships formalized by a treaty in biblical texts? Unhappily, there is no way to know. I have identified several such friendships on the basis of the presence of both unmistakable treaty idioms and strong indicators of a friendship in the texts describing them. It is possible, however, that biblical texts assume that the formalization of friendships is a broader phenomenon even though treaty idioms are not always present in depictions of friendships. As I have discussed, the purpose of formalizing a friendship through covenanting may have been to reassure each party that his expectations would be met, given the severity of typical curses directed at treaty violators.

How do women's friendships compare with those of men? Our main sources representing female friendship are the book of Ruth and the story of Jephthah's daughter and her friends (Judg 11:37–38). As with narrative portrayals of particular male friendships (e.g., that of Jonathan and David), the technical terminology of friendship familiar from psalms of individual complaint, wisdom texts, and prophetic sources is mainly absent from prose representations of women's friendships. Nonetheless, narratives of women's friendships emphasize characteristics of biblical friendship seen in other texts concerned with the friendship of men (e.g., friendship as a voluntary association, mutual feelings of affection, loyalty, behavioral parity). Like male friendships, the friendship between Naomi and Ruth is portrayed as a voluntary association. There is evidence in the Ruth story of an emotional bond shared by both parties to the friendship (e.g., Ruth 1:14 in tandem with 3:1). Although Ruth and Naomi are not said explicitly to pay back that which is good (*ṭôbâ*) for good treatment received, the two certainly seek one another's welfare and reciprocate generous treatment, thereby manifesting behavioral parity as male friends are expected to do according to other biblical sources. Jephthah's daughter's friends are loyal and remain with her at the time of her calamity, accompanying her on her journey before her death. They appear to play the role of comforter for her, joining in her mourning—they weep with her according to Judg 11:37—just as male friends would be expected to do for their friend at a time of personal catastrophe, illness, or the death of a close family member (e.g., Job 2:11–13; Ps 35:13–14). Not unlike some male friends, Jephthah's daughter and her friends appear to be peers in every respect; as with other friendships between men, Ruth and Naomi's friendship is characterized by some formal differences (in this case, generation and status [mother-in-law/daughter-in-law]).[6] Although friendship between women is not well represented in biblical materials, the stories of Ruth and Naomi and Jephthah's daughter and her companions suggest implicitly a set of norms for friendship that are not dissimilar to those we can reconstruct for male friends according to a wide range of biblical sources. One difference, however, between the representation of women's friendships and men's friendships is a lack of evidence for formalization in women's friendships. From my perspective, this is hardly surprising, given that women are not portrayed in biblical texts as treaty partners.

One combination of friends that is not attested in biblical representations of friendship is friendship between men and women. This may be because the relationships of women and men, with the exception of those between female and male family members, are most often cast in sexual, or at least erotic, terms. On the infrequent occasions when friendship terminology is used in contexts describing the erotic or sexual relations of women and men, as in the Song of Songs, it appears to function, like the familial terminology in that text, to enrich the poet's rhetoric metaphorically, adding yet another axis of emotional intimacy to the portrait of the relationship of the male and female lover, as I argued in the Introduction.[7] I believe that the same is true of texts such as Jer 3:4, in which Yhwh is cast as Israel's husband and addressed by Israel as both "my father" and "the friend ['*allûp*] of my youth." In both examples, the poet draws upon the rhetoric of friendship and of familial relations in order to create a more emotionally complex relationship between male and female lovers or husband and wife. But these texts tell us nothing about constructions of friendship or familial relations in themselves. Just as familial relationships are routinely represented as nonsexual and nonerotic, so are friendships, and this may explain why friendships between women and men are unattested in biblical texts. There may be exceptions to the nonerotic, nonsexual pattern of representing friendships (e.g., 2 Sam 1:26), but these do not invalidate the pattern itself.[8]

Neither the technical vocabulary of friendship nor its representation in different types of biblical literature suggests that friends need be peers in all respects. Various texts suggest in fact that inequality of wealth, social status, life stage, treaty status, or other personal characteristics does not preclude the establishment of a friendship. The wealthy may have friends who are not well-to-do (Prov 19:4, by implication); friends may differ with respect to social status (Ruth and Naomi, Jonadab and Amnon), treaty status (David and Jonathan), or life stage (Naomi and Ruth). In some cases, friends might be equals in most or all respects (e.g., Jephthah's daughter and her friends; the psalmist and his friend in Ps 55:14–15, 21; Job and his three comforters); in other instances, friends are peers in some respects but unequal in others (David and Jonathan); and some friends might be equal in few respects (Naomi and Ruth are both widows, but Naomi remains Ruth's mother-in-law and is a generation older than Ruth). Nonetheless, all biblical friendships evidently share the assumption of behavioral parity, whether this is suggested implicitly or stated explicitly. Whatever the differences between friends, all friends must reciprocate that which is good (*ṭôbâ*) to their friends through various manifestations of loyalty. Like friends, fictive friends are not necessarily peers in most or all respects. The "friend of the king" is likely not the king's equal in any way but possibly life stage, just as the vassal is mainly not a peer of his suzerain, even though he might be called his suzerain's friend (Isa 41:8; *EA* 288). But as with friends who are unequal, suzerains and vassals are expected to treat one another appropriately, demonstrating loyalty and honoring their treaty partners (see, e.g., Exod 20:6 par. Deut 5:10; 1 Sam 2:30; and 2 Sam 19:6–8 for the suzerain's obligations).

What does the diachronic dimension add to our portrait of biblical friendship? Comparison of friendship in earlier materials with friendship in Ben Sira allows for the development of a diachronic perspective. We see earlier biblical ideas reproduced without significant change (e.g., regarding the expectation of behavioral parity or friends sharing an implicit common classification with family members) as well as developed and extended (e.g., regarding gradations of friendship). Rhetoric familiar from earlier texts is frequently employed and sometimes elaborated. We also see new ideas that seemingly appear for the first time in biblical materials, some possibly of Greek origin (e.g., the "good friend" as fighting friend), as well as vocabulary and idioms absent from earlier biblical texts ("good friend," "true friend"). Some earlier ideas make no appearance in Ben Sira (e.g., women's friendship, friendship formalized by treaty), and some earlier vocabulary and idioms are absent (e.g., "to pay back that which is evil [instead of what is good]"). Although it is possible to identify differences between Ben Sira's ideas about friendship and his vocabulary and idioms of friendship on the one hand and the ideas, vocabulary, and idioms of earlier biblical texts on the other, it is often difficult or impossible to determine instances in which Ben Sira himself is innovating and instances in which he is not. In some cases, he may simply be reproducing ideas, vocabulary, or idioms that were current in his early-second-century BCE Palestinian environment but not current earlier, or avoiding earlier ideas, vocabulary, or idioms because they are not in use in his own time and place. That he uses the word *ḥābēr* of the friend in 37:6 (B, D) is likely not his innovation, given the similar usage in Eccl 4:10, another biblical text of Hellenistic date. In contrast, Ben Sira's avoidance of the earlier biblical idiom "to pay back that which is evil [instead of what is good]," whatever its motivation, and his use of the novel expression "good friend" may well be his innovations, though it is difficult to determine this in any convincing way. Although we cannot be certain when Ben Sira is innovating and when he mirrors vocabulary, idioms, and ideas of his context, embracing a comparative perspective allows us to form an impression of a number of the ways in which the ideas, idioms, and vocabulary of biblical friendship developed in the late first millennium BCE.

Biblical friends are distinct social actors enjoying a special, even privileged, status. Although they are often compared to relatives explicitly or implicitly, sharing many of the same expectations (e.g., loyalty, behavioral parity, mutual affection), and though friends, like relatives, might be more emotionally intimate with one another or less so, the relationship of two friends differs fundamentally from that of two family members related by blood in that it is voluntary and more easily terminated.[9] In addition, friends do not share a number of the obligations incumbent upon certain relatives (e.g., the role of Levir or redeemer). The importance of friendship in the Hebrew Bible, something seldom acknowledged by biblical scholars, comes into relief not only from the commonly attested comparison and shared classification of friends with family members, but also when we consider how friendship is deployed fictively to characterize treaty relationships that are entirely political.[10] Just as two kings in a treaty might describe themselves as fictive kin (e.g., "brother," "father," "son"), underscoring by so doing the central importance of familial relations in the world of the biblical text, they might also refer to one another as "friend," suggesting the significance of friendship as a social phenomenon. That friends are compared to family members but rarely if ever cast as fictive kin themselves also highlights the distinct place of friendship in biblical society, as does the phenomenon of relatives as friends. At the same time, however, biblical texts suggest that friendship, though it is important, ranks below familial relations, communicating this through the consistent pattern of comparing friends to family members but never likening relatives to friends. Thus, it would not be unreasonable to suggest that friendship matters more to the authors of the Hebrew Bible than is typically acknowledged by specialists, but that the Hebrew Bible's paradigmatic social relationships are familial.

What does the Hebrew Bible's representation of friendship contribute to the contemporary, incipient, cross-disciplinary theorization of friendship? It constitutes yet another data set to consider, not only enriching our understanding of the representation of social relationships in antiquity, an area of research that has been overly focused on Greco-Roman evidence up to the present, but also providing additional ancient material to those who study friendship cross-culturally from the perspective of a variety of disciplines. Contemporary, cross-disciplinary attempts to theorize friendship often begin with Aristotle or cite him early on, as if Aristotle's views were somehow definitive for antiquity. An example of this is Ethan J. Leib's *Friend v. Friend: The Transformation of Friendship and What the Law Has to Do with It*.[11] Yet such work would be considerably enriched if it took other ancient sources such as the Hebrew Bible into account as well, given that biblical perspectives and Aristotle's views differ in a number of respects (e.g., what characterizes the preeminent form of friendship [typically loyalty and intimacy in biblical texts versus shared virtue or excellence (*aretē*) according to Aristotle]). For Leib in particular, biblical friendships formalized by treaty and, presumably, subject to treaty sanctions would have provided a very interesting adumbration of or even a model for his own argument that contemporary U.S. law ought to recognize friendship formally and, along with legal institutions and public policy, "be oriented toward promoting and facilitating friendships."[12] As Leib himself acknowledges, there is nothing quite like this in Aristotle.[13]

Examples of how biblical representations of friendship could contribute to contemporary, cross-cultural theorizing of friendship from the perspective of a single discipline also abound.[14] Consideration of the biblical evidence might have given pause to social scientists such as Steven M. Graham and Margaret S. Clark, who acknowledge "cross-cultural differences in friendship" but nonetheless theorize that "friends are expected to be mutually responsive to one another's welfare by providing help" although "such responsiveness ought to be given voluntarily and it should occur on a noncontingent rather than a tit-for-tat basis."[15] This is certainly not the assumption of a text such as Ps 35:12–14, where the sufferer castigates friends who did not come to his aid in time of need, although he had been there for them when they were sick, as I have discussed in detail. Others, such as Bettina Beer, have also sought to theorize friendship cross-culturally from the perspective of a single discipline, arguing that it is an "informal social relationship."[16] Once again, consideration of the biblical evidence calls such a generalization into question, given the association of friendship with covenant-making in at least some instances.[17]

Much more could be said about how biblical data might contribute to contemporary interdisciplinary and disciplinary theorizing of friendship. As others seek to understand friendship cross-culturally, I urge them to engage with the rich materials of the Hebrew Bible.

Notes

Introduction

1. Nor can I presuppose much about friendship in contemporary non-Western societies, whether developed (e.g., Japan), developing (e.g., China or India), or traditional (e.g., the pastoral Fulbe in Cameroon). On friendship patterns in contemporary non-Western societies, see, e.g., the discussions of Bettina Beer, "Friendship, Anthropology of," in *International Encyclopedia of the Social and Behavioral Sciences* (ed. Neil J. Smelser and Paul B. Baltes; Oxford: Elsevier, 2001), 9:5805–8; Monika Keller, "A Cross-Cultural Perspective on Friendship Research," *International Society for the Study of Behavioural Development Newsletter* 46 (2004): 10–11, 14; Tilo Grätz, Barbara Meier, and Michaela Pelican, "Freundschaftsprozesse in Afrika aus socialanthropologischer Perspektive: Eine Einführung," *Afrika Spectrum* 39 (2004): 9–39; Michaela Pelican, "Friendship Among Pastoral Fulbe in Northwest Cameroon," *African Study Monographs* 33 (2012): 165–88; and the essays in *The Anthropology of Friendship* (ed. Sandra Bell and Simon Coleman; Oxford: Berg, 1999). Some of the studies cited in this note bring into relief differences between common contemporary Western notions of friendship and the ways in which friendship is conceived in a variety of contemporary non-Western contexts. For a recent review of research on friendship in anthropology and sociology by a biblical scholar, see Jonathan Y. Rowe, *Sons or Lovers: An Interpretation of David and Jonathan's Friendship* (New York: Bloomsbury T & T Clark, 2012), 83–90.
2. See, e.g., Baruch Halpern, *David's Secret Demons: Messiah, Murderer, Traitor, King* (Grand Rapids, MI: Eerdmans, 2001), 283, who concludes that the relationship of Jonathan and David was "probably invented or inferred" by the authors of 1 Sam, "not recollected."
3. Examples include Alexander A. Fischer, "Freundschaft (AT)," *Das wissenschaftliche Bibellexikon im Internet* (www.wibilex.de; updated 2007); Diether Kellermann, "*rēaʿ*," *TDOT* 13:522–32; Richard S. Hess, "*rʿh* II," *NIDOTTE* 3:1144–49; J. Kühlewein, "*rēaʿ* companion," *TLOT* 3:1243–46; Andreas Scherer, "Is the Selfish Man Wise? Considerations of Context

117

in Proverbs 10.1–22.16 with Special Regard to Surety, Bribery and Friendship," *Journal for the Study of the Old Testament* 76 (1997): 59–70, esp. 67–69; Reinhard G. Kratz, "'Abraham, mein Freund': Das Verhältnis von inner- und außerbiblischer Schriftauslegung," in *Die Erzväter in der biblischen Tradition: Festschrift für Matthias Köckert* (ed. Anselm C. Hagedorn and Henrik Pfeiffer; BZAW 400; Berlin: De Gruyter, 2009), 115–36, esp. 119–25; Thomas Römer, "L'amitié selon la Bible hébraïque," *Transversalités* 113 (2010): 31–45; Graham Davies, "The Ethics of Friendship in Wisdom Literature," in *Ethical and Unethical in the Old Testament: God and Humans in Dialogue* (ed. Katharine J. Dell; New York: T & T Clark, 2010), 135–50; Davies, "The Friendship of Jonathan and David," in *Studies on the Text and Versions of the Hebrew Bible in Honour of Robert Gordon* (ed. Geoffrey Khan and Diana Lipton; VTSup 149; Leiden: Brill, 2012), 65–76; and most recently, Jan Dietrich, "Von der Freundschaft im Alten Testament und Alten Orient," *Die Welt des Orients* 44 (2014): 37–56, and "Friendship with God: Old Testament and Ancient Near Eastern Perspectives," *Scandinavian Journal of the Old Testament* 28 (2014): 157–71 (my thanks to Matthew Rutz for bringing Dietrich's essay "Von der Freundschaft im Alten Testament und Alten Orient" to my attention). See also Susan Ackerman, *When Heroes Love: The Ambiguity of Eros in the Stories of Gilgamesh and David* (New York: Columbia University Press, 2005), which analyzes material relevant to this study but with a focus on gender and the erotic rather than on dynamics of friendship. Note that the six-volume *Anchor Bible Dictionary* (ed. David Noel Freedman; New York: Doubleday, 1992) lacks an entry on friendship.

4. E.g., Gabriel Herman, "Friendship, Greece," *OCD* (3rd ed., 1996): 611; David Konstan, *Friendship in the Classical World* (Cambridge: Cambridge University Press, 1997); and the essays in John T. Fitzgerald, ed., *Friendship, Flattery, and Frankness of Speech: Studies on Friendship in the New Testament World* (Leiden: Brill, 1996); Fitzgerald, ed., *Greco-Roman Perspectives on Friendship* (Atlanta: Society of Biblical Literature, 1997); and recently, Craig A. Williams, *Reading Roman Friendship* (New York: Cambridge University Press, 2012) (I am grateful to David Konstan for bringing Williams's book to my attention). For contemporary legal studies, see, e.g., Ethan J. Leib, *Friend v. Friend: The Transformation of Friendship and What the Law Has to Do with It* (New York: Oxford University Press, 2011); for sociology, see, e.g., Rebecca G. Adams and Graham Allan, eds., *Placing Friendship in Context* (Cambridge: Cambridge University Press, 1998); Ray Pahl, *On Friendship* (Cambridge: Polity, 2000); Pahl, "Toward a More Significant Sociology of Friendship," *European Journal of Sociology* 43 (2002): 410–23; Liz Spencer and Ray Pahl, *Rethinking Friendship: Hidden Solidarities Today* (Princeton, NJ: Princeton University Press, 2006); for social anthropology, see, e.g., Sandra Bell and Simon Coleman, "The Anthropology of Friendship: Enduring Themes and Future Possibilities," in *Anthropology of Friendship*, 1–19; Beer, "Friendship," 5805–8; Grätz, Meier, and

Pelican, "Freundschaftsprozesse," 9–39; Pelican, "Friendship," 165–88; for developmental psychology, see, e.g., Keller, "Friendship Research," 10–11, 14; for philosophy, see, e.g., James O. Grunebaum, *Friendship: Liberty, Equality, and Utility* (Albany, NY: SUNY Press, 2003); Alexander Nehamas, "The Good of Friendship," *Proceedings of the Aristotelian Society* 110 (2010): 267–94 (my thanks to Nathaniel B. Levtow for the Nehamas reference); for medicine and public health, see, e.g., Carla M. Perissinotto et al., "Loneliness in Older Persons: A Predictor of Functional Decline and Death," *Archives of Internal Medicine* 172 (2012): 1078–84; Julianne Holt-Lunstad et al., "Social Relationships and Mortality Risk: A Meta-Analytic Review," *PLoS Medicine* 7 (2010) (www.plosmedicine.org/article/info:doi/10.1371/journal.pmed.1000316); Renee B. Cadzow and Timothy J. Servoss, "The Association Between Perceived Social Support and Health Among Patients at a Free Urban Clinic," *Journal of the National Medical Association* 101 (2009): 243–50.

5. On this, see Konstan, *Friendship in the Classical World*, 38.
6. Those who consider the evidence for Greek influence on Ben Sira include Fischer, "Freundschaft (AT)," passim; Jeremy Corley, *Ben Sira's Teaching on Friendship* (BJS 316; Providence, RI: Brown Judaic Studies, 2002), 1, 12, 14–15 n. 54, 213, and passim; Otto Kaiser, "Was ein Freund nicht tun darf: Eine Auslegung von Sir 27,16–21," in *Freundschaft bei Ben Sira: Beiträge des Symposions zu Ben Sira Salzburg 1995* (ed. Friedrich V. Reiterer; BZAW 244; Berlin: De Gruyter, 1996), 107; and Kaiser, *Weisheit für das Leben: Das Buch Jesus Sirach übersetzt und eingeleitet* (Stuttgart: Radius, 2005), 140–43 (the latter brought to my attention by Fischer).
7. A recent contribution with cross-disciplinary interests is Leib, *Friend v. Friend*. I engage this book in the Conclusion.
8. On the literary representation of institutions, social practices, rites, and so on in the Hebrew Bible, see recently the astute comments of Jeffrey Stackert, *A Prophet like Moses: Prophecy, Law, and Israelite Religion* (New York: Oxford University Press, 2014), 50–51. Such representations are not a simple, unproblematic window into real-life practice in the past; rather, they reflect literary and ideological needs of authors and may include what Stackert refers to as "creative reimaginations of social conventions and religious practices known to the author and his or her audience" (51). Thus, literary representations have a complex relationship to historically situated practice. On the one hand, they are not generated in a vacuum and must resonate in some way with their intended audiences; on the other, they are intended to shape the way in which audiences think. On this issue, see further my comments in *Disability in the Hebrew Bible: Interpreting Mental and Physical Differences* (New York: Cambridge University Press, 2008), 3–4.
9. I do not include the Hebrew text of Ben Sira in this survey. Its vocabulary and idioms of friendship will be considered in Chapter 4 and compared there to usages in the earlier biblical materials considered here.

10. Contrast modern Hebrew *yĕdîdût* and *rēʿût* ("friendship"). The former occurs in Jer 12:7 with the meaning "beloved" in reference to Judah in relationship to Yhwh; the latter is a noun that is attested in rabbinic texts (e.g., y. Berakot 4, 7d; b. Ketubbot 8a; b. Yebamot 14b). Also, contrast the rich vocabulary of Akkadian: *ṭābūtu, ruʾūtu, rāʾimūtu, i/ebrūtu*, all appropriately translated "friendship" in at least some contexts. (All translations in this volume are my own unless otherwise indicated.) The lack of an extant word meaning "friendship" in biblical Hebrew is most likely the result of the limited vocabulary of the Hebrew Bible and nothing more, given the various words that can be translated "friendship" in Akkadian.

11. E.g., for *rēaʿ*, Deut 13:7; Mic 7:5; Job 2:11; Prov 17:17; for *rēʿâ*, Judg 11:38 (on Judg 11:37 see ahead at n. 40); for *rēʿeh*, 2 Sam 16:16; 1 Kgs 4:5, evidently a political office or role (Kühlewein, "*rēaʿ* companion," 1244; Herbert Donner, "Der 'Freund des Königs,'" *Zeitschrift für die alttestamentliche Wissenschaft* 73 [1961]: 269–77, on the office's probable Egyptian origin; P. Kyle McCarter, Jr., *II Samuel: A New Translation with Introduction, Notes and Commentary* [AYB 9; Garden City, NY: Doubleday, 1984], 372); for *mērēaʿ*, Prov 19:4, 7. The word *rēʿeh* is probably derived from a root *r ʿ h*, as is *raʿyâ*. I have argued elsewhere that *mērēaʿ* is a Hi masculine-singular participle from a geminate root *r ʿʿ* ("A Suggestion Regarding the Derivation of the Hebrew Noun *mērēaʿ*," *Journal of Semitic Studies* 56 [2011]: 217–19). John Huehnergard has suggested to me that *rēaʿ* may also be derived from *r ʿʿ*, its form not unlike that of *lēb* (< *libb*) (e-mail communication, 7 October 2010; see H. Bauer and P. Leander, *Historische Grammatik der hebräischen Sprache* [Hildesheim: Olms, 1965], 454–55, for this *qill* noun type; contrast Davies, who suggests a derivation from *r ʿ h*, following BDB ["The Ethics of Friendship," 137]). Understanding *rēaʿ* as a *qill* noun from *r ʿʿ* seems more cogent than positing a contraction from *rēʿeh* (e.g., GKC par. 84ai). The word *rēʿâ* is apparently the feminine of *rēaʿ*, so also presumably derived from *r ʿʿ* (see Bauer and Leander, ibid., on this feminine noun type). A verbal form derived from the root *r ʿʿ* is *lĕhitrōʿēaʿ* in Prov 18:24; verbal forms from *r ʿ h* are attested in texts such as Judg 14:20; Prov 13:20; 22:24.

12. As in Pss 38:12; 88:19; Prov 17:17; 18:24.

13. Mic 7:5; Ps 55:14. Alternatively, it has been argued that *ʾallûp* is related to the verb *ʾlp*, "to learn" (Prov 22:25), with a meaning "one who is learned," not unlike *mĕyuddāʿ* in meaning (see ahead on *mĕyuddāʿ*). For this argument, see E. H. Merrill, "*ʾlp*," *NIDOTTE* 1:415, as well as Hess, "*rʿh* II," 1145, who translates *ʾallûp* as "familiar, confidant."

14. E.g., Jer 20:10; Pss 7:5; 41:10; 55:21. The expression *ʾîš/ʾĕnôš šālôm* is used of both friends (see, esp., Ps 41:10) and treaty partners (Obad 1:7, with distinct treaty language [*bĕrît*]). The usage in Obad 1:7 has apparently led translators such as those of NJPS to miss the friendship content in a text such as Ps 41:10, which betrays no distinct treaty idioms and describes the friend (*ʾîš šālôm*) as one

"whom I trusted, who ate my food." (NJPS renders "ally.") Ps 28:3 suggests that friends ought to communicate their goodwill or speak positively (*dbr šālôm*) with one another, as does Ps 35:20. On this, see also Jer 9:7, where the friend says the right thing (lit., "he speaks goodwill") but is full of secret machinations.

15. The word *mĕyuddāʿ* occurs in 2 Kgs 10:11; Pss 31:12; 55:14; 88:9, 19; and Job 19:14. It appears that it is never clearly used of family members and is evidently used of friends in two passages: 2 Kgs 10:11 and Ps 55:14. 2 Kgs 10:11 suggests that "those known" to Ahab (*mĕyuddāʿāyw*) are nonfamilial associates. They are listed separately from Ahab's "house," along with his magnates and his priests: "Jehu struck down all who remained of the house of Ahab in Jezreel and his magnates and his intimates [*mĕyuddāʿāyw*] and his priests." In Ps 55:14, the *mĕyuddāʿ* is also referred to as *ʾallûp*, another term of friendship, and no familial terminology is present in that context.

16. Job 19:13 is the only occurrence of this word, which is derived from the same root as *mĕyuddāʿ*. Although it seems likely that *yōdēaʿ* is a term of friendship rather than a familial term, the evidence for this is less clear than it is for *mĕyuddāʿ* (on the latter, see my discussion in the previous note).

17. On hendiadys constructions, see Williams par. 72. Well-known examples include *tōhû wābōhû*, "a formless void" (Gen 1:2), and *nāʿ wānād*, "a restless wanderer," used of Cain (Gen 4:14). On *ʾallûp* possibly as "one who is learned," see previously, n. 13. If this understanding of *ʾallûp* is correct, the hendiadys could be translated as "my learned intimate."

18. The verb *ʾmn* (Hi), "to trust," is also associated with friends in Mic 7:5, suggesting that trust is a norm of friendship.

19. *HALOT* 655 and 745. Sir 6:6 (A; Beentjes 6:5) refers to a friend who is a trusted intimate as *baʿal sôd*. On versification in Ben Sira as well as the citation of the book's Hebrew manuscripts, see Chapter 4, n. 3.

20. Gen 44:30 is the only other occurrence of the expression *qšr nepeš*. Significantly, it is not attested as an idiom of covenant (see my discussion in Chapter 3).

21. Ps 38:21 likely refers to both disloyal friends and unfaithful family members, given that both are mentioned explicitly in 38:12. The word *ḥābēr* is used of peers (Ps 45:8), allies (Judg 20:11), and associates (Ezek 37:16, 19), among others, but it seems unlikely that it is used of friends in texts predating the Hellenistic period. I discuss the term and its uses in Ben Sira in Chapter 4. On the possible use of the verbal root *ḥbr* for the relationship of David and Jonathan, see ahead, n. 34.

22. "One who affiliates himself" is very likely the literal meaning of *mērēaʿ* (see Olyan, "Derivation of the Hebrew Noun *mērēaʿ*," 219).

23. Hebrew "love" always has positive connotations, as "love" does in English, though its precise meaning (e.g., loyalty, sexual-emotional desire, nonsexual emotional bonding) must be determined from context, as I discuss ahead.

24. See n. 13.

25. Several texts warn not to trust friends with confidences (Jer 9:3; Mic 7:5), and the disloyal friend of the psalms of individual complaint, sometimes characterized as an enemy who repays that which is evil instead of what is good (Ps 35:12), is a prominent topos in that corpus. On this, see my treatment in Chapter 2.
26. Interestingly, nothing in the biblical vocabulary of friendship suggests that equality of wealth, social status, life stage, or other personal characteristics is required of friends or even desirable in a friendship, and several narratives and some wisdom texts suggest the same idea implicitly. For example, Jonathan, a prince and the heir to Saul's throne, can be David's friend, though David does not share his rank and is represented as Jonathan's vassal in a text such as 1 Sam 20:41, where David bows down three times before Jonathan. A friendship can develop between Naomi and Ruth, although Naomi is a generation older and is Ruth's mother-in-law. Finally, Prov 19:4 states that "wealth adds many friends," suggesting implicitly that these friends have less and stand to gain in some manner—either materially or less tangibly (e.g., by acquiring greater social capital)—from a friendship with a wealthy man. In contrast to its inattention to axes of personal equality or inequality, biblical friendship vocabulary foregrounds the expectation of behavioral parity in a friendship (reciprocity of treatment), an assumption that is evidenced in narratives, the psalms of individual complaint, and wisdom texts. I say more about behavioral parity in the following chapters. Contrast the position of Dietrich, who claims that biblical friendship is normally assumed to be between peers: "Freundschaften entstehen zumeist zwischen Gleichrangigen, vor allem zwischen Menschen gleichen Alters, gleichen Geschlechts und gleicher sozialer Stellung" ("Von der Freundschaft," 53–54; see also 45–46, 48–51). Dietrich ignores the behavioral dimension of biblical friendship, where expectations of parity are most pronounced.
27. The same observation applies to the Akkadian vocabulary of friendship. E.g., *bēl ṭābti* can mean "friend" or "patron"; similarly, *ebru* can mean "friend," "fellow merchant," or "partner."
28. A comparable usage is attested for the feminine noun *rēʿût* in Esth 1:19.
29. Other meanings, such as "legal adversary," have been proposed for *rēaʿ*, though not cogently (e.g., Friedrich Horst, *Hiob 1–19* [BKAT 16.1; Neukirchen-Vluyn: Neukirchener Verlag, 1969], 253, regarding Job 16:20–21).
30. This translation is preferable to the common "groomsman," "wedding companion," or "best man," none of which clearly communicates the fact that the companions are strangers to Samson rather than his friends (cf., e.g., Kühlewein, "*rēaʿ* companion," 1244; Kellermann, "*rēaʿ*," 525).
31. 1 Sam 30:26 states: "When David came to Ziklag, he sent part of the spoil to his friends, the elders of Judah, saying, 'Here is a present for you from the spoil of the enemies of Yhwh.'" These "friends" are clearly David's political allies rather than his personal friends, as the list of Judean towns receiving booty from David is rather long. Though it might be appropriate to translate *rēaʿ* as "friend" in 1 Sam 30:26 and related texts instead of "ally" in order to capture the use of

friendship idioms in contexts of political alliance, this extension of friendship rhetoric into the sphere of politics should always be kept in mind. A vassal may also be a "friend" of his suzerain according to some texts. Isa 41:8 refers to Abraham as Yhwh's "friend" (*ʾōhēb*) in an obvious treaty context—other treaty terms such as "servant" are used—and *EA* 288 casts the vassal as "friend" (ᴸᵁ́ *ru-ḫi*) at the same time that he is a "son," "servant," and "tribute bearer" (William L. Moran, *The Amarna Letters* [Baltimore: Johns Hopkins University Press, 1992], 331; *The Assyrian Dictionary of the Oriental Institute of the University of Chicago* [Chicago: University of Chicago Press, 1956–2010], 14:439 [*ruʾu*]; my thanks to Nathaniel DesRosiers for reminding me of the Amarna evidence). Similarly, a king may refer to himself as a "friend" of his god or to his god as his "friend," as in Code Hammurapi 2:69, where Hammurapi describes Erra as his friend (*ru-šu*; Martha T. Roth, *Law Collections from Mesopotamia and Asia Minor* [Atlanta: Scholars Press, 1995], 78). On friendship with God, see further Römer, "L'amitié selon la Bible hébraïque," 44–45; Dietrich, "Von der Freundschaft," 48–51, and "Friendship with God," 157–71. Dietrich notes that friendships between deities and humans are rarely encountered in ancient West Asian texts, in contrast to friendships between deities or those between humans.

32. Note the NRSV's rendering "as one speaks to a friend," and similarly that of William H. C. Propp, *Exodus 19–40: A New Translation with Introduction and Commentary* (AYB 2A; New York: Doubleday, 2006), 583; Römer, "L'amitié selon la Bible hébraïque," 45; and Dietrich, "Von der Freundschaft," 50. Contrast Davies, who argues that it is "much more likely" that the best translation is not unlike that of NJPS ("The Ethics of Friendship," 138).

33. Nor is the Siloam Tunnel Inscription from Jerusalem (late eighth century BCE), in which *rʿw* (*rēʿô*) occurs three times with reference to the tunnel builders (lines 2–4). Context suggests that the word is best translated "his fellow" or "his colleague," not "his friend," as some render it (e.g., Gary A. Rendsburg and William M. Schniedewind, "The Siloam Tunnel Inscription: Historical and Linguistic Perspectives," *Israel Exploration Journal* 60 [2010]: 191).

34. For the verb "to love" and its derivatives in treaty settings, see, e.g., Exod 20:6 par. Deut 5:10; 1 Kgs 5:15; Lam 1:2; and William L. Moran, "The Ancient Near Eastern Background of the Love of God in Deuteronomy," *CBQ* 25 (1963): 77–87. For *rēaʿ* used in reference to an ally, see 1 Sam 30:26 and Lam 1:2. For *ṭôb/ṭôbâ* in covenant contexts, see, e.g., Deut 23:7; 2 Sam 2:6; Ezra 9:12; cuneiform and other parallels (e.g., *ṭābtu, ṭābūtu, ṭūbtu*; epigraphic Aramaic *ṭābtāʾ*); Moran, "A Note on the Treaty Terminology of the Sefire Stelas," *Journal of Near Eastern Studies* 22 (1963): 173–76; and Michael Fox, "*Ṭôb* as Covenant Terminology," *BASOR* 209 (1973): 41–42. For *šālôm* and *ʾiš/ʾĕnôš šālôm* as treaty terms, see, e.g., Deut 23:7; 1 Kgs 5:26; Jer 38:22; Obad 1:7; and Moshe Weinfeld, "*bĕrîth*," *TDOT* 2:259. Note also the cuneiform treaty idiom *ṭūbtu u sulummû*, which brings together Akkadian cognates of *ṭôb/ṭôbâ* and *šālôm*. Interestingly, the common biblical covenant term *ḥesed* ("loyalty") does not appear to be much used for nonpoliti-

cal relationships, including friendships. An exception is Job 6:14 (MT). Though the text is clearly disturbed at this juncture, the sense is fairly clear: the friend may spurn (*m's* < *lms* [?]) loyalty (*ḥesed*) and abandon the fear of Shadday, and brothers may act deceptively. (On the evidence supporting this reconstruction, see Chapter 1, n. 13. In 2 Sam 16:17, *ḥesed*, used of Hushay, the "friend of David," is political. On its use in the Jonathan-David narratives, see my discussion in Chapter 3.) On "loyalty" (*ḥesed*) in the settings of family, friendship, and treaty, see Frank Moore Cross, "Kinship and Covenant in Ancient Israel," in Cross, *From Epic to Canon: History and Literature in Ancient Israel* (Baltimore: Johns Hopkins University Press, 1998), 5–7, 9, and n. 12. There are a number of other treaty-related idioms that are rarely if ever used of friendship. Examples include the verb *bḥr*, "to choose," and its opposite, *m's*, "to spurn" (as in Jer 33:24, regarding Yhwh's covenants with David and Levi); the verb *ʿzb*, "to abandon" (e.g., Deut 29:24, with *bĕrît* as object); and the verb *škḥ*, "to forget" (e.g., Deut 4:23, 31, with *bĕrît* as object). The verb *ʿzb* is used once of friendship in Prov 27:10 and *škḥ* once in Job 19:14, and *m's* may be reconstructed in MT Job 6:14, as mentioned above. Though *bḥr* is used of the relationship of Jonathan and David in the MT of 1 Sam 20:30, LXX suggests *ḥbr*, and many see this as the better reading (e.g., McCarter, *1 Samuel*, 339. See also Ps 119:63).

35. See, e.g., the use of *ʾāḥ*, "brother," for an ally in 2 Sam 1:26; 1 Kgs 9:13; 20:32–33. Amos 1:9 refers to a *bĕrît ʾaḥîm*. Similar usage is attested for "father" and "son" in texts that assume a suzerain-vassal relationship between treaty partners. Note also that fellow Israelite males are sometimes referred to as "brother" (e.g., Exod 4:18; Deut 15:12), as are fellow tribesmen (e.g., 2 Sam 19:13), suggesting that a parity bond is assumed in at least some texts for adult male members (household heads?) of larger communal units such as the tribe or the people as a whole.

36. In 1 Kgs 9:13, Hiram addresses David's son and successor Solomon as "brother," suggesting that his treaty with Solomon is a treaty of equals. The same seems likely to be the case with respect to Hiram's treaty with David.

37. Moran, "Love of God," 78. Adding to the challenge of interpreting biblical "love" idioms is the fact that "love" rhetoric can also be used in the Hebrew Bible to describe a sexual-emotional bond between a man and a woman, as in Gen 25:28 and 2 Sam 13:4.

38. On the treaty idiom "to love *x* as oneself," see, e.g., Lev 19:18 and Esarhaddon's Vassal Treaty (D. J. Wiseman, "The Vassal Treaties of Esarhaddon," *Iraq* 20 [1958]: 49–50 [col. 4, lines 266–68]: "[You swear] that you will love Ashurbanipal, the crown-prince, son of Esarhaddon, king of Assyria, your lord as [you do] yourselves"; Wiseman's translation). There is a slight variation in the biblical manifestations of the idiom between *kĕnapš-* in 1 Sam 18:1, 3 and *kāmô-* in Lev 19:18. The word *ḥesed* ("loyalty") occurs a number of times in the David-Jonathan narratives (1 Sam 20:8, 14, 15; 2 Sam 9:1, 3) and is a common treaty idiom elsewhere, but it, in itself, does not necessarily point to the formalized na-

ture of the relationship between Jonathan and David, since *ḥesed* is mentioned on occasion as an expectation of familial relations and friendships that do not otherwise evidence the rhetoric of treaty-making (e.g., Ruth 1:8; Job 6:14).

39. The word *rēʿîm* in Jer 3:1 refers to divine rivals of Yhwh with whom Yhwh's "wife" Israel prostitutes herself. Compare texts such as 1 Sam 15:28; 28:17; 2 Sam 12:11, where *rēaʿ* appears to mean "peer who is a rival," specifically for the throne. In the case of Jer 3:1, the rivals are other male deities. See also the use of *rēaʿ* in Hos 3:1, which is similar to Jer 3:1.
40. The *qěrê* is *rēʿōtay*, from *rēʿâ*, and a form of the same word also occurs in the next verse. The *qěrê* may therefore be harmonizing in its suggestion of *rēʿōtay*.
41. On traditional and skeptical wisdom (or, for some, didactic and critical wisdom), see, e.g., the comments of Michael V. Fox, *Proverbs 1–9: A New Translation with Introduction and Commentary* (AYB 18A; New York: Doubleday, 2000), 17–19, as well as John J. Collins, *Jewish Wisdom in the Hellenistic Age* (OTL; Louisville, KY: Westminster John Knox, 1997), 13–15, 224. Some have challenged this widely embraced contrast, emphasizing instead continuities between Proverbs on the one hand and Ecclesiastes or Job on the other (e.g., Choon-Leong Seow, *Ecclesiastes: A New Translation with Introduction and Commentary* [AYB 18C; New York: Doubleday, 1997], 68–69). Collins's treatment of skeptical and traditional wisdom recognizes both their contrasting characteristics and their continuities (e.g., ibid., 10, for an example of the latter).

Chapter 1: Friends and Family

1. On theorizing social actors in sociology, see, e.g., Alain Touraine, "A Method for Studying Social Actors," *Journal of World-Systems Research* 6 (2000): 900–918.
2. The leader of a group of prophets may also be addressed as a "father" by the king, as in 2 Kgs 13:14. My thanks to Nathaniel Levtow for this reference.
3. The implication is that a married woman has become part of her husband's family. Note Naomi's words to Ruth regarding Boaz in Ruth 2:20: "The man is close to us; he is one of our redeemers [*qārôb lānû hāʾîš miggōʾălēnû hûʾ*]." This is the case only because of the marriages of Naomi and Ruth into the family of Elimelek, kinsman of Boaz. The idiom *haqqārōb/haqqěrôbâ ʾēlāyw* stands in apposition to *šěʾērô* in Lev 21:2 and *ʾăḥōtô* in 21:3, further defining these terms; similar constructions are found in Lev 25:25 (regarding the redeemer) and Num 27:11. In 2 Sam 19:43; Ruth 2:20; 3:12, the adjective *qārôb* functions as a predicate and clearly refers to family members. Finally, *qārôb* may stand alone as a substantive that we might translate as "intimate," as in Exod 32:27; Pss 15:3; 38:12; Job 19:14; and Neh 13:4. In this latter usage, its familial sense is sometimes less clearly established, in contrast to the other usages I have mentioned above, where a familial sense is clear. I discuss *qārôb* further in n. 18.
4. Note that no other women are potential heirs according to this text.
5. See Gen 44:20 for another example of a father's love for his son. Also Prov 13:24, which one might describe as "love with a twist": "He who withholds his rod

hates his son,/ But he who loves him is careful to discipline him." A metaphorical application of such love is to be found in Hosea 11:1.

6. The translation of *nepeš* is daunting, as many have observed. For the range of possibilities, see, e.g., *HALOT* 711–13; C. Westermann, "*nepeš* soul," *TLOT* 2: 743–59; H. Seebass, "*nepeš*," *TDOT* 9:497–519. I prefer "life" or "self" in this context, rather than "soul."
7. Literally, "compassion grows warm toward." See H. J. Stoebe, "*rḥm* pi. to have mercy," *TLOT* 3:1226, who speculates that the idiom points to the "physiological phenomena of strong emotion."
8. Ps 109 assumes that love is something to be reciprocated and may refer to disloyal family members who not only fail to return love, but act as the complainant's adversaries instead: "In place of my love they act as adversaries against me" (v. 4; *taḥat 'ahăbātî yiśṭĕnûnî*). It is equally possible that this psalm refers to disloyal friends, or even to a mix of both ex-friends and hostile relatives, as in Ps 38:12.
9. Literally, "could not speak good will to him." I have emended the text of Gen 37:4 slightly to make sense of it (*dabbĕrô lĕšālôm* > **dabbēr lô šālôm*, supported by LXX *lalein autōi ouden eirēnikon*). To communicate one's good will or speak positively is expected of family members (Esth 10:3) and friends (Jer 9:7; Pss 28:3; 35:20). For another example of emotionally intense hatred of a family member, see 2 Sam 13:15. My thanks to Nathaniel Levtow for drawing my attention to Lev 19:17.
10. On covenant love, see especially the classic treatment of William L. Moran, "The Ancient Near Eastern Background of the Love of God in Deuteronomy," *CBQ* 25 (1963): 77–87.
11. By privileging his personal feelings and mourning for his dead rebel son Absalom even after his army has defeated Absalom's forces, David has, in effect, shamed and rejected his army according to Joab: "You have shamed all your servants today who saved your life . . . and have said that you do not have officers and servants"; vv. 6–7).
12. In Exod 20:6 and Deut 5:10, Yhwh states that he is loyal "to the thousands, to those who love me, that is, those who keep my commandments." Here I read epexegetical waw before "those who keep my commandments." On this, see Williams par. 434 and W.-O. 39.2.4.
13. The text of Job 6:14–15 is difficult but the sense of the passage seems clear enough: Just as a friend spurns (*m's* < *lms* [?]) loyalty and abandons the fear of Shadday, Job's brothers act deceptively (*bgd*) toward him. The reconstruction *mā'as* is supported by the LXX rendering *apeipato*. The verb *apeipein* ("refuse," "renounce," "disown") is used in two other LXX Job passages where the MT has a form of *mā'as*, which was likely also in the translator's *Vorlage* (10:3 and 19:18). The text implies that the brothers are disloyal just as the friend is, and their disloyalty is made manifest through deception.
14. The acts that constitute the loyalty of Ruth and Orpa to Naomi and to their dead husbands according to Ruth 1:8 are not specified.

15. 2 Sam 10:2: "I will be loyal to [lit., 'do loyalty with'] Hanun, son of Nahash, just as his father was loyal to me."
16. Frank Moore Cross, "Kinship and Covenant in Ancient Israel," in Cross, *From Epic to Canon: History and Literature in Ancient Israel* (Baltimore: Johns Hopkins University Press, 1998), 5, 6. See also Mark S. Smith, "'Your People Shall Be My People': Family and Covenant in Ruth 1:16–17," *CBQ* 69 (2007): 254–55, who points out that Cross was anticipated on this point by Paul Kalluveettil, *Declaration and Covenant: A Comprehensive Review of Covenant Formulae from the Old Testament and the Ancient Near East* (AnBib 88; Rome: Biblical Institute Press, 1982), 7–16.
17. The use of the verb *dābaq* in Ruth 1:14 will be considered in Chapter 3.
18. The adjective *qārôb/qĕrôbâ* is used of both kin and certain non-kin. When used of non-kin, it seems to refer only to the attendants of a ruler, e.g., Yhwh's priests in Lev 10:3; Ezek 42:13; 43:19; the Persian king's advisers in Esth 1:14. It is commonly used of kin, as in texts such as Lev 21:2, 3; 25:25; Num 27:11; 2 Sam 19:43; Ruth 2:20; 3:12; Neh 13:4; 1 Chr 12:41. Israel as Yhwh's ʿ*am qārōb* in Ps 148:14 suggests to me a metaphorical extension of the familial usage not unlike the common designation of Yhwh as Israel's redeemer. Because there is no biblical passage in which *qārôb* is used clearly of friends, I think it likely that it refers to family members in contexts such as Exod 32:27; Pss 15:3; 38:12; Job 19:14, where its referent is not wholly clear, even if the parallel term is one of friendship. Such pairings of friendship and familial terms are commonplace in poetic texts. See, e.g., *CAT* 5.9 I 8, 10 (ʾaḫ // rʿ); Job 30:29; Prov 17:17; Ps 122:8 (ʾāḫ // rēaʿ); and my discussion ahead.
19. It is likely that the ideal also includes petitionary acts, as I shall discuss.
20. The rhetoric of Ps 109:4–5 is similar, though it is unclear whether those accused of disloyalty are family members, ex-friends, or a combination of both, as in Ps 38:12.
21. The opposite of such behavior is "to seek that which is evil" or "destructive," or "to speak evil" or "destructive things." In Ps 38:13, "those who seek my undoing" (*dōrĕšê rāʿātî*, lit., "those who seek my evil") may well be family members; the same is true of "those who speak evil" or "destructive things against my life" (*haddōbĕrîm rāʿ ʿal napšî*) in Ps 109:20.
22. See the Aramaic text of 3.48–4.49; 4.51–52 in Bezalel Porten and Ada Yardeni, *Textbook of Aramaic Documents from Ancient Egypt* (Jerusalem: Hebrew University, 1993), 30, 32. Literally, "as a man with his brother" (*kʾyš ʾm ʾḥwhy*).
23. For the superlative understanding of *neʾĕmān hûʾ* in this context, see Baruch A. Levine, *Numbers 1–20: A New Translation with Introduction and Commentary* (AYB 4A; New York: Doubleday, 1993), 331. See also 342, where he compares 1 Sam 22:14. For a different understanding—Moses as the only reliable member of Yhwh's household—see Jeffrey Stackert, *A Prophet like Moses: Prophecy, Law, and Israelite Religion* (New York: Oxford University Press, 2014), 115, with citations.

128 Notes to Pages 18–21

24. It has been argued that honoring parents in the Decalogue refers to demonstrations of reverence for them after their death, which might include the provision of ancestral rites (Herbert Chanan Brichto, "King, Cult, Land and Afterlife—A Biblical Complex," *Hebrew Union College Annual* 44 [1973]: 30–31). Although possible, this understanding of the commandment to honor parents is at best a speculation, as honoring living parents is a habitual social practice according to Mal 1:6, not unlike a slave honoring his master.

25. The Marduk Prophecy states that when social order is restored to Babylon, a son will reverence his father as a god (Rykle Borger, "Gott Marduk und Gott-König Šulgi als Propheten: Zwei prophetische Texte," *BO* 28 [1971]: 11 for the text).

26. The verbs *kbd* and *qll* are antonyms, as are their Akkadian cognates *kabātu* and *qalālu*. On this, see further Saul M. Olyan, "Honor, Shame and Covenant Relations in Ancient Israel and Its Environment," *JBL* 115 (1996): 203–4 nn. 5–6 with bibliography.

27. In 1 Sam 2:30, Yhwh states that "those who honor me I will honor and those who despise me will be diminished [*kî mĕkabbĕday' ăkabbēd ûbōzay yēqāllû*]."

28. On this, see Olyan, "Honor, Shame and Covenant Relations," 205–6, 211–12, 216–17, for examples.

29. See Lev 18:6–7, 9, 10, 11, 12, 13; 20:17, 19, 20, for sexual relations with close female relatives; for such relations with the wives of male kinsmen, see Gen 35:22; 49:4; Lev 18:8, 14, 15, 16; 20:11–12, 21.

30. Borger, "Gott Marduk," 8, 11, for the text.

31. Num 35:19; see also vv. 20–21; Deut 19:11–13; Josh 20:1–9; 2 Sam 14:4–11.

32. Literally, "he shall do the brother-in-law's duty for her [*wĕyibbĕmāh*]."

33. In the idiom of the text, he "destroyed earthward [*wĕšiḥēt 'arṣāh*] so as not to give progeny to his brother."

34. Needless to say, Onan's acts have been, and continue to be, understood very differently by many later, nonacademic interpreters. For a recent example from a conservative Catholic context, see Brian W. Harrison, "The Sin of Onan Revisited," *Living Tradition* (1996): article 67 (www.rtforum.org/lt/lt67.html).

35. Why the property of Elimelek must be redeemed is unclear, and the combination of the roles of redeemer and Levir in Ruth is otherwise unattested in extant biblical materials (Edward F. Campbell, Jr., *Ruth: A New Translation with Introduction, Notes, and Commentary* [AYB 7; Garden City, NY: Doubleday, 1975], 132–33).

36. Lawrence E. Stager, "The Archaeology of the Family in Ancient Israel," *BASOR* 260 (1985): 22–23; Elizabeth Bloch-Smith, *Judahite Burial Practices and Beliefs About the Dead* (Journal for the Study of the Old Testament Supplement Series 123; Sheffield: Sheffield Academic Press, 1992), 111, 150.

37. The idea that a deceased person's afterlife might be affected positively or negatively by his or her burial status is suggested by cuneiform evidence. On this,

see, e.g., Saul M. Olyan, "Unnoticed Resonances of Tomb Opening and Transportation of the Remains of the Dead in Ezekiel 37:12–14," *JBL* 128 (2009): 495–98.
38. Andrew R. George, *The Babylonian Gilgamesh Epic: Introduction, Critical Edition and Cuneiform Texts* (2 vols.; Oxford: Oxford University Press, 2003), 1: 734.
39. E.g., Gen 50:10 for the seven-day mourning period.
40. See GKC par. 157b on *kî* introducing direct narration. For a close Ugaritic parallel to this text, see El's symbolic descent when he hears of Baal's death: "I will descend to the underworld, to Baal's place [*ʾaṯr bʿl ʾarḍ b ʾarṣ*]," *CAT* 1.5 VI 24–25.
41. On friends as the focus of Ps 35, see ahead n. 86.
42. The Aqhat epic from Ugarit, which lists the responsibilities of the son for his dead father, includes among these the erection of a standing stone (*skn ʾilʾib*) but does not mention an obligation to invoke the father's name (*CAT* 1.17 I 26).
43. On ancestral cultic rites in cuneiform cultures, see, e.g., Miranda Bayliss, "The Cult of Dead Kin in Assyria and Babylonia," *Iraq* 35 (1973): 115–25; A. Skaist, "The Ancestor Cult and Succession in Mesopotamia," in *Death in Mesopotamia* (ed. Bendt Alster; Copenhagen: Akademisk Forlag, 1980), 123–28; and Karel van der Toorn, "Gods and Ancestors in Emar and Nuzi," *Zeitschrift für Assyriologie* 84 (1994): 38–59. In cuneiform texts, the principal heir often functions as the custodian (*pāqidu*) who has the responsibility to perform such rites, which might include pouring fresh water (*mê naqû*), making offerings (*kispa kasāpu*), and invoking the name of the dead (*šuma zakāru*). In the absence of an heir, others may play the role of the custodian, including strangers.
44. Van der Toorn, *Family Religion in Babylonia, Syria and Israel: Continuity and Change in the Forms of Religious Life* (Leiden: Brill, 1996), 211–18.
45. On this, see my discussion in n. 24 above.
46. 2 Sam 18:18 suggests that they took place away from the tomb while Gen 35:20 may suggest that they took place at the tomb.
47. On the "Nehemiah Memoir," see Jacob L. Wright, *Rebuilding Identity: The Nehemiah-Memoir and Its Earliest Readers* (BZAW 348; Berlin: De Gruyter, 2004).
48. There has been much discussion of—and speculation about—the possible nuances of each of these idioms and how their meanings might differ. For general discussion, see, e.g., Theodore J. Lewis, *Cults of the Dead in Ancient Israel and Ugarit* (HSM 39; Atlanta: Scholars Press, 1989), 164–65 and nn. 11 and 12, who also provides bibliography. It is clear that the idiom "to lie down with" one's "ancestors" is not used exclusively of kings, as some have suggested. See Gen 47:30, where the expression is used of Jacob, and Deut 31:16, where it is used of Moses.
49. E.g., those said to be "gathered to" their "people" are not necessarily buried in a family tomb (e.g., Deut 32:50, regarding both Aaron and Moses), suggesting that the biblical usage of the idiom in at least some cases is broader than might

have originally been the case. Nor is everyone described as "lying down with" his "ancestors" interred immediately (e.g., Gen 47:30), which raises questions about the exact meaning of the idiom.

50. I follow Michael V. Fox (*Proverbs 10–31: A New Translation with Introduction and Commentary* [AYB 18B; New Haven, CT: Yale University Press, 2009], 647) in understanding *lĕhitrōʿēaʿ* as a Hitpolel infinitive construct from a root *rʿʿ*. The root means something like "to associate with," "to affiliate with," or in Fox's view, "to be a friend." It is evidently the root of *mērēaʿ*, as I have argued elsewhere ("A Suggestion Regarding the Derivation of the Hebrew Noun *mērēaʿ*," *Journal of Semitic Studies* 56 [2011]: 217–19), and may also be the root of *rēaʿ* (see further n. 11 in the Introduction). Fox translates *lĕhitrōʿēaʿ* as "for socializing with," a translation not unlike my own. The first word of the verse, *ʾyš*, ought to be understood as *ʾiš*, "there is," a word attested elsewhere in biblical Hebrew (2 Sam 14:19; Mic 6:10) with cognates in Ugaritic (*ʾiṯ*) and Aramaic (*ʾit, ʾitay*), as Fox points out (647). On *ʾiš*, see also *HALOT* 92.

51. That the verb "to cling to" (*dbq*) might have physical connotations is suggested by Ruth 2:8, 21, 23.

52. This is not unlike mourning the dead as the paradigmatic form of mourning to which other, non-death-related forms of mourning are compared (e.g., mourning during petition of the deity or at a time of calamity). On this, see, e.g., the explicit comparison of petitionary mourning rites to those of mourning a parent in Ps 35:14 and my argument in *Biblical Mourning: Ritual and Social Dimensions* (Oxford: Oxford University Press, 2004), 141–45.

53. On this tendency in the contemporary West, see, e.g., Pahl, *On Friendship*, 8, who states that "our expectations and aspirations are growing, and we are even prepared to judge the quality of our relationships with kin on the basis of some higher ideal of whether we can be closer to them as friends." See also Keller, "Friendship Research," 10, who notes that as a result of historical change, parent-child relationships in the West have become more symmetrical, in other words, more like friendships.

54. The verse is constructed as an a fortiori argument with *ʾap kî*. On this construction, see Williams par. 387 with citations.

55. The closest biblical parallel to this expression is 1 Sam 18:1, 3, where Jonathan is said to love David "as himself" (*kĕnapšô*). On the challenges of translating *nepeš*, see my discussion earlier in n. 6. Note that the treaty idiom "to love *x* as oneself" differs from the idiom "to be as oneself," which has demonstrable emotional resonance in passages such as Deut 13:7 and Sir 37:2 (B, D). The primary difference is the presence of the verb "to love" in the treaty idiom and its absence from the expression "to be as oneself."

56. For the idiom "to bear reproach," see Jer 15:15 and Ps 69:8. My translation has been influenced by NJPS, which captures the likely meaning of the text well. Though some translations render *qārōb* as "neighbor(s)" (e.g., NJPS, NRSV, RSV), this understanding seems unlikely given the common use of substantive

qārôb/qĕrôbâ elsewhere as a familial term when it is not used of a ruler's attendants, and the lack of evidence that it is used of friends or neighbors. (The use of *qārōb* as a predicate in Exod 12:4 suggests proximity: "His neighbor who is close [*haqqārōb*] to his house.") On *qārôb/qĕrôbâ* and its usages, see earlier nn. 3 and 18.

57. James L. Kugel, *The Idea of Biblical Poetry: Parallelism and Its History* (New Haven, CT: Yale University Press, 1981), 29.
58. Ibid., 29.
59. I read ʾ*ōhăbay wĕrēʿay* as a hendiadys construction ("loving friends") rather than as two separate groups of friends ("those who love me and my friends"). The use of ʾ*ōhăbîm*, literally "those who love," may be sarcastic, given the context.
60. Such implicit shared classification through parallelism is attested also in cuneiform and other extrabiblical materials. See, e.g., Lambert, *BWL* 34:84–86: "My brother [*a-ḫi*] has become a stranger, / My friend [*ib-ri*] a malevolent demon" (my translation and interpretation; contrast Lambert's rendering of *a-ḫi* as "friend"). A Ugaritic example is *CAT* 5.9 I 8, 10.
61. The idiom is *dbr šālôm*.
62. On *qārôb/qĕrôbâ* meaning "relative," see my earlier discussion in nn. 3, 18, and 56.
63. See Kugel, *Idea of Biblical Poetry,* 76–87, for a discussion of parallelism in what most refer to as prose. (Kugel is not convinced that the poetry/prose binary is useful for understanding biblical literature, as "the categories of prose and poetry imply too sharp, and total, a polarity," 86.)
64. The fact that the text is concerned with intimates suggests that *rēaʿ* be understood as "friend" here, not "neighbor" or something similar.
65. Some of the Hebrew of v. 29 is challenging, as many have noted (NJPS; William H. C. Propp, *Exodus 19–40: A New Translation with Introduction and Commentary* [AYB 2A; New York: Doubleday, 2006], 546). For the understanding of the preposition *bĕ-* as "at the cost of," see, e.g., Williams par. 246 (*bet* of price or exchange). NRSV captures this sense in its rendering, as does Brevard Childs, *The Book of Exodus: A Critical, Theological Commentary* (OTL; Philadelphia: Westminster, 1974), 555, 557 (cf. NJPS; Propp, ibid., 540). Deut 33:9 may allude to the narrative of Exod 32:27, 29, as Zackary Wainer has pointed out to me (oral communication).
66. The one possible exception is 2 Sam 1:26, in which David addresses Jonathan as "my brother Jonathan," though it is likely that this reflects a friendship cast in terms of a treaty of equals, as I discuss in Chapter 3.
67. See also 1 Sam 30:26 for political allies as "friends" (*rēʿîm*) and my comments about this text in the Introduction, n. 31. An ally or friend is expected to send "comforters" who join the mourner in contexts of death (e.g., 2 Sam 10:2), petition, or calamity; the allies of personified Jerusalem not only fail to fulfill this expectation, but become her enemies, not unlike the ex-friends of the psalms of individual complaint.

68. On fictive kinship, see, e.g., Parker Shipton, "Fictive Kinship," in *The Dictionary of Anthropology* (ed. Thomas Barfield; Oxford: Blackwell, 1997), 186–88, and Helen Rose Ebaugh and Mary Curry, "Fictive Kin as Social Capital in New Immigrant Communities," *Sociological Perspectives* 43 (2000): 189–209. The idea of fictive friends is obviously modeled on the commonplace notion of fictive kin. Zeba Crook speaks of fictive friendship in a recently published essay on gift-giving and friendship in classical contexts, though his usage is not the same as mine ("Fictive Giftship and Fictive Friendship in Greco-Roman Society," in *The Gift in Antiquity* [ed. Michael L. Satlow; Chichester: Wiley-Blackwell, 2013], 61–76). For him, fictive friendship is not genuine friendship in the sense that it does not conform to the routine expectations of Greco-Roman friendship (e.g., it is not symmetrical, in contrast to genuine friendship in classical contexts). In contrast, fictive friendship of West Asian political allies is symmetrical, given that allies are bound by a parity treaty; what is missing, and what makes it fictive in my view, is a personal, affective dimension to the relationship, a characteristic of many friendships in biblical representation. My thanks to Michael L. Satlow for bringing Crook's essay to my attention.
69. The exception is 2 Sam 13:3, which describes David's son Amnon's first cousin Jonadab as his "friend" (*rēaʿ*). I shall have more to say about the narrative of Amnon and Jonadab in Chapter 3.
70. The idiom is nearly identical in Hebrew: *wĕnepeš yĕhônātān niqšĕrâ bĕnepeš dāwīd* in 1 Sam 18:1 versus *wĕnapšô qĕšûrâ bĕnapšô* in Gen 44:30.
71. See further my discussion in Chapter 3.
72. In contrast to the binding of two selves or lives together, a second familial idiom accenting the emotional dimension of love, "to be overcome with emotion toward [*kmr* (Ni) *raḥămîm ʿal-/ʾel-*]," as in Gen 43:30 and 1 Kgs 3:26, is not used of friends in any extant text.
73. On "loyalty" (*ḥesed*), see my previous discussion, including n. 16, with citations. I treat the use of *ḥesed* in the David-Jonathan narratives in Chapter 3.
74. For the reading *mʾs (with LXX) for *lms* (?), see my discussion in n. 13.
75. It is not clear whether Ps 109 refers to friends, relatives, or a combination of the two.
76. On Ruth fulfilling all expectations of familial loyalty, see 1:8, which suggests that she has practiced *ḥesed* both with Naomi and with her dead husband Mahlon. Her release from such obligations is made clear by Naomi's command in that verse that Ruth and Orpa return to their natal houses. Verses 11–13 elaborate upon Naomi's argument that the two women are in no way obliged to remain with her and ought to leave her.
77. One potential difficulty for my interpretation is that Ruth continues to be referred to as Naomi's daughter-in-law by the narrator (e.g., in 1:22) and by Naomi (e.g., 2:20), even though the writer has taken pains to emphasize Ruth's complete lack of further obligation to Naomi. I address this in my in-depth analysis of the Ruth narrative in Chapter 3.

78. I read ʾōhēb wārēaʿ as a hendiadys. It is probably used sarcastically in this context.
79. On friends as the focus of Ps 35, see ahead, n. 86.
80. The meaning of the idiom *hlk rākîl* is not entirely clear. Though it is often understood to mean "to slander," Prov 11:13 suggests a meaning more like "to be untrustworthy": "The untrustworthy person reveals a confidence [*hôlēk rākîl mĕgalleh sôd*]." See also Prov 20:19.
81. Obviously, assumptions about who might play the Levir role vary from text to text, as Deut 25:5–10, Gen 38, and Ruth 3 and 4 indicate. See my comments earlier on the Levir role in the book of Ruth.
82. See also 2 Sam 3:31–37, the narrative of Abner's funeral in Hebron, in which David plays the role of lead mourner, walking behind the bier.
83. Kerry M. Sonia argues that benevolent transportation of the remains of the dead is an ancestor cult practice unrecognized by scholars ("The Enduring Dead: The Cult of Dead Kin in Ancient Israel," PhD diss., Brown University, 2016). If she is correct, then David's transfer of the remains of Saul, his sons, and his grandsons to the Saulide ancestral tomb in Benjamin (2 Sam 21:12–14) suggests that according to this text, an ally—or would-be ally in this instance—can play a role in ancestor cult, presumably in the absence of relatives.
84. Contrast the request of Patroclus to Achilles that their bones be interred together, sharing a single urn (*Iliad* 23.82–92). I discuss Ruth's statement in Ruth 1:17 that she will die and be buried where Naomi dies in Chapter 3.
85. Texts are not consistent with regard to who should play the role of comforter and who should play the role of mourner. Though Lev 21:2–4 casts close family members (parents, children, siblings) as mourners, Gen 37:35, in contrast, suggests that a man's children play the role of his comforters in a context in which their brother is believed to have died.
86. The meaning of the third colon of v. 13 is opaque ("As for my prayer, it returned to my bosom"). Though the first colon of v. 14 is challenging, it is not impossible. It reads *kĕrēaʿ kĕʾāḥ lî*, which might best be translated "the same for a friend as for my brother," with the double *kĕ-* understood as an identity construction (W.-O. 11.2.9b; Williams par. 256; Joüon par. 174i). It is likely that a verb such as "to mourn" is assumed, given the context: "(I mourned) the same for a friend as for my brother, / I walked around as would one mourning (his) mother." As in Ps 35:14, identity constructions with double *kĕ-* frequently lack a verb (Lev 7:7; Josh 14:11; 1 Kgs 22:4). This colon is the primary datum suggesting that the petitioner's adversaries in Ps 35 are ex-friends rather than relatives, as it indicates that the psalmist mourned for friends, comparing that petitionary mourning to mourning dead relatives such as a brother or mother. Furthermore, the psalm makes no explicit mention of family members.
87. Literally, "(As) one who is dark, I was prostrated." See similarly Pss 38:7; 42:10; 43:2 for this use of *qdr* for the mourner.
88. Sickness and petition for the restoration of health is a topos of the psalms of individual complaint (e.g., Pss 30; 32:3–7; 38; 42:10–12).

89. For *dbq* with a sense of physical proximity, see Ruth 2:8, 21, 23.
90. Evidence from the Neo-Assyrian royal ancestor cult may suggest that such reciprocal expectations extended to dead kin and predecessors as well as to the living. On this, see Bayliss, "Cult of Dead Kin," 124.
91. Note the exceptions mentioned in nn. 66 and 69. The fellow tribesman or Israelite is also described fictively as a brother on occasion (e.g., Num 16:10; Deut 15:12; 17:15).
92. The one possible exception to this pattern of nonerotic intimacy among friends is to be found in 2 Sam 1:26, which I address in Chapter 3. In this text, Jonathan's love for David is said to "surpass" the love of women.
93. We know few details of the expectations of maternal kin, though some biblical evidence is suggestive. According to 2 Sam 13:37, after Amnon's murder, Absalom flees Jerusalem and is given asylum by his maternal grandfather, Talmay, king of Geshur. Talmay's willingness to take Absalom in suggests a strong bond characterized by personal loyalty, especially given Talmay's apparent treaty relationship with David, evidenced by David's marriage to his daughter Maacah, Absalom's mother (2 Sam 3:3). A second example of a maternal relative providing shelter to a fugitive is the story of Jacob's flight to Laban, his maternal uncle, at his mother's suggestion (Gen 27:43–45). Later in the narrative, Laban describes Jacob as "my bone and my flesh" (29:14). Abimelek uses the same idiom of himself in relation to maternal kin in Shechem in Judg 9:2, and the Shechemites describe him as their "brother" (9:3). Thus, idioms familiar from texts that speak of patrilineal kinship relations (e.g., 2 Sam 19:13) are used of matrilineal kin as well, and the expectation of loyalty and support, particularly in times of need, is also evidenced for kin on the mother's side in biblical narratives.

Chapter 2: Failed Friendship

1. Rykle Borger, "Gott Marduk und Gott-König Šulgi als Propheten: Zwei prophetische Texte," *BO* 28 (1971): 3–24.
2. E.g., *BWL* 34:84, 92 (Ludlul Bel Nemeqi) for a cuneiform parallel to the topoi of disloyal friend and unfaithful family member.
3. On *ʾōhăbay wĕrēʿay* as a hendiadys, see the discussion in Chapter 1, n. 59.
4. See also Ps 88:19: "You made far from me (my) loving friend [*ʾōhēb wārēaʿ*]." For *mĕyuddāʿ* as "friend" in Ps 88:9, see the discussion in n. 15 in the Introduction.
5. For this meaning of *qĕrôbay*, see Chapter 1, n. 18.
6. See also Pss 10:1; 22:12, 20; 35:22; 38:22 for this motif. The abandonment of the sufferer by his gods while his oppressors are helped by their gods is a topos in cuneiform texts such as Ludlul Bel Nemeqi (*BWL* 32:43–46; 34:95–98).
7. On *ḥdl*, "cease/fail to be present," see *HALOT* 292, citing Job 14:7, in which a tree that has been cut down nevertheless sends off shoots: "If it is cut down, it nonetheless regenerates, its shoots do not fail to appear [*ḥdl*]." The verb is also

used of leaving a person alone (e.g., Exod 14:12). For *qārôb* as "relative" in this context, see Chapter 1, n. 18.

8. Reading **měraḥemet* here for MT *měraḥēm* (see, e.g., *HALOT* 1217).

9. Yhwh is said to forget about the dead in Ps 88:6. In contrast to Yhwh failing to remember the living petitioner in other psalms of individual complaint, Yhwh's forgetting of the dead in Ps 88 is not cast as an illegitimate act but rather as a natural result of the dead's departure to a locus beyond Yhwh's interest or even power: "I am reckoned with those who descend to the Pit, / I am like a man without help, / Among the dead . . . / Those who lie in the grave, / Whom you do not remember anymore, / And they for their part are cut off from your hand" (Ps 88:5–6). Along with Yhwh's failure to remember the dead in Ps 88:6 is the forgetfulness of the dead themselves, mentioned in Ps 88:13, where the underworld is called "the land of forgetfulness" (*'ereṣ nĕšiyyâ*), and in Ps 6:6. Contrast Ruth 2:20, where it is assumed that Yhwh has not abandoned his loyalty to the dead.

10. It seems likely that the third generation refers to the descendants of male immigrants from these two groups. On this, see my discussion in "'Sie sollen nicht in die Gemeinde des Herrn kommen': Aspekte gesellschaftlicher Inklusion und Exklusion in Dtn 23,4–9 und seine frühen Auslegungen," in Saul M. Olyan, *Social Inequality in the World of the Text: The Significance of Ritual and Social Distinctions in the Hebrew Bible* (JAJSup 4; Göttingen: Vandenhoeck & Ruprecht, 2011), 175–76, 181. One component of the permanent exclusion of Moabites and Ammonites from the community according to Deut 23:7 is that Israelites "shall not seek their welfare [*šālôm*] or their well-being [*ṭôbâ*]" ever. This has often been understood to be a statement about treaty-making, given the technical terms employed (*šālôm, ṭôbâ*), though I have noted in the Introduction that these terms are also used in friendship contexts. Given this, it seems likely that "to abominate" the friend in texts such as Ps 88:9 and Job 19:19 includes ceasing to pursue his well-being and welfare (*ṭôbâ, šālôm*). The meaning of entering the assembly of Yhwh in Deut 23:2–9 is not clear. At least some early interpreters understood it to mean entering the temple (e.g., Lam 1:10). On this, see ibid., 176–77.

11. In Deut 7:26, derivatives of the roots *tʿb*, "abominate," and *šqṣ*, "abhor," occur in apposition. Ps 119:163 is similar, pairing the roots *tʿb*, "abominate," and *śnʾ*, "hate."

12. In contrast to an idiom such as "abominate," used both of friends who reject friends and of treaty violators, the verb Ni *bʾš* ("to make oneself odious," lit. "to make oneself stink") is used of treaty breakers and may well be an idiom of treaty violation (e.g., 2 Sam 10:6; 16:21; perhaps also 1 Sam 13:4), but it is never used of friends who abandon a friendship in surviving materials.

13. The identity of these malevolent agents as friends is suggested by the first colon of v. 14, *kěrēaʿ kěʾāḥ lî*, perhaps best rendered "the same for a friend as for my brother," referring evidently to the manner in which the petitioner mourned

when his friends were sick. On this colon and its interpretation as an identity construction, see further Chapter 1, n. 86, with citations and discussion. The meaning of the second colon of v. 12 is opaque. For *ḥāmās* as "violent" or "false" in this context, see *HALOT* 329.

14. The word *šōlēm* likely has the same meaning as the more common *ʾîš/ʾĕnôš šālôm*, "one with whom I enjoy good relations." The latter refers clearly to friends in Ps 41:10, as I discuss in the Introduction, n. 14.
15. In Ps 109:5, the verb *śym* is used instead of Pi *šlm* or *gml*.
16. E.g., both "loyalty" (*ḥesed*) and "love" (*ʾāhēb*) in treaty contexts are assumed to be reciprocal, even when the treaty is one of unequals. In Exod 20:6 (par. Deut 5:10), Yhwh states that he practices loyalty (*ḥesed*) with those who love him, meaning those who obey his commandments. (On epexegetical waw here, see n. 27 ahead.) Conversely, Israel in its youth is characterized as practicing loyalty (*ḥesed*) with Yhwh according to Jer 2:2. On loyalty (*ḥesed*) in treaty settings, see, e.g., Frank Moore Cross, "Kinship and Covenant in Ancient Israel," in Cross, *From Epic to Canon: History and Literature in Ancient Israel* (Baltimore: Johns Hopkins University Press, 1998), 5–7, 9, and n. 12. Just as vassals owe their suzerain "love" (Deut 6:5), so the suzerain is obligated to love his vassals (2 Sam 19:6–7). On covenant love, see William L. Moran, "The Ancient Near Eastern Background of the Love of God in Deuteronomy," *CBQ* 25 (1963): 77–87. Treaty partners are also obligated to honor one another. On honor as a reciprocal treaty obligation, see my discussion in "Honor, Shame and Covenant Relations in Ancient Israel and Its Environment," *JBL* 115 (1996): 201–18.
17. Related to the idiom "to pay back that which is evil instead of what is good" is the expression "those who seek my undoing [*dōrĕšê rāʿātî*]," rendered literally, "those who seek my evil" (Ps 38:13), the opposite of loyal treatment. The latter is exemplified by Mordecai in the book of Esther, who is said to be "one who seeks that which is good on behalf of his people [*dōrēš ṭôb lĕʿammô*]" (Esth 10:3). Similar to *dōrĕšê rāʿātî* is *mĕbaqšê rāʿātî* (Ps 71:13, 24).
18. Elsewhere in Job's poetic core, Job accuses his three friends of being "troubling" or "mischievous comforters [*mĕnaḥămê ʿāmāl*]," as in 16:2, and "worthless healers [*rōpĕʾê ʾĕlîl*]," as in 13:4.
19. The seekers of the petitioner's undoing are also mentioned in v. 24.
20. Reading *kĕtîb šōḥēṭ* ("slaughtering") instead of *qĕrē šāḥûṭ* ("sharpened"), with LXX and Vg. On this, see further the discussion of *HALOT* 1459–60 and William McKane, *Jeremiah. Volume I: Introduction and Commentary on Jeremiah I–XXV* (2 vols.; International Critical Commentary; Edinburgh: T & T Clark, 1986), 202–3. I translate *bĕqirbô*, literally "in his midst," idiomatically as "privately."
21. Friends are expected to speak positively or communicate their good will (*dbr šālôm*, lit., "speak good will"; Jer 9:7; Pss 28:3; 35:20), as are family members (Esth 10:3; cf. Gen 37:4).

22. For the motif of the rejoicing enemy, see, e.g., Mic 7:8; Lam 1:21; 2:17.
23. On this, see Gary A. Anderson, *A Time to Mourn, A Time to Dance: The Expression of Grief and Joy in Israelite Religion* (University Park: Pennsylvania State University Press, 1991), 49–53. Further elaboration of this argument may be found in Saul M. Olyan, *Biblical Mourning: Ritual and Social Dimensions* (Oxford: Oxford University Press, 2004), 13–19.
24. Isa 61:1–4 is similar in its illustration of the relationship of acts of rejoicing to those of mourning.
25. On the evidence that the enemies of Ps 35 are ex-friends, see my discussion in n. 13 and Chapter 1, n. 86. I understand *šeqer* as an adverbial accusative here as well as in Pss 38:20; 69:5. On this, see GKC par. 131q n. 3.
26. E.g., "At all times the friend loves," Prov 17:17; see also the friend as "lover" in Pss 38:12; 88:19; Prov 18:24. Various texts speak of parents loving their children (e.g., Gen 22:2; 25:28; 37:3–4).
27. Reading epexegetical waw before "those who keep my commandments" (Williams par. 434; W.-O. 39.2.4).
28. The meaning of the last three words of v. 21 is opaque, and therefore I have not translated them. The MT reads *taḥat rodpi ṭôb*, with *qĕrê rodpî* (*kĕtîb rdwpy*). The colon might be translated "Acting as an adversary toward me because I pursued what is good." The preposition *taḥat* can have a causal sense, though it is generally followed by *ʾăšer* or *kî* when it does, as in Num 25:13; Deut 4:37; 2 Kgs 22:17; Jer 29:19; Prov 1:29 (Williams par. 353, 534), and this is not the case here. Nonetheless, a causal understanding of *taḥat* is supported by the LXX (*epei katediōkon dikaiosunēn*) and makes more sense in context than understanding *taḥat* to have a sense of exchange, as it does in the previous colon ("instead of"), though to act as an adversary toward the psalmist because he pursued what is good does not make much sense to me either.
29. In Zech 3:1, the heavenly adversary ("the Satan") apparently stands to the right of the defendant to accuse him (*lĕśiṭnô*).
30. In Ps 69:5, the legal context in which "those who hate me without justification" and "wrongful enemies" accuse the sufferer is made clear in the final cola: "That which I did not steal must I now restore?"
31. On human and divine adversaries, see, especially, T. J. Wray and Gregory Mobley, *The Birth of Satan: Tracing the Devil's Biblical Roots* (Gordonsville, VA: Palgrave Macmillan, 2005). An older work on the topic is Peggy L. Day, *An Adversary in Heaven: Śāṭān in the Hebrew Bible* (HSM 43; Atlanta: Scholars Press, 1988). Ryan Stokes has recently argued that the noun *śāṭān* and verbal reflexes of the root *śṭn* always suggest physical attack or even execution rather than accusation or, more generally, adversarial behavior ("Satan, YHWH's Executioner," *JBL* 133 [2014]: 251–70). Though Stokes's argument may well be cogent for passages such as Num 22:32–33 and 1 Sam 29:4, his understanding of 2 Sam 19:23—that David rejects Abishai's proposal to be Shimi's executioner—is no

more likely than the view that David rebukes Abishai for opposing his leniency toward Shimi. Stokes himself acknowledges that "attack" physically is only one possible meaning for *śṭn/śāṭān* in Pss 38:21; 71:13; and 109:4, 6, 20, 29 and that other understandings might even include accusation (258). I am not convinced by his treatment of Zech 3 and Job 1–2.

32. See n. 13 on *ḥāmās* as "violent" or "false" in this context.
33. On adverbial *ʾak* with a sense of "completely" or "entirely," see also Deut 16:15; Jer 32:30.
34. On the idiom *nāzōrû ʾāḥôr*, see Joseph Blenkinsopp, *Isaiah 1–39: A New Translation with Introduction and Commentary* (AYB 19; New York: Doubleday, 2000), 179–80. He translates "they have fallen away." One might also render "they have turned away," given the combination of *nāzōrû*, "they have become estranged," and the substantive *ʾāḥôr* with adverbial function, best rendered "backward."
35. Literally, "The zeal of your house has consumed me." The reference to Yhwh's house is obscure, as is the relationship of "zeal" to the sufferer. Is it his own zeal? That is how I have rendered it, though this understanding is a guess.
36. While treaties between equal parties are typically portrayed as voluntary, suzerain-vassal treaties often are not. For an example of a vassal who submits to a suzerain by choice, see 2 Kgs 16:7–9; for those coerced into vassalage, usually through military defeat, see, e.g., 2 Sam 10:19. Marriage is frequently represented as a voluntary association, though it has its own unique dynamics in comparison to friendship or alliances, with termination an option only for one party (the husband) and the reasons needed to justify it not always very clear (e.g., Deut 24:1). Furthermore, an offense such as adultery results in the wife's execution, not simply the termination of the bond (e.g., Deut 22:20–21, 23–24).
37. Military defeat is suggested by "Let them be driven back and be shamed"; exile is suggested by "Let them be like chaff before the wind."
38. Examples of undoing or not enforcing curses are rare, though attested, in the biblical text (Judg 17:1–4; 1 Sam 14:24–30, 36–45).
39. See similarly Deut 20:12; Josh 10:1, 4; 11:19. In contrast, 1 Kgs 22:45 may not suggest capitulation by one party but rather a peace established by the mutual agreement of equal partners. For debates about the nature of Jehoshaphat's making peace with the king of Israel, see Mordechai Cogan, *1 Kings: A New Translation with Introduction and Commentary* (AYB 10; New York: Doubleday, 2000), 501, who notes that there has been much disagreement about the nature of the peace. The text simply states that Jehoshaphat "made peace with the king of Israel."
40. E.g., 1 Kgs 8:30, 34, 36, 39, 50.
41. In contrast, several texts entertain the possibility of reconciliation between formerly married people, even if they forbid it under certain circumstances (e.g., after a divorced woman's marriage to a second man, as in Deut 24:4 and Jer 3:1). Hos 2:16–25, utilizing the marriage metaphor, envisions a reconciliation between Yhwh and his "wife" Israel.

42. Execution of children who strike or curse parents is mentioned in Exod 21:15, 17, though nothing is said of disowning them.
43. Scholars who assume a relationship of some kind between Deut 33:9 and Exod 32:27–29 include Bernard M. Levinson (NJPS ad loc., 447); Frank Moore Cross, *Canaanite Myth and Hebrew Epic* (Cambridge, MA: Harvard University Press, 1973), 200; and Richard D. Nelson, *Deuteronomy* (OTL; Louisville, KY: Westminster John Knox, 2002), 389, among others. Nelson, anticipating my argument here, comments in passing that the rhetoric of v. 9 "sounds like a formal legal proclamation of familial severance" (390).
44. What exactly do Abraham and Israel represent, and why would they—even metaphorically—disown "us"? See the discussion of Joseph Blenkinsopp, *Isaiah 56–66: A New Translation with Introduction and Commentary* (AYB 19B; New York: Doubleday, 2003), 263, who considers various possible interpretations but does not reach a firm conclusion on the meaning of the verse. He chooses to translate counterfactually ("Were Abraham not to know us, Israel not to acknowledge us"; 252) as opposed to rendering as an indicative. Even if one were to render the verse thus, the rhetoric of termination is unaffected. Note that Ps 27:10 may also suggest the possibility of terminating familial bonds.
45. It is implicit in the Marduk Prophecy and other texts that suggest that divine influence has brought about social decline characterized by conflict—sometimes violent—between intimates, including friends.
46. Needless to say, one does not seek to shame one's loyal friends, treaty partners, and relatives. This principle is well illustrated by 2 Sam 10:1–5 for allies and 19:6 for vassals.
47. The curses of Deut 28:25 and 48 mention military defeat, nudity, and famine as punishments for Israelites should they violate their covenant with Yhwh. For military defeat and flight before the enemy as shaming, see, e.g., 2 Sam 19:4; Jer 9:18; Ezek 7:18; and Ps 35:4. For nudity as a humiliation, see, e.g., 2 Sam 10:4–5; Isa 20:4; 47:3; and Lam 1:8. For famine as a source of disgrace, see, e.g., Ezek 36:29–30. To shame those who are loyal is a serious offense, as these texts illustrate.
48. There is a change from plural to singular in v. 6 with the beginning of the curses.
49. Hebrew *mōšēk ḥesed*, literally "one who maintains (lit., prolongs) loyalty." The idiom *mšk ḥesed* also occurs in Ps 36:11 and Jer 31:3, with Yhwh as the agent who maintains loyalty.
50. In v. 7, *šht rištām* is difficult, and other interpretations are certainly possible.
51. See, e.g., Lev 26:17, 33, 37–38; Deut 28:25, 31, 36, 43–44.
52. E.g., Sefire I C 16–25; II C 13–17. See also statements such as "And if you do not do this, you will have been disloyal (lit., false) to all the gods of this treaty in this document" (III 3–4). Joseph Fitzmyer, *The Aramaic Inscriptions of Sefire* (Biblica et orientalia 19; Rome: Pontifical Biblical Institute, 1967), 20, 82, 96, for the text; my translation. D. J. Wiseman, "The Vassal Treaties of Esarhaddon," *Iraq* 20 (1958): 59–69 (col. 6, line 414, to col. 7, line 529).

53. E.g., Deut 28:18; *KAI* 13.7; 14.8; A. Kirk Grayson, *Assyrian Rulers of the Early First Millennium BC I (1114–859 BC)* (Toronto: University of Toronto Press, 1991), 282 (A.0.101.26, line 72); 342 (A.0.101.70, lines 17–18).
54. E.g., Deut 28:21–22, 27, 35.
55. E.g., Deut 28:16–17, 18, 23–24; Mic 6:15; Grayson, *Assyrian Rulers I*, 254 (A.0.101.17, col. 5, line 94).
56. E.g., Deut 28:25; Grayson, *Assyrian Rulers I*, 342 (A.0.101.70, line 16); Sefire I A 38–39 (Fitzmyer, *Aramaic Inscriptions*, 14).
57. E.g., Deut 28:36, 41.
58. E.g., Deut 28:28–29; Sefire I A 39 (Fitzmyer, *Aramaic Inscriptions*, 14).
59. E.g., Deut 28:26; *KAI* 14.8.
60. E.g., Grayson, *Assyrian Rulers I*, 282 (A.0.101.26, line 72); 342 (A.0.101.70, lines 17–18); Sefire I C 24–25; II A 4 (Fitzmyer, *Aramaic Inscriptions*, 20, 80).
61. E.g., *KAI* 13.8; 14.8.
62. See, e.g., Job 6:14–15 on the obligation of friends and brothers to practice loyalty (*ḥesed*). Treaty partners are also obliged to do the same, as texts such as Exod 20:5–6 (par. Deut 5:9–10) and 2 Sam 10:1–2 illustrate, but they do not seem to be at issue in Ps 109.
63. That loyalty extends beyond the death of one to whom another is committed, either formally or informally, is well illustrated by 2 Sam 9:1, where David asks, "Does there remain a survivor belonging to Saul's house, that I might demonstrate loyalty to him (lit., "do loyalty [*ḥesed*] with him") on account of Jonathan?" Treaties themselves assume that loyalty is an obligation that continues after the death of a treaty partner. On this, see, e.g., Sefire III 9–14, esp. line 11: "If they slay me, you yourself must come and avenge my blood from the hand of those who hate me" (Fitzmyer, *Aramaic Inscriptions*, 96, 98, for the text; my translation).
64. On the death-related obligations of kin and friends, see my discussion in Chapter 1.
65. ŠEŠ (*aḫu*) ŠEŠ (*aḫā*)-*šú* GU₇ (*ikkal*) *ru-u₈-a ru-u₈-a-šú ina* GIŠ.TUKUL (*kakki*) *i-ra-si-ib* (Borger, "Gott Marduk," 8, for the text; my translation).
66. [*ib*]-[*ru*] *ib-ra-šu ina* GIŠ.TUKUL (*kakki*) *ú-šam-qat* [*ru-u₈*]-*a ru-u₈-a-šú ina* GIŠ.TUKUL (*kakki*) *ú-ḫal-laq* (Borger, "Gott Marduk," 15, for the text; my translation).
67. Deut 28:4, 11.
68. Deut 28:5, 8, 11; Grayson, *Assyrian Rulers I*, 253 (A.0.101.17, col. 5, lines 52–54); Hayim Tadmor and Shigeo Yamada, *The Royal Inscriptions of Tiglath-Pileser III (744–727 BC) and Shalmaneser V (726–722 BC), Kings of Assyria* (Winona Lake, IN: Eisenbrauns, 2011), 142 (53, lines 27–28).
69. Grayson, *Assyrian Rulers I*, 282 (A.0.101.26, lines 68–69).
70. Deut 4:26; 22:7; 1 Kgs 3:14.
71. Deut 28:7; Grayson, *Assyrian Rulers I*, 253 (A.0.101.17, col. 5, lines 50–51).
72. Tadmor and Yamada, *Royal Inscriptions*, 142 (53, lines 26–28).

73. On the psalms of individual complaint, see, e.g., the brief survey of Erich Zenger, "Das Buch der Psalmen," in Zenger, *Einleitung in das Alte Testament* (3rd ed.; Stuttgart: Kohlhammer, 1998), 318–20, and the discussion and bibliography in Olyan, *Biblical Mourning*, 72–76 and n. 22. A work of particular note on the subject is Erhard Gerstenberger, *Der bittende Mensch: Bittritual und Klagelied des Einzelnen im Alten Testament* (Wissenschaftlichen Monographien zum Alten und Neuen Testament 51; Neukirchen-Vluyn: Neukirchener, 1980). For the disloyal friend in the psalms of individual complaint, particularly in Ps 22, see Michaela Bauks, *Die Feinde des Psalmisten und die Freunde Ijobs: Untersuchungen zur Freund-Klage im Alten Testament am Beispiel von Ps 22* (Stuttgarter Bibel Studien 203; Stuttgart: Katholisches Bibelwerk, 2004). On the mixing of psalm genres in the exile, see Rainer Albertz, *Die Exilszeit: 6. Jahrhundert v. Chr.* (Stuttgart: Kohlhammer, 2001), 130–35.
74. For intervention as the goal of petitionary rites, see further Olyan, *Biblical Mourning*, 75–76, 79–81. See also Gerstenberger, *Der bittende Mensch*, 158, and Bauks, *Die Feinde*, 78.
75. The meaning of the second colon of v. 17 is not entirely clear, and therefore my translation is abridged. Following *ḥāśîbāh napšî* ("save my life") is *miššōʾêhem*, possibly "from their ravages," assuming a noun **šwʾ*, which is otherwise unattested (cf. *šôʾâ*, "ruin, devastation, waste," which is relatively common). LXX *apo tēs kakourgias autōn* could be construed to support **šwʾ*.
76. See the similar images in *BWL* 34:71–72.
77. Enemies without a previous, positive association can be described as "haters," as in Exod 1:10; Esth 9:1, 5, 16, though they are obviously never said to "hate" instead of "love," as they never owed love in the first place.
78. On this idiom, see n. 49.

Chapter 3: Friendship in Narrative

1. The Joban poetic core mentions both anonymous friends (e.g., 19:13–14, 19) and Job's three named comforters; the narrative prologue and epilogue mention only the latter. I treat friendship in the prologue and epilogue in this chapter, with reference to the poetic core.
2. For a skeptical view of the historicity of the relationship of David and Jonathan, see the assessment of Baruch Halpern, who does not believe that David ever served at Saul's court (*David's Secret Demons: Messiah, Murderer, Traitor, King* [Grand Rapids, MI: Eerdmans, 2001], 283). Similarly, Jacob L. Wright sees the relationship as a creation of writers who lived much later than the tenth century BCE (*David, King of Israel, and Caleb in Biblical Memory* [New York: Cambridge University Press, 2014], 40). Contrast this with the treatment of Steven L. McKenzie, who entertains the possibility that David and Jonathan might have been friends, while rejecting the historicity of obvious apologetic claims, e.g., that Jonathan actively conspired against his father or willingly

gave up his right to succeed him (*King David: A Biography* [New York: Oxford University Press, 2000], 84–85). On the literary genres of Job, see C. L. Seow, *Job 1–21: Interpretation and Commentary* (Grand Rapids, MI: Eerdmans, 2013), 47–65. For Ruth as fiction, see, e.g., Edward F. Campbell, *Ruth: A New Translation with Introduction, Notes, and Commentary* (AYB 7; Garden City, NY: Doubleday, 1975), 10.

3. Among scholars who also speak of the relationship of Ruth and Naomi as a friendship are Alexander A. Fischer, "Freundschaft (AT)," *Das wissenschaftliche Bibellexikon im Internet* (www.wibilex.de; updated 2007), who offers no arguments to support this interpretation of their relationship, though he recognizes Ruth's choice to take profound risks to remain with Naomi as well as the reciprocal nature of their support of one another. A more developed and insightful treatment is that of Christian Frevel, who states that Ruth's unconditional commitment to Naomi and Naomi's grateful acceptance of it make the book a story of women's friendship (*Das Buch Rut* [Neuer Stuttgarter Kommentar Altes Testament 6; Stuttgart: Katholisches Bibelwerk, 1992], 37). Elsewhere, Frevel underscores the reciprocal nature of their relationship, demonstrated by the help they offer one another (*Rut*, 36, 88). Though I agree with Frevel's emphasis on free choice and reciprocity, we disagree on the role of their common connection to Elimelek's family and what it will allow them to accomplish together, as I will show. I also miss in Frevel's treatment an explanation for the continued use of familial terminology throughout the story, even after all familial obligations have been satisfied. Note also Renate Jost, who speaks of Ruth and Naomi having a lifelong friendship and understands Ruth's oath (1:17) as functioning to transform her from a dependent daughter-in-law into a "partner" of Naomi ("Partnerin Noomis"). Unfortunately, Jost provides little or no argument to support her assertions (*Freundin in der Fremde: Rut und Noomi* [Stuttgart: Quell, 1992], 5, 29).

4. Neither Ruth nor Naomi is ever referred to as *rěʿût*, possibly "female companion" in some contexts (e.g., Jer 9:19), or as *rēʿâ/raʿyâ*, "friend," and other technical vocabulary of friendship is in the main lacking in the text, though Ruth is said to love Naomi on one occasion (4:15). (Ruth's "loyalty" [*ḥesed*] to Naomi, mentioned in 1:8, is familial and precedes the beginning of their friendship.) Though some have speculated that the name Ruth (*rût*) is related to the noun *rěʿût*, this has not been demonstrated convincingly (for this view, see, e.g., Fischer, "Freundschaft [AT]"; Jost, *Freundin in der Fremde*, 18–19). As Campbell notes, though the Peshitta "renders [the name] *rʿût*, 'woman companion,' throughout the book . . . no LXX or Latin evidence supports the presence of a consonant *ʿayn* [sic] in the name; for a West Semitic word to lose this guttural sound is unlikely in the extreme" (*Ruth*, 56; similarly, Jack M. Sasson, *Ruth: A New Translation with a Philological Commentary and a Formalist-Folklorist Interpretation* [2nd ed.; Sheffield: Sheffield Academic Press, 1989], 20–21). Many others have

noted that Ruth chooses to remain with Naomi (e.g., Fischer, "Freundschaft [AT]"; Frevel, *Rut,* passim); still others have underscored the significance of reciprocity for the book of Ruth (e.g., Campbell, *Ruth,* 66), though reciprocity in Ruth *as a component of friendship* has not been much recognized (Frevel is an exception [*Rut,* 36, 88]). Finally, on Ruth as a novella, see, e.g., Erich Zenger, "Das Buch Rut," in *Einleitung in das Alte Testament* (3rd ed.; Stuttgart: Kohlhammer Verlag, 1998), 205.

5. In other words, without a male protector, supporter, or authority figure.
6. The syntax here is difficult. As Campbell, *Ruth,* 66, points out, the jussive that precedes the imperative has no stated object. A jussive followed by an imperative with *wāw* copulative is a construction known from other passages in which the imperative expresses "a consequence which is to be expected with certainty, and often a consequence which is intended" (GKC par. 110i, cited by Campbell, ibid., 66). Campbell's solution, to reconstruct *maśkōret,* "recompense," is rather speculative, when the versions support *ḥesed,* though if *ḥesed* is reconstructed, v. 9 essentially repeats the wish expressed in v. 8. My translation is not unlike that of NJPS. An alternative approach would be to assume that the syntax of the clause has been interrupted (e.g., Jeremy Schipper, "The Syntax and Rhetoric of Ruth 1:9a," *VT* 62 [2012]: 643–44, who cites and builds upon the argument of Robert D. Holmstedt, *Ruth: A Handbook on the Hebrew Text* [Waco, TX: Baylor University Press, 2010], 66, 75).
7. This point is often made. See, e.g., Frevel, *Rut,* 60.
8. Many believe that there is an allusion to a Levir of some kind here (see, e.g., Campbell, *Ruth,* 73, 83–84, 132–33; Zenger, "Das Buch Rut," 203; Irmtraud Fischer, *Rut: Übersetzt und ausgelegt* [Herders Theologischer Kommentar zum Alten Testament; Freiburg: Herder, 2001], 140–41). Fischer's understanding of the Levir allusion in 1:11 is particularly striking and worthy of comment. For her, Naomi "sieht die Leviratsehe nicht als Erhaltung der Genealogie ihrer verstorbenen Söhne, deren Name nicht ausgelöscht werden soll, sondern als eine Rechtsinstitution zur Witwenversorgung ihrer beiden Schwiegertöchter." If she is correct, Naomi's views stand in stark contrast to those of Boaz, whose words in 4:10 focus on providing an heir to Mahlon: "Ruth the Moabite woman, the wife of Mahlon, I acquire as a wife in order to raise up the name of the dead man upon his inalienable property [*naḥălâ*], that the dead man's name not be cut off from his brethren and from the gate of his place" (see also 4:5). Contrast Sasson, who states that the story "tells us *nothing* about the workings of this institution" (*Ruth,* 229).
9. "Where you die" is the best option for translating the somewhat ambiguous *ba'ăšer tāmûtî,* given that *wěšām 'eqqābēr* ("and there I will be buried") follows it. For this reasoning, see, e.g., Sasson, *Ruth,* 30, and Mark Smith, "Your People Shall Be My People": Family and Covenant in Ruth 1:16–17," *CBQ* 69 (2007): 243. The alternative, to translate the statement instrumentally ("in the manner you die"), seems fanciful to me.

10. Some understand the oath differently: "if anything but death parts us" (Sasson, *Ruth*, 28; similarly NJPS and others). But this understanding of *kî hammāwet yaprîd bênî ûbênēk* is more difficult to defend than "if (even) death separates me from you" on account of the words directly preceding the oath: "Where you die, I will die and there I will be buried." If Ruth has already made clear that she will remain with Naomi in death, why would she state in her oath that only death will part the two of them? Rather, it seems more likely that she is simply affirming her previous statement that they will remain together even at death. See similarly Tod Linafelt in Tod Linafelt and Timothy K. Beal, *Ruth and Esther* (Berit Olam; Collegeville, MN: Liturgical Press, 1999), 16. Though I agree with Campbell's rendering and his view regarding the relation of Ruth's oath to her preceding statement, I cannot accept his speculation that the oath tells us something about secondary burial customs (*Ruth*, 74–75).
11. A classic study of adoption formulae is Shalom M. Paul, "Adoption Formulae: A Study of Cuneiform and Biblical Legal Clauses," *Maarav* 2 (1979–80): 173–85. Another useful survey of cuneiform evidence may be found in Paul Kalluveettil, *Declaration and Covenant: A Comprehensive Review of Covenant Formulae from the Old Testament and the Ancient Near East* (AnBib 88; Rome: Biblical Institute Press, 1982), 108–9 (brought to my attention by Smith, "Your People Shall Be My People"). Neither Paul nor Kalluveettil refers to Ruth 1:16.
12. The adoption is then restated as follows: "As for Ephraim and Manasseh, they shall be mine like Reuben and Simeon."
13. Ezek 36:28 is similar in construction to Jer 31:33.
14. Zech 13:9 is similar to Hos 2:25, with Yhwh saying "You are my people" and Israel saying "Yhwh is my god."
15. For the latter, see, e.g., Hos 1:9, "You are not my people and I am not your (god)," and the discussion in Paul, "Adoption Formulae," 179–80.
16. It is especially close in style to Hos 2:25 and Zech 13:9, which, like it, are verbless. On "solemn declarations" as a component of the establishment and termination of adoptions and other formal ties such as marriages, see Paul, "Adoption Formulae," 179 and n. 10. That adoption-like rhetoric might occur outside of the setting of a formal adoption is illustrated also by Gen 28:20–21, where the context is a vow. Jacob states: "If God is with me and watches over me on this journey which I am undertaking and gives me food to eat and a garment to wear and I return safely to the house of my father, then Yhwh shall become my god [*wĕhāyâ yhwh lî lēʾlōhîm*]." The style here is quite close to the adoption rhetoric of 2 Sam 7:14 (*ʾānî ʾehyeh lô lĕʾāb wĕhûʾ yihyeh lî lĕbēn*).
17. For the tradition that a god is worshiped in his territory, see, e.g., 1 Sam 26:19, which suggests that when David leaves Yhwh's patrimony, he must worship other gods. See also the question posed by Ps 137:4, "How do we sing a song of Yhwh in an alien land?" The Naaman story provides an elaborate solution to the problem of wanting to worship a deity outside of his territory: import earth from that god's land and sacrifice to that god on it. According to this ideology

of territorial cult, the Elimelek family would be expected to worship Chemosh while residing in Moab, as Moab is his land. Yet Naomi's words to Ruth in 1:15 seem to suggest otherwise: "Your sister-in-law has returned to her people and her god(s)." One possible explanation is that the author simply does not subscribe to the territorial bounding of Yhwh worship and suggests implicitly that when joining a Judahite family, the Moabite wives have left their gods as well as their natal families, even if that Judahite family resides temporarily in Moab itself. If this is the case, Ruth's declaration and the oath by Yhwh that follows it function to formalize what had already been the case in practice according to the author.

18. When Orpa leaves Naomi, she returns to her people and her god(s) according to 1:15. This suggests that as long as she is connected to Elimelek's family, she has embraced his people and his god.
19. Mark Smith sees "covenantal language" in Ruth 1:16–17, with Ruth establishing "a family relationship with Naomi that transcends the death of the male who had connected them, and in fact this relationship represents a family tie closer than that expressed by the formal status of former in-laws" ("Your People Shall Be My People," 247). He goes on to characterize the new relationship as that of mother and daughter on the basis of Naomi's use of "my daughter" for Ruth (ibid., 258), even though the narrative continues to use in-law terminology. He does not speak of adoption with respect to Ruth and Naomi, or of adoption-like rhetoric in Ruth 1:16, preferring to compare the rhetoric of covenanting in texts such as 1 Kgs 22:4 and 2 Kgs 3:7. In my view, the adoption rhetoric of texts such as Hos 2:25 and Zech 13:9 is closer to that of Ruth 1:16 than is the treaty rhetoric cited by Smith.
20. On the oath formula, see, e.g., Campbell, *Ruth*, 74; Sasson, *Ruth*, 30–31.
21. For the former, see my discussion ahead. The indirect evidence for the possibility of a widow's burial in the tomb of her natal family is to be found in a text such as Lev 22:13, which allows a priest's childless, widowed daughter who has returned to her father's house to eat of the holy foods, something forbidden to nondependents but permitted to the priest's dependents, including his slaves (Lev 22:11). Such a widow, a dependent of her father once again and a resident in his house, would presumably be buried in her natal family's tomb.
22. Whether Ruth's statement suggests anything about a shared afterlife is, unfortunately, unclear.
23. On the evidence for perpetuation of such ties even after the widow's husband's death, see Paula S. Hiebert, "'Whence Shall Help Come to Me?': The Biblical Widow," in *Gender and Difference in Ancient Israel* (ed. Peggy L. Day; Minneapolis: Fortress, 1989), 129–30, and Hennie J. Marsman, *Women in Ugarit and Israel: Their Social and Religious Position in the Context of the Ancient Near East* (Oudtestamentische Studiën 49; Leiden: Brill, 2003), 308–9. Evidence of a widow's continuing ties to her husband's family includes Gen 38:24–26, according to which Tamar is still under her father-in-law's authority, even as a

widow (he can order her execution, even though she has returned to her father's household). This observation is made by Hiebert, who is followed by Marsman. Compare Frevel, who argues that widows normally return to their natal families and claims that all ties to the dead husband's family are sundered at his death (*Rut*, 55, 87). Clearly, this is not the case according to Gen 38:24–26, where a father-in-law continues to exercise authority over a widow. According to the narrative in Ruth, the link to the family of the dead husband continues if the widow desires it, though here, the father-in-law is no longer living nor are there any other closely related males—sons, brothers-in-law—present to act as protectors, providers, or authority figures.

24. Frevel does not recognize this point (*Rut*, 83). The absorption of wives into the families of their husbands is perhaps best illustrated by the words of Rachel and Leah in Gen 31:15, who speak of their relationship to their father after they have married: "Are we not considered alien women [*nokriyyôt*] by him [*lô*]?" On this text, see the discussion of Hiebert, "Biblical Widow," 132–33. For the lamed of agent, see, e.g., Williams par. 280.

25. Interestingly, the roles of redeemer and Levir are evidently combined in Ruth, as many have remarked. Campbell notes: "From the story's point of view, the combination of redemption and levirate marriage is a *presupposition*" (*Ruth*, 132; italics in the original). Furthermore, no other biblical text combines the two in such a way, as not a few have noted (e.g., ibid., 132–33).

26. In some of these examples, the ideal is implicit.

27. Many have understood the four occurrences of the verb to suggest a leitmotif (e.g., Campbell, *Ruth*, 97; Sasson, *Ruth*, 28, 50).

28. That the verb "to cling to" and its derivatives also have treaty resonances has been discussed in Chapter 1. Campbell finds such resonances in Ruth's clinging in 1:14, though I believe that its familial and friendship resonances are far more likely in this context (*Ruth*, 31, 81). Likewise, the relevance of Gen 2:24, where a man is said to leave his parents and "cling" to his wife, becoming "one flesh," is questionable, given the more likely friendship and familial resonances of "to cling" discussed above. Thus, I cannot accept the argument of Jutta Hausmann that because both Ruth 1:14, 16 and Gen 2:24 employ the verbs "to cling to" and "to abandon," "Rut tritt damit faktisch an die Stelle des Mannes von Naomi" (*Rut: Miteinander auf dem Weg* [Biblische Gestalten 11; Leipzig: Evangelische Verlagsanstalt, 2005], 66). Like Hausmann, others interpreting Ruth 1:14 also privilege the clinging of man to wife in Gen 2:24 while ignoring the clinging of friend to friend and family member to family member assumed by a text such as Prov 18:24 (e.g., Jost, *Freundin in der Fremde*, 27; Linafelt, *Ruth and Esther*, 15).

29. These observations have been made by others, e.g., Adele Reinhartz in NJPS (1582). Jost understands "my daughter" to be a term of endearment (*Freundin in der Fremde*, 26). Smith, as noted, assigns significance to the use of the term

"daughter" by Naomi though he says little about its use by Boaz ("Your People Shall Be My People," 258).

30. Contrast Ruth's interactions with Boaz, where the narrator brings into relief status differences through the use of terms of submission such as "my lord" and "your maidservant" by Ruth (2:13; 3:9) and through Ruth's acts of prostration before Boaz (2:10). Jeremy Schipper finds an indicator of Naomi's continuing authority over Ruth in the use of the preposition ʿim in 1:7, 11, 22 and 2:6, though I am not convinced, given that ʿim is most easily understood to indicate simply accompaniment in these contexts ("Translating the Preposition ʿm in the Book of Ruth," *VT* 63 [2013]: 663–69). See also Fischer, *Rut*, 139, who argues that "my daughters" in 1:11 suggests the authority of Naomi over her daughters-in-law, though the use of the expression may be nothing more than affectionate and an acknowledgment of age difference in that context. The same is true of "my daughter" when used of Ruth by Boaz and Naomi in chapters 2 and 3.

31. Compare this approved abandonment of her natal family and home with her refusal to "abandon" Naomi (1:16). Note also Naomi's statement that Yhwh has not "abandoned" his loyalty (*ḥesed*) to the living and the dead (2:20), just as Ruth has been loyal (ʿāśâ ḥesed) both to Naomi and to her dead husband (1:8).

32. Contrast the many commentators who have argued for a date in the sixth or fifth century on the basis of the book's assumed anti-xenophobic response to texts such as Deut 23:4–9 and Neh 13:1–3. On this, see, e.g., Zenger, "Das Buch Rut," 205–7; Frevel, *Rut*, 34, 38; Jost, *Freundin in der Fremde*, 8–9, 11–13; and Thomas Römer, "L'amitié selon la Bible hébraïque," *Transversalités* 113 (2010): 36. For a useful discussion of dating that reaches no firm conclusion, see Sasson, *Ruth*, 240–52.

33. On the "woman of strength" of Prov 31:10, see Michael V. Fox, *Proverbs 10–31: A New Translation with Introduction and Commentary* (AYB 18B; New Haven, CT: Yale University Press, 2009), 891, whose rendering of ʾēšet ḥayil I adopt here. As Fox states regarding the ideal woman of Prov 31, "her primary strength is in character, because even her practical competencies are not simply technical skills but manifestations of her focus, selflessness, and determination." Fischer sees an intertextual allusion here with Prov 31:10 (*Rut*, 215).

34. Naomi's change of mood and tone has been observed by others, e.g., Campbell, who states that "her passivity gives way to activity" as the narrative develops (*Ruth*, 32). See similarly Kristin Moen Saxegaard, *Character Complexity in the Book of Ruth* (FAT 2.47; Tübingen: Mohr/Siebeck, 2010), 96: "From being passive and, most of all, silent, Naomi now is the one who takes the initiative."

35. Hebrew *mēšîb nepeš* may be rendered "one who lifts spirits" given the sense of *wĕnepeš ʾădōnāyw yāšîb* in Prov 25:13 (what a trustworthy envoy does) and *mēšîb nepeš* in Lam 1:16 (what a comforter should do). Elsewhere, the idiom *yšb* (Hi) *nepeš* seems to refer to physical revival (e.g., Lam 1:11, 19, of those who are starving by means of food). See also Ps 19:8, where Yhwh's teaching is *tĕmîmâ mĕšîbat nāpeš*.

36. Others have noted Ruth's consistency as a character, e.g., Saxegaard, *Character Complexity*, 142. Saxegaard also makes a case for Naomi's complexity (ibid., 75–104). If Ruth develops at all as a character, her growth is to be discerned in her movement from deference and self doubt in her interaction with Boaz (2:10) to confident assertion with him (3:9). Contrast my reading with that of Linafelt, who finds complexity in Ruth's character, including a lack of candor (e.g., *Ruth and Esther*, xv).

37. It is not at all clear to me what the nature of Ruth's "latter [act of] *ḥesed*" mentioned by Boaz in 3:10 is. He says that it is greater than her "former" *ḥesed*, which must refer to her loyalty to Naomi. Could it be her choice of Boaz as redeemer and husband? This makes sense in context, though why would Ruth owe Boaz *ḥesed* in the form of marriage, and why would her choice of Boaz be construed as superior to her loyalty to Naomi? I remain perplexed by this verse.

38. Theories abound regarding the hypothetical sources and the development of 1 and 2 Sam. According to many contemporary scholars, the narratives about Jonathan and David are embedded in a larger, hypothetical, apologetic work, the "History of David's Rise" (HDR) comprising approximately 1 Sam 16 to 2 Sam 5, a work the Deuteronomists used as a source when they constructed their history (e.g., P. Kyle McCarter, Jr., *I Samuel: A New Translation with Introduction, Notes and Commentary* [AYB 8; Garden City, NY: Doubleday, 1980], 27–30; Michael B. Dick, "The 'History of David's Rise to Power' and the Neo-Babylonian Succession Apologies," in *David and Zion: Biblical Studies in Honor of J. J. M. Roberts* [ed. Bernard F. Batto and Kathryn L. Roberts; Winona Lake, IN: Eisenbrauns, 2004], 3; Thomas Römer, *The So-Called Deuteronomistic History: A Sociological, Historical and Literary Introduction* [London: T & T Clark, 2007], 95). There is, however, no consensus among advocates of an HDR regarding its dating. Compare McCarter's arguments for a tenth-century date to those of Römer, who advocates a late-seventh-century date and sees the HDR as pro-Josianic propaganda (McCarter, ibid., 29; Römer, ibid., 95–97). Dick, for his part, brings into relief HDR's parallels with the apologies of Neo-Babylonian usurpers (ibid., 3–19). McCarter provides a useful survey of various views of the HDR and its provenance up to 1980, Dick up to 2004. Others take a different approach, understanding the development of 1 and 2 Sam as a result of combining hypothetical sources with supplementation, the latter continuing as the text developed (e.g., Wright, *David, King of Israel*).

39. There is also 2 Sam 1:19–26, David's Lament over Saul and Jonathan, which is a poem, not a narrative. I treat this text below, in note 40, and in the appendix at the end of this section in the chapter.

40. For an explication of the different treaty relationship combinations assumed in the Jonathan-David narratives, see the study of Jerzy Wozniak, "Drei verschiedene literarische Beschreibungen des Bundes zwischen Jonathan und David," *Biblische Zeitschrift* 27 (1983): 213–18. Wozniak does not treat 2 Sam 1:26, and his understanding of the nature of the treaty in each prose narrative sometimes

differs from mine, as I shall note. 2 Sam 1:26 likely presumes a treaty of equals, given that David refers to Jonathan as "my brother," which is typical treaty rhetoric (Saul M. Olyan, "'Surpassing the Love of Women': Another Look at 2 Samuel 1:26 and the Relationship of David and Jonathan," in Olyan, *Social Inequality in the World of the Text: The Significance of Ritual and Social Distinctions in the Hebrew Bible* [JAJSup 4; Göttingen: Vandenhoeck & Ruprecht, 2011], 86–87). On the other hand, Jonathan as David's "brother" could perhaps be a familial usage, given the relationship of Jonathan and David as brothers-in-law according to some narratives (e.g., 1 Sam 18:27; 19:10–17; 25:44). But this latter interpretation would require us to assume that the poet presumes such a familial relationship, something that cannot be demonstrated. Fischer, for his part, understands the use of "brother" in David's Lament to reflect the formulaic address of lamentation for the dead, citing Jer 22:18 ("Freundschaft [AT]"), but this is unconvincing, given the David-Jonathan relationship's strong treaty associations in the prose narratives, and given that Jer 22:18 is specifically concerned with the death of a king, who is also addressed as "sister," "lord," and "his majesty."

41. Although an in-law relationship might be presupposed by some of the Jonathan-David narratives, it is not necessarily presumed by all. The narrative in 1 Sam 18:1–4 precedes David's marriage to Michal in 18:27, and the other narratives I discuss do not make reference to an in-law relationship.

42. The word *rēaʿ* occurs twice in the David-Jonathan narrative in 1 Sam 20:41 in the fixed reciprocal expression *ʾîš ʾet rēʿēhû*, used here to modify each of two verbs: "They kissed one another and wept together." On this construction, see GKC par. 139e. Obviously, *rēaʿ* in this usage is not to be translated "friend." Those who describe the Jonathan-David relationship as a friendship include Martti Nissinen, "Die Liebe von David und Jonatan als Frage der modernen Exegese," *Biblica* 80 (1999): 250–63; Steven L. McKenzie, *King David: A Biography* (New York: Oxford University Press, 2000), 84–85; Patricia K. Tull, "Jonathan's Gift of Friendship," *Interpretation* (April 2004): 130–43; Thomas Römer and Loyse Bonjour, *L'homosexualité dans le Proche-Orient ancien et la Bible* (Geneva: Labor et Fides, 2005), 68–79; Fischer, "Freundschaft (AT)"; Römer, "L'amitié selon la Bible hébraïque," 37–44; Graham Davies, "The Friendship of Jonathan and David," in *Studies on the Text and Versions of the Hebrew Bible in Honour of Robert Gordon* (ed. Geoffrey Khan and Diana Lipton; VTSup 149; Leiden: Brill, 2012), 65–76; Jonathan Y. Rowe, *Sons or Lovers: An Interpretation of David and Jonathan's Friendship* (New York: Bloomsbury T & T Clark, 2012). A number of authors suggest the friendship is atypical (e.g., Fischer, who describes it as "unique" ["einzigartig"], or Römer and Bonjour, who refer to it as "exceptional" ["la relation exceptionnelle," "une relation hors de commun"], underscoring its strength and intimacy [70, 79]). Many who assume a friendship offer few if any arguments in defense of this viewpoint. My thanks to Jacob L. Wright for the Tull reference.

43. As Römer and Bonjour state, "contre toutes les conventions de l'Antiquité, Jonathan choisira David et s'opposera à son père" (*L'homosexualité*, 72). Others have noted the obvious, apologetic purpose of narratives that claim that Jonathan chose fidelity to David over loyalty to his father. Such narratives seek to make David's rise to the throne seem legitimate, inevitable, and desirable to all, including Saul's own heir. On this, see, e.g., McKenzie, *King David*, 84–85. Jonathan choosing David over his father is likely intended to suggest a strong personal commitment to David as well as to serve an apologetic purpose.

44. Many have noted that the MT of 18:1–4, like 17:12–31, 41, 48b, 50, 55–58 and 18:5, 10–11, 17–19, 29b–30, are missing from LXX^B. McCarter has made a case for their likely absence not only from the Hebrew underlying the Old Greek, but from "the primitive text of Samuel itself." Thus, the text of 18:1–4 ought to be seen as part of a larger, late addition to the Hebrew text of Samuel (*I Samuel*, 306). For the content of the interpolation and how it differs from that of the core of chapters 17 and 18, see McCarter, ibid., 307–9.

45. D. J. Wiseman, "The Vassal Treaties of Esarhaddon," *Iraq* 20 (1958): 49–50 (col. 4, lines 266–68). Wiseman's translation.

46. Wozniak believes that 18:1–4 suggest a parity treaty ("Drei verschiedene literarische Beschreibungen," 217).

47. E.g., Moshe Weinfeld, "*bĕrîth*," *TDOT* 2:263; Wozniak, "Drei verschiedene literarische Beschreibungen," 215; McCarter, *I Samuel*, 305. Fischer understands the exchange as an act that "strengthens" the covenant ("Freundschaft [AT]"). A number of scholars have seen in it a symbolic renunciation of the throne, focusing on what they believe to be the royal status of the garment (*mĕ'îl*) and—according to some—other items given over by Jonathan (e.g., Römer and Bonjour, *L'homosexualité*, 69; McCarter, among others, is also not averse to this understanding [ibid., 305]). But I am reluctant to embrace this interpretation of Jonathan's gift of clothing and other personal items to David for several reasons. First, the *mĕ'îl* is worn by everyone from Job to Aaron to Samuel's ghost and therefore lacks a distinctly royal association. And with regard specifically to the exchange of personal items, including weapons, the same scenario is present in 17:38–39, where Saul gives David his weapons and armor to fight Goliath. But in this narrative, David cannot make use of the weapons and armor, and does not do so. It seems implausible that the author of 17:38–39 wants the reader to understand David's refusal of Saul's weapons and armor as a rejection of the throne. More likely in my view, those responsible for 17:38–39 and 18:4 do not imagine that the giving of personal items such as clothing (including the *mĕ'îl*) and weapons represents a symbolic renunciation of the throne.

48. The renderings of the idiom are nearly identical in Hebrew: *wĕnepeš yĕhônātān niqšĕrâ bĕnepeš dāwīd* in 1 Sam 18:1 versus *wĕnapšô qĕšûrâ bĕnapšô* in Gen 44:30.

49. Nothing is said directly about David's feelings for Jonathan in 18:1–4, though David does participate in the covenant-making rite (v. 3). In contrast, David's emotions are brought into relief in 20:41 and 2 Sam 1:26.

50. Elsewhere, Saul interprets acts such as this as treasonous. This is demonstrated by his words to Jonathan in 20:30 and to his Benjaminite vassals in 22:7–8. Not only do Jonathan's acts of loyalty to David instead of Saul constitute rebellion in Saul's eyes; the withholding of information about the existence of the David-Jonathan treaty by Saul's vassals is also treasonous according to 22:8 (*kî qĕšartem kullĕkem ʿālay*).
51. The love of Saul's servants for David in 18:22 is clearly political and refers back to the love of all Israel and Judah for David as military commander mentioned in 18:16. On this, see, among others, William L. Moran, "The Ancient Near Eastern Background of the Love of God in Deuteronomy," *CBQ* 25 (1963): 81, and Römer and Bonjour, *L'homosexualité*, 71. In 2 Sam 15:25–26, David raises the possibility that Yhwh no longer "delights in" him when his son Absalom has rebelled against him.
52. See also Ps 112:1, where the idiom is used of Yhwh's worshipers: "Happy is the man who reverences Yhwh, / Who delights exceedingly in his commandments [*bĕmiṣwōtāyw ḥāpēṣ mĕʾōd*]."
53. Are David and Jonathan equals in 19:1–7? Is one or the other subordinate? No idioms of inequality appear in this Jonathan-David narrative, in contrast to others such as 1 Sam 20:1–10, 18–22, 24–41; 21:1; or 23:14–18. Wozniak, for his part, sees a treaty in which David is subordinate in 19:1–7 ("Drei verschiedene literarische Beschreibungen," 217). In 1 Sam 22:8, Saul makes reference to a treaty between Jonathan and David, seems to assume it was initiated by Jonathan as in 18:1–4 and 20:8, and understands David to be the subordinate, who is incited to rebel by Jonathan himself ("my son has incited my servant against me"). As noted, David is also portrayed as vassal in 20:1–10, 18–22, 24–41 and 21:1.
54. Note that Ps 35:27 does not use the preposition *bĕ* with *ḥāpēṣ*, though Ps 109:17 does.
55. An emotional resonance may also be present with the enemies of the psalmist who delight in his undoing (40:15; 70:3).
56. Contrast Römer and Bonjour, who see an erotic side to Jonathan's delighting in David, citing several instances where the verb has such a resonance (e.g., Gen 34:19; *L'homosexualité*, 72).
57. McCarter sees vv. 11–17, 23, 40–42 as a likely interpolation (*I Samuel*, 342, 343), but v. 41 suggests that vv. 40–41 belong with the original narrative, given David's subservience to Jonathan in that verse (he bows three times). Thus, the seam appears to be between v. 41 and v. 42, not between v. 39 and v. 40, as McCarter would have it. Verse 42 refers directly to the mutual oath mentioned in v. 23 and seems to assume the oath of v. 13, though the oath of v. 13 is taken only by Jonathan. In v. 42, Jonathan says to David, "Go in peace [*lēk lĕšālôm*]"; in v. 13, he had promised as part of his oath that David would go in peace: "you will go in peace [*wĕhālaktā lĕšālôm*]." Cf. Wozniak, who views 20:1–21:1 as a unit and

understands David to be the subordinate partner throughout ("Drei verschiedene literarische Beschreibungen," 217).

58. McCarter favors the latter reading, though his reasons for doing so—"David would not credit Saul with being concerned with his son's feelings at this point"—are not convincing. Both MT *pn y'ṣb* and LXX[B] *mē ou bouletai* (**pn yw'ṣ*) are equally plausible in context. For McCarter's treatment, see *I Samuel*, 335.

59. As many have noted, this statement seems to adumbrate David's generous treatment of Jonathan's surviving son Meribbaal for Jonathan's sake in 2 Sam 9:1–13 and 21:7 (e.g., McCarter, *I Samuel*, 344). The oath of v. 17 is difficult to untangle. The MT has Jonathan making David swear "because he loved him for (with) the love of his (own) self he loved him." Though Jonathan having David swear an oath in this context makes sense, given that he has just exacted a commitment from David to deal loyally with his house (v. 15), the statement that he made him swear "because he loved him for (with) the love of his (own) self he loved him" is odd, given that a similar statement is made in 18:3 about Jonathan: Jonathan and David cut a covenant "when" or "because he loved him as himself." Furthermore, Jonathan took an oath earlier in the passage, committing himself to report to David any malevolent intentions of Saul toward David (v. 13), and some textual evidence suggests that it is Jonathan who swears in v. 17 as well (e.g., LXX[B]; see McCarter, ibid., 337).

60. The meaning of the final part of the verse—ʿ*ad dāwīd higdîl*—is wholly obscure and I therefore leave it untranslated.

61. Susan Ackerman has noted the reciprocal nature of Jonathan's and David's "feelings" as expressed in this passage (*When Heroes Love: The Ambiguity of Eros in the Stories of Gilgamesh and David* [New York: Columbia University Press], 184–85).

62. Fischer notes the association of kissing with familial greeting and leave-taking ("Freundschaft [AT]"), as do Zehnder ("Exegetische Beobachtungen zu den David-Jonathan-Geschichten," *Biblica* 79 [1998]: 163) and others.

63. Others have noted the strong emotions expressed in v. 41, emotions that suggest a "deep friendship" according to Römer and Bonjour (*L'homosexualité*, 76). Ackerman speaks of the shared emotional commitment of David and Jonathan and their "mutual affection and devotion" (*When Heroes Love*, 185). Zehnder's suggestion that the kissing in 1 Sam 20:41 has political connotations on account of Samuel kissing Saul in 1 Sam 10:1 ignores the reciprocal nature of the act and its strong emotional associations in 1 Sam 20:41 and in passages such as Gen 33:4 and Ruth 1:9, 14, though I believe he is correct to argue against an erotic interpretation in 1 Sam 20:41 ("Exegetische Beobachtungen," 162–64). Though both kissing and weeping can be used to express political affiliation, in the context of 1 Sam 20:41, they seem to have a nonpolitical purpose, as in Gen 33:4 and Ruth 1:9, 14. On weeping as a ritual expression of political affiliation, see, e.g.,

Ezra 10:1 and my discussion in *Biblical Mourning: Ritual and Social Dimensions* (Oxford: Oxford University Press, 2004), 68–69, 90–91, 107. For weeping as emotional expression, see, e.g., 2 Sam 19:1–2, where David's politically inappropriate weeping over his dead rebel son Absalom is not only disruptive but a threat to his reign, as his commander Joab points out to him in vv. 6–8. On kissing as a political act, see, e.g., Gen 41:40; 1 Sam 10:1; 2 Sam 15:5; 19:40; Ps 85:11. Several scholars have noted that kissing can have political or emotional resonances, depending on the context, and cite 1 Sam 20:41 as an instance in which kissing is an expression of friendship (e.g., John Ellington, "Kissing in the Bible: Form and Meaning," *Bible Translator* 41 [1990]: 410; K.-M. Beyse, "*nāšaq*," *TDOT* 10:75).

64. For the *mišneh lammelek* or *mišnēh hammelek*, evidently a high royal position, see Esth 10:3 and 2 Chr 28:7. In Esth 10:3, it is Mordecai who occupies this office for Ahasuerus. On Jonathan as subordinate to David in this narrative, see Wozniak, "Drei verschiedene literarische Beschreibungen," 218.

65. See, e.g., Römer, *Deuteronomistic History*, 96, who sees in 23:16–18 a text supporting Benjaminite submission to Judah in Josiah's era. Compare McKenzie's treatment in *King David*, 84–85.

66. As noted, 19:1–7 may also bear witness to a relationship with an emotional dimension, given the range of meaning of the idiom *ḥāpēṣ bĕ-*, but this remains unclear.

67. Others find evidence for an emotional—and even erotic—connection between Jonathan and David in other passages in the prose narratives, as well as in 2 Sam 1:26. See, e.g., Römer and Bonjour, who understand Jonathan's removal of his clothing and weapons in 18:4 as an act bearing witness to "un sentiment personnel et sans doute érotique à l'égard de David," just as they see an erotic resonance to Jonathan's delighting in David in 19:1 (*L'homosexualité*, 70, 72). Ackerman's views are similar. She speaks of "many passages that seem to depict the two heroes' relationship as eroticized or sexualized in nature" (*When Heroes Love*, 166; the argument is developed on 173–74, 176–78, 181, 183–84, 189, 192). I am reluctant to assign an emotional resonance, much less an erotic character, to idioms and actions that are more readily explained in other ways. Aside from 1 Sam 18:1 and 20:41, prose texts that unambiguously evidence a friendship, I believe that the poetry of 2 Sam 1:26 bears witness to an emotional bond between David and Jonathan and is the most cogent evidence suggesting a homoerotic relationship between the two men. On this, see my discussion ahead.

68. MT *bišlōmāyw* > **bĕšōlĕmô*, an apparent case of a rare but contextually appropriate word (*šōlēm*) replaced during the process of textual transmission by a common word (*šālōm*) that makes little sense in context. NJPS appears to read **šōlēm*, translating "ally": "He harmed his ally, he broke his pact." NRSV is similar in its rendering "a friend." LXX *en tōi apodidonai* and Vg. *in retribuendo* seem to assume **lĕšallēm*.

69. NJPS correctly identifies the agent of v. 21 with the friend of v. 14 in a note. It is not clear to me who else the aggressor of v. 21 might be, though the change of person from second ("you ... my friend") to third ("he sent forth his hand") is a bit jarring. Presumably, the victim of v. 21 is the psalmist himself.
70. Women's friendships are never portrayed in this manner, likely because women are not understood to be treaty partners in biblical texts.
71. Note the various curses against violators of treaties (e.g., Deut 27:15–26; 28:15–69; Jer 34:18–19).
72. Note the evidence for cursing disloyal friends *after* their acts of betrayal (Ps 35:4–7; perhaps also Ps 109:8–9, 11–12, 16). Are these curses to be understood as a reaction to disloyalty in the context of a nonformalized friendship or a reiteration of imprecations stated previously, when a friendship was formalized as a treaty relationship? Unhappily, there is no way to answer this question.
73. "Surpassing," 90–91. The quotation is from *EA* 17:24–26, translated by William L. Moran, *The Amarna Letters* (Baltimore: Johns Hopkins University Press, 1992), 41. For the Akkadian text in transliteration, see Hans-Peter Adler, ed., *Das Akkadische des Königs Tusratta von Mitanni* (Neukirchen-Vluyn: Neukirchener; Kevelaer: Butzon & Bercker, 1976), 122. I provide other examples in "Surpassing," including those of a comparable type to 2 Sam 1:26 ("The love of *x* is greater than the love of *y*"). Marriage, like treaty relations, requires fidelity of the wife, so the comparison in Jer 2:2 is apt.
74. See, further, "Surpassing," 93–95, for a more detailed treatment. Marriage may be cast explicitly as a covenant beginning in sixth-century texts, but this remains unclear. The texts in question are Ezek 16:8; Mal 2:14; and Prov 2:17, and Moshe Greenberg, among others, has argued that passages such as Mal 2:14 and Prov 2:17 "may be otherwise interpreted" and that "nowhere is marriage expressly called a covenant" (*Ezekiel 1–20: A New Translation with Introduction and Commentary* [AYB 22; Garden City, NY: Doubleday, 1983], 278). Andrew E. Hill provides a useful summary of the debate in the field about the referent of the word *bĕrit* in Mal 2:14 (marriage itself or Yhwh's treaty with Israel; *Malachi: A New Translation with Introduction and Commentary* [AYB 25D; New York: Doubleday, 1998], 243). Even if marriage is cast as a covenant in texts such as Mal 2:14, my generalization about women as partners in political treaties remains the case: They are not evidenced in this role.
75. "Surpassing," 85–99. Others who address the issue of a possible homoerotic relationship between Jonathan and David from a variety of different perspectives include Ackerman, *When Heroes Love*, 165–99; Römer and Bonjour, *L'homosexualité*, 68–79, 93–102; Nissinen, "Die Liebe von David und Jonatan," 250–63; Zehnder, "Exegetische Beobachtungen," 153–79; Silvia Schroer and Thomas Staubli, "Saul, David und Jonatan—eine Dreiecksgeschichte?" *Bibel und Kirche* 51 (1996): 15–22; and, most recently, James E. Harding, *The Love of David and Jonathan: Ideology, Text, Reception* (Sheffield: Equinox, 2013),

esp. 51–121. I comment on the views of a number of these scholars in "Surpassing," passim.
76. See n. 40. It is possible to render ʾahăbat nāšîm as "the love of wives" rather than "the love of women" and to attempt to make a case that fidelity is at issue in 2 Sam 1:26, since wives cannot commit adultery and David is said to have had multiple wives. But this argument founders when its implications are considered. Comparison of Jonathan's love to the love of wives still suggests something sexual, given the association of marriage and the erotic. And if the mention of "my brother" is understood as a reference to a parity treaty between the two men, as seems likely, the comparison to the love of wives fails, given that the husband-wife relationship is consistently constructed as hierarchical rather than a relationship of equals ("Surpassing," 93).
77. Römer and Bonjour also see erotic overtones in 2 Sam 1:26, as do others (*L'homosexualité*, 77–78).
78. I leave aside the narrative of Hushay the Archite and David in 2 Sam 15:32–37 and 16:16–19. Though Hushay is called "David's friend" (rēʿeh dāwīd) in 16:16, and David is repeatedly referred to as Hushay's "friend" by David's rebel son Absalom (16:17), Hushay is a political appointee occupying an office known as "the friend of the king." (See 1 Kgs 4:5, where "the friend of the king" appears in a list of Solomon's royal officials.) Hushay is the king's servant (ʿebed) and owes him "loyalty" (ḥesed) as does any other courtier (15:34; 16:17). This is why he can say to Absalom, "Whomever Yhwh, this people, and all the men of Israel have chosen, I am his and with him I will stay" (16:18) and "Whom shall I serve [ʿbd]? Shall it not be his son? As I served your father, thus I shall (serve) you" (16:19). Though Hushay's words are part of a ruse concocted by David himself to trick Absalom into accepting bad advice (15:34), they are believable enough that Absalom is taken in by them. Thus, the narrative itself suggests that the "friend of the king" might potentially serve any king, irrespective of his personal feelings and preferences. In a word, the relationship of Hushay and David or Hushay and Absalom is one of master and servant. On the office of "friend of the king," see further the citations in n. 11 in the Introduction. On fictive friendship and fictive kinship, see my discussion in Chapter 1.
79. "To move back and forth" (nûd) is a mourning gesture mentioned elsewhere (e.g., Jer 16:5; 22:10; Ps 69:21; Job 42:11).
80. The distinction between who is obligated to be a mourner and who is expected to be a comforter is not always clear, as I discuss in Chapter 1, n. 85.
81. Reading wlʾ yprsw lḥm for MT wlʾ yprsw lhm on the basis of LXX artos (*leḥem) and the fact that the idiom pāras leḥem is otherwise known (Isa 58:7).
82. For comforters in these three settings of mourning, see further my discussion in *Biblical Mourning*, 46–49, 88–89, 99.
83. The word ʿāmāl, "trouble" or "mischief," is often associated with ʾāwen, "wrongdoing," "trouble" in Job (e.g., 4:8; 5:6; 15:35) and once with šāwʾ, "worthlessness," "falseness" (7:3).

84. Healing and comforting are brought together in Lam 2:13, with healing as the goal of comforting in that text. On the relationship of comforting and consolation, see my discussion in *Biblical Mourning*, 48. Generally, "to comfort" in the context of mourning means one of three things: to join the mourner and embrace mourning rites (e.g., Isa 51:19; Job 2:11); to end the mourner's mourning period (e.g., Gen 37:35; Isa 61:2–3); and to offer consolation to the mourner in various ways, including by means of speech (Job 16:5; Lam 1:16). On these, see ibid., 47–48.
85. Noted also by C. L. Seow, *Job 1–21: Interpretation and Commentary* (Illuminations; Grand Rapids, MI: Eerdmans, 2013), 795.
86. See, similarly, Abraham in Gen 20:7, who is to intercede for Abimelek of Gerar.
87. See, e.g., 8:3–7; 15:17–35; 20:1–29 and the discussion in Seow, *Job 1–21*, 92–97.
88. See the discussion in Seow, *Job 1–21*, 27–29, who cites Wolf-Dieter Syring, *Hiob und sein Anwalt: Die Prosatexte des Hiobbuches und ihre Rolle in seiner Redaktions- und Rezeptionsgeschichte* (BZAW 336; Berlin: De Gruyter, 2004), 25–50. Syring considers the evidence for one or the other as the earlier composition and reviews the history of the discussion since the seventeenth century. Seow makes a case for the literary integrity of the book, arguing that the contrasts between narrative and poetry "do not necessarily suggest different authorship but may rather point to a single composer utilizing different genres and styles" (ibid., 28). He also notes a variety of literary connections between the poetry and the narrative, which he interprets to suggest single authorship, though in my view, these links are as easily understood to suggest that the prose is derived secondarily from the poetic core (ibid., 28).
89. Obviously, I find this viewpoint most compelling, given the evidence.
90. Seow, *Job 1–21*, 27, 28, citing the classic study of H. L. Ginsberg, "Job the Patient and Job the Impatient," *Congress Volume, Rome, 1968* (VTSup 17; Leiden: Brill, 1968), 98–107.
91. In other words, for precisely the reasons that the characters of the poetic core appeal more to many readers today.
92. Literally, "that I might go and descend upon the mountains." On this, see the discussion of Jack M. Sasson, *Judges 1–12: A New Translation with Introduction and Commentary* (AYB 6D; New Haven, CT: Yale University Press, 2014), 441. The expression *yārad ʿal-* occurs in association with a mountain in Exod 19:18, though the sense is somewhat different: "All of Mt. Sinai was smoldering because Yhwh had descended upon it [*yārad ʿālāyw*] in fire" (see also v. 20). The *qĕrê rēʿôtay* is the plural of *rēʿâ*, the feminine form of *rēaʿ*; the *kĕtîb raʿyôtay* is the plural of *raʿyâ*. See my discussion of these words in the Introduction. Given the supportive role of the daughter's *rēʿôt/raʿyôt*, I render the word "friends." See ahead for discussion of the ways they might support Jephthah's daughter. Sasson considers the identity of the daughter's companions and the reasons they might accompany her but does not mention friendship as a possibility (ibid., 442).

93. The meaning of the verb *lĕtannôt* is obscure. LXX, Vg., and the Targum suggest "mourn" or "bewail" as the meaning, yet the use of what appears to be the same root (*tnh*) in Judg 5:11 suggests a meaning more like "to recount" (see the discussion in *HALOT* 1759–60; also BDB 1072). Sasson translates "commemorate," citing the use of the verb in Judg 5:11 (*Judges 1–12*, 443 and 532 n. 33); similarly, Michaela Bauks renders "gedenken" (*Jephtas Tochter: Traditions-, religions- und rezeptionsgeschichtliche Studien zu Richter 11,29–40* [FAT 71; Tübingen: Mohr/Siebeck, 2010], 6). The link between the two-month journey of the story and the four-day observance of v. 40 is not readily apparent, suggesting that the observance and the narrative were not originally connected. On the possible purpose of the festival itself, see, e.g., the comments of Bauks, ibid., 66–67, and Peggy L. Day, "From the Child Is Born the Woman: The Story of Jephthah's Daughter," in *Gender and Difference in Ancient Israel*, 58–74.

94. In both v. 37 and v. 38, one could make a case that the mention of Jephthah's daughter's friends is a secondary addition to the story. In v. 37, "I and my friends" reads as a supplemental gloss at the end of the verse that is not unlike "the adulterer and the adulteress" at the end of Lev 20:10. In both instances, the focus of the verse is a single individual: Jephthah's daughter in the case of v. 37 and the adulterer in the case of Lev 20:10. But the focus in each case is expanded by a gloss to include others: Jephthah's daughter's friends in Judg 11:37 and the adulteress in Lev 21:10. In Judg 11:38, "she and her friends" disrupts a narrative that speaks only of Jephthah's daughter: "He sent her off for two months and she went—she and her friends—and she wept over her virginity on the mountains." The possibility that the two mentions of the friends are supplemental glosses, however, does not diminish the importance of the friends in the final form of the narrative.

95. On the separation of mourner and comforter from daily life, see my discussion in *Biblical Mourning*, 35–39, 47, 88–91, 98–101. Though women are not described using the technical term "comforter" in any biblical text, they are said to comfort others and be comforted by them. In Isa 66:13, Yhwh will comfort Israel as a mother comforts her son. In Job 42:11, Job's sisters are among those who comfort him. In 2 Sam 12:24, Bathsheba is comforted by David. And in Ruth 2:13, Ruth states that Boaz has comforted her. Interestingly, in none of these examples do women comfort women, in apparent contrast to the story of Jephthah's daughter.

96. The only mention of comforting in Ruth is 2:13, and Boaz is the agent of the comforting there, not a woman.

97. I translate *ḥākām* "worldly" in this context, given its range of meaning and given the positive connotations of English "wise," which would not be an appropriate rendering here. Other passages where *ḥākām* might be rendered "worldly" include 2 Sam 14:2; 20:16; 1 Kgs 2:9. It is unlikely that Jonadab occupies an official position comparable to "the friend of the king," given that 13:3 implies

that Amnon has other "friends" (*lěʾamnôn rēaʿ ûšěmô yônādāb;* see McCarter, *II Samuel*, 321, for this point). I also note that the word used is *rēaʿ*, the standard word for "friend," not *rēʿeh*, used in the expressions *rēʿeh dāwīd* (2 Sam 16:16) and *rēʿeh hammelek* (1 Kgs 4:5), though this point is not decisive, given Absalom's use of *rēaʿ* instead of *rēʿeh* in his chiding of Hushay (2 Sam 16:17).

98. When Amnon threatens Tamar, she pleads with him to marry her (v. 13); later, she calls his attempt to expel her (*šlḥ* Pi) after he has raped her worse than his initial act of violence (v. 16). Some understand this to suggest that she already views herself as married to Amnon, given the use of "expel" (*šlḥ* Pi) for divorce in Deut 22:28, a text that does not permit divorce to a man who has raped a virgin (McCarter, *II Samuel*, 324). Whether such restrictions are presupposed by the author of 2 Sam 13 remains unclear, though it does seem likely that marriage between brother and sister is at least conceivable to the author, given Tamar's words in v. 13: "Now then, speak to the king, for he will not withhold me from you." Contrast the restrictions of sister-brother sexual acts in Lev 18:9, 11; 20:7; Deut 27:22, precluding such marriages. Deut 22:13–21 suggests that acquiring a virgin as a wife was both desirable and expected. Should a woman turn out not to be a virgin after she has married and her husband accuses her accordingly, she is to be executed by the community "for she has committed an outrage [*něbālâ*] in Israel, whoring [*znh*] (while resident in) the house of her father."

99. Even though Absalom's plan was unknown to David, David's reluctance to allow Amnon to attend is made clear in v. 26, suggesting distrust of Absalom's intentions. The secret nature of Absalom's plan is suggested by the statement in v. 22 that Absalom said nothing to Amnon, either bad or good, after he raped Tamar, "though Absalom hated Amnon because he had raped Tamar his sister."

100. Friends, like family members, embrace mourning rites when their friend mourns, thereby affirming and perpetuating their relationship with the mourner. Conversely, they rejoice when their friend rejoices. On this, see further Olyan, *Biblical Mourning*, 56–57, 93–94, 106–7.

101. Compare Saul's interpretation of the concealment of Jonathan's treaty with David by Saul's courtiers as treasonous (1 Sam 22:8).

102. See 2 Sam 19:1–5 on vassals embracing their lord's ritual stance even if it is inappropriate to the occasion. Contrast this with Benjaminite Shimi's public ritual acts of disaffiliation from David in 2 Sam 16:5–8, which include a refusal to embrace mourning rites during David's catastrophic retreat from Jerusalem. On this, see further, Olyan, *Biblical Mourning*, 92–93.

103. Frequently but not always: Job's three comforters of the Job prologue and epilogue, as well as Jephthah's daughter's friends, are mainly without complexity, in contrast to more complex characters such as David, Jonadab, and Naomi.

104. For the reading **běšōlěmô* instead of MT *bišlōmāyw*, see earlier, n. 68.

105. It is worth noting that we learn more in Ps 55 about the former relationship of the complainant and his ex-friend than we normally do in the psalms of individual complaint. See vv. 14–15, where the now disloyal friend is described as "you, a man like myself [*ĕnôš kĕʿerkî*], my gentle intimate [*ʾallûpî ûmĕyuddāʿî*]," and their activities are said to have included visits together to the temple during which they made "sweet fellowship." Nonetheless, the portrait of the disloyal friend in Ps 55 is not much different from similar evocations of ex-friends in comparable psalms.
106. Prov 19:4 is an exception to this pattern in its claim that "wealth adds many friends," a statement implicitly suggesting material inequality between the wealthy man and the "many friends" attracted by his wealth, who must stand to gain in some way from association with him, whether materially, in terms of status enhancement, or from access to valuable resources, including social capital.
107. An exception to this pattern is Ps 55:14, in which the complainant refers to his disloyal friend as "you, a man like myself [*ĕnôš kĕʿerkî*]." The expression *ĕnôš kĕʿerkî* suggests comparable value, thus, equality by whatever measure the psalmist has in mind.
108. No indicators of hierarchy are present in the texts narrating the actions of Job's comforters or those of the friends of Jephthah's daughter. Job and his three friends even wear the same type of garment (the *mĕʿîl*), which they each tear (1:20; 2:12), a fact that may be intended to suggest parity of social status and/or wealth. Jan Dietrich also sees Job's friends as his peers, although he provides little argument to support this viewpoint ("Von der Freundschaft im Alten Testament und Alten Orient," *Die Welt des Orients* 44 [2014]: 45–46).
109. One combination not attested in narrative sources or elsewhere is friendship between men and women as distinct from metaphorical use of friendship and familial rhetoric to describe lovers in texts such as the Song of Songs. I treat this unattested combination in the Conclusion.

Chapter 4: Friendship in Ben Sira

1. For the various renderings of the title in Christian Bibles and their derivations, see the comments of Patrick W. Skehan and Alexander A. Di Lella, *The Wisdom of Ben Sira* (AYB 39; New York: Doubleday, 1987), 3. As Skehan and Di Lella note, the original Hebrew title is lost, along with the Hebrew text of the beginning of the book and much of what follows. (Less than 70 percent of the Hebrew text survives in manuscript.) The title of the book in most manuscripts of the Greek translation is the Wisdom of Jesus, Son of Sirach. The work is referred to in the Talmud as the Book of Ben Sira (e.g., b. Hagigah 13a; b. Niddah 16b). Many modern scholars refer to the text as the Book of Ben Sira (e.g., Moshe Zvi Segal, *sēper ben sîrāʾ haššālēm* [Jerusalem: Mossad Bialik, 1958]) or the Wisdom of Ben Sira (e.g., Skehan and Di Lella, ibid.; Jeremy Corley, *Ben*

Sira's Teaching on Friendship [BJS 316; Providence, RI: Brown Judaic Studies, 2002], 1). For simplicity's sake, I refer both to the author (named in 50:27 and after 51:30 [B]) and to the work itself as Ben Sira.

2. Roman Catholics and Eastern Orthodox Christians consider Ecclesiasticus or Sirach one of a number of deuterocanonical writings (Catholics) or *anaginōskomena* (Orthodox Christians). On the deuterocanonical books in the Catholic context, see further the comments of Skehan and Di Lella, *Wisdom*, 17–20; for the status of the *anaginōskomena* in Eastern Orthodoxy, see Eugen Pentiuc, *The Old Testament in Eastern Orthodox Tradition* (New York: Oxford University Press, 2014), 132–34. My thanks to Susan A. Harvey for the latter reference.

3. Throughout this chapter, I make reference when necessary to several of the versification schemas embraced by scholars of Ben Sira. E.g., when I refer to what many scholars designate as Sir 6:6 in the Hebrew (e.g., Skehan and Di Lella, *Wisdom*, or Corley, *Teaching*, following LXX), I also supply the verse as it is numbered in Pancratius C. Beentjes, *The Book of Ben Sira in Hebrew: A Text Edition of All Extant Hebrew Manuscripts and a Synopsis of All Parallel Hebrew Ben Sira Texts* (VTSup 68; Atlanta: Society of Biblical Literature, 2006), in this case, 6:5. In addition, I routinely note the Hebrew manuscript to which I refer. On the various versification schemas, see further Beentjes, "'Ein Mensch ohne Freund ist wie eine linke Hand ohne die Rechte': Prolegomena zur Kommentierung der Freundschaftsperikope Sir 6,5–17," in *Freundschaft bei Ben Sira: Beiträge des Symposions zu Ben Sira Salzburg 1995* (ed. Friedrich V. Reiterer; BZAW 244; Berlin: De Gruyter, 1996), 1 n. 2. On the paraphrastic character of the Greek translation at points, see, e.g., the discussion of Otto Kaiser, "Was ein Freund nicht tun darf: Eine Auslegung von Sir 27,16–21," in *Freundschaft bei Ben Sira*, 112, 119, whose focus is 27:16, 17, and 21. Martin Hengel characterizes the translation as "relatively free" (*Judaism and Hellenism: Studies in Their Encounter in Palestine During the Early Hellenistic Period* [2 vols.; trans. John Bowden; Philadelphia: Fortress, 1981], 1:131).

4. For *ʾōhēb*, see 6:5, 7, 8, 9, 10, 13, 14, 15, 16 (A; Beentjes 6:4, 6, 7, 8, 9, 12, 13, 14, 15); 7:18 (A); 9:10 (A); 12:8 (A); 14:13 (A); 37:1 (D), 4 (B, D), 5 (B, D); for *rēaʿ*, see 6:17 (A; Beentjes, 6:16); 7:12 (A); 9:14 (A); 12:9 (A); 13:21 (A); 37:2 (B, D); for *mērēaʿ*, see 13:21 (A). For *ʾōhēb* in earlier texts, see, e.g., Pss 38:12; 88:19; Prov 17:17; 18:24; for *rēaʿ* in earlier passages, see, e.g., Deut 13:7; Mic 7:5; Job 2:11; Prov 17:17; Ps 38:12; for *mērēaʿ*, see, e.g., Prov 19:4, 7. It may be that *ʾōhēb* and *rēaʿ* have slightly different nuances in Ben Sira's usage, as suggested by 33:20 (E), although these are difficult to pin down and the two words are apparently used interchangeably in some passages of the book (6:16–17 [A; Beentjes 6:15–16]; 12:8–9 [A]; 31:2 [B]). On the possibility of different meanings for *rēaʿ* and *ʾōhēb*, see the detailed discussion of Lutz Schrader, "Unzuverlässige Freundschaft und verläßliche Feindschaft: Überlegungen zu Sir 12,8–12," in *Freundschaft bei Ben*

Sira, esp. 25–28, 39, who is not convinced but cites the views of others (e.g., 26 n. 19).

5. For the ex-friend or false friend as a *śōnēʾ*, see, e.g., 6:9 (A; Beentjes 6:8); 12:8–9 (A), and compare Ps 41:8.
6. Some have taken the expression *ʾanšê šĕlômĕkā* to refer not to one's friends but to "acquaintances" (Skehan and Di Lella, *Wisdom*, 186, 187) or "those at peace with you" (Corley, *Teaching*, 38, 47), given the contrast with the "trusted intimate" (*baʿal sôd*) in Sir 6:6 (A; Beentjes 6:5). But earlier sources such as Ps 41:10 suggest that *ʾîš/ʾĕnôš šālôm* can refer to a friend: "Even my friend whom I trusted, who ate my food" (*gam ʾîš šĕlômî ʾăšer bāṭaḥtî bô ʾôkēl laḥmî;* for *gam* as "even," see Williams par. 379). Furthermore, the contrast with the "trusted intimate" in Sir 6:6 (A; Beentjes 6:5) need not suggest that the *ʾanšê šālôm* are not friends; they are simply not unusually trustworthy friends as is the "trusted intimate." That *ʾîš/ʾĕnôš šālôm* can also be used of treaty partners is evidenced in Obad 1:7 (*ʾanšê bĕrîtekā / ʾanšê šĕlōmekā*). Segal understands the expression to refer to friends in Sir 6:6 (A; Beentjes 6:5): "You should have many friends [*yĕdîdîm rabbîm*] but trust only one of them" (*sēper ben sîrāʾ haššālēm*, 36; my translation). Beentjes, "'Ein Mensch ohne Freund,'" 9–11, interprets similarly ("viele Freunde—aber nur ein Vertrauter," 9). Segal, too, notes that *ʾanšê šĕlômĕkā* is a treaty idiom as well as a term of friendship (*sēper ben sîrāʾ haššālēm*, 36).
7. For the use of the verb *bāṭaḥ* of friends in earlier materials, see, e.g., Mic 7:5; Ps 41:10; and Jer 9:3 (by implication). See also Mic 7:5 for the use of Hi *ʾmn* with reference to friends. For friends condemned for standing at a distance, see Ps 38:12, which Corley believes Sir 37:4 (B) seeks to echo (*Teaching*, 78). Sir 6:11 (A; Beentjes 6:10) uses the verb Hit *ndh*, "remove oneself," and 6:12 (A; Beentjes 6:11) uses Ni *str*, "conceal oneself," in contrast to Sir 6:8 (A; Beentjes 6:7) and 37:4 (B), which use *ʿmd* and *ʿmd minneged*, the latter a common idiom in earlier biblical texts.
8. Job 19:19 states that "those whom I loved have turned against me [*nehpĕkû bî*]."
9. Friends who forget their friend are mentioned in Job 19:14, and the friend who abandons his friend (and the friend of his father) is spoken of in Prov 27:10. These expressions are rarely used of friends in earlier materials though they are commonly used in treaty contexts, as I have noted in the Introduction (n. 34). Sir 37:6 (B, D) speaks of forgetting and abandoning friends specifically in the context of battle, a departure from earlier materials, as I shall discuss.
10. Deut 13:7 speaks of the particularly intimate friend as "your friend who is as yourself" (*rēʿăkā ʾăšer kĕnapšĕkā*), implicitly classifying him with intimate family members, as I have discussed. Note that 37:2 (D) reads *rēaʿ kĕnepeš*, in contrast to *rēaʿ kĕnapšĕkā* (B), which is closer to the expression in Deut 13:7. Corley notes the parallel between Deut 13:7 and Sir 37:2 but cites only manuscript D's reading *rēaʿ kĕnepeš*; he also mentions Lev 19:18 and 1 Sam 18:1, although these latter texts use two variants of a different idiom, "to love *x* as oneself," thus rendering

a less compelling parallel (*'āhēb kāmô-l' āhēb kĕnapš-*). Corley does not mention the fact that "to love *x* as oneself" is a treaty idiom where it occurs (*Teaching*, 74). On this usage, see my previous discussion in the Introduction, n. 38, and in Chapter 3, at n. 45.

11. As I have discussed, *ḥābēr* is used of peers (Ps 45:8), allies (Judg 20:11), and associates (Ezek 37:16, 19) in biblical texts antedating Ben Sira, but no earlier text suggests an association with friendship, in contrast to Ben Sira and other Hellenistic-era materials (e.g., Eccl 4:10; see the Introduction, n. 21). The fact that *ḥābēr* is used of friends in Eccl 4:10 suggests that the usage is likely not an innovation of Ben Sira.

12. This statement may be building on Ps 41:10 (*'îš šĕlômî . . . 'ôkēl laḥmî*), which casts the disloyal friend as a person who benefits from one's hospitality. If this reading is correct, it suggests that Ben Sira understands Ps 41:10 to refer to the friend rather than an ally. Yet there are differences. In Sir 6:10 (A; Beentjes 6:9), the friend is described as a "companion of the table" and is unreliable at a time of trouble; in Ps 41:10 the friend is said to "eat my food" and is actively hostile. Corley mentions Ps 41:2, 10 in his discussion but does not suggest directly that Sir 6:10 (A; Beentjes 6:9) builds on 41:10 (*Teaching*, 53–54).

13. The Hebrew of Sir 7:12 (A) has *rēaʿ wĕḥābēr*, which may refer to two separate individuals rather than a hendiadys; in contrast, the Greek translation has simply *philos*. This may indicate that the translator understood *rēaʿ wĕḥābēr* as a hendiadys construction if it is indeed in the translator's Hebrew *Vorlage*; alternatively, the Hebrew manuscript used by the translator may have read only *rēaʿ* or *ḥābēr* rather than both. The Greek text of Sir 40:23 has *philos kai hetairos* as double subject, possibly a rendering of a *Vorlage* with **rēaʿ/'ôhēb wĕḥābēr*. If this is the case, then we have an example of *ḥābēr* rendered *hetairos*, "companion," a word used of friends in classical Greek materials (David Konstan, *Friendship in the Classical World* [Cambridge: Cambridge University Press, 1997], 32–33). The surviving, fragmentary Hebrew of Sir 40:23 suggests a plural subject (*ynhgw*).

14. Another possible example of Ben Sira distinguishing between *rēaʿ* and *ḥābēr* is Sir 40:23 if the Greek *philos kai hetairos* renders a *Vorlage* with *rēaʿ/'ôhēb wĕḥābēr* (see the previous note).

15. Skehan and Di Lella, *Wisdom*, 197, 201.

16. Gradations are also suggested by the idea of the existence of an intimate friend who is described as a "friend who is as yourself" (37:2 [B]) and by expressions such as "good friend" (*'ôhēb ṭôb*).

17. See also *mtq* (Hi) *sôd*, literally, "make sweet fellowship," understood by *HALOT* 655, 745 to mean "to keep close company" or "conduct confidential business," something friends are said to have done together in Ps 55:15 (*yaḥdāw namtiq sôd*).

18. Though note the related idiom *hpk bĕ-*, "to turn against," used in Sir 6:12 (A; Beentjes 11) as well as Job 19:19.

19. Corley, *Teaching*, 148. Although Ps 22:12 speaks of a "helper" (*'ōzēr*), his identity is unclear. He could as easily be a relative as a friend, given the mention of disloyal relations in texts such as Ps 38:12.
20. Corley does not notice that *smk* is not used of friends in earlier materials but notes its use, along with *'zr*, of Yhwh, as in Isa 63:5; Ps 54:6 (*Teaching*, 147).
21. The *ba'ălê laḥmĕkā* are not unlike the *'ōkēl laḥmî* of Ps 41:10, though the expression is different. Both expressions suggest that the friend benefits from one's largesse.
22. The word *mĕyuddā'* is typically rendered *gnōstos* in the LXX (e.g., in 4 Kgs 10:11 [= 2 Kgs 10:11] and Ps 54:13 [= 55:14]). This word occurs only once in the Greek text of Ben Sira and in a context that does not reference friendship (Sir 21:7).
23. Sir 13:20 speaks of the poor person as an abomination to the rich, but this usage is not about friends, as the point of the passage is that rich and poor cannot be friends.
24. For Ben Sira's concern with unfaithfulness in friendship, see, e.g., 6:8–13 (A; Beentjes 6:7–12).
25. E.g., Prov 17:17; Job 19:19; Sir 13:15–16; 22:20 [*philia*]; 27:18 [*philia*]; 37:1 (D).
26. See, e.g., Pss 38:12; 88:9; Prov 19:7 as well as Sir 6:11, 12 (A; Beentjes 6:10, 11); 13:21–22; 22:25; 37:4 (B), 6 (B, D).
27. See Sir 13:22 [A; Beentjes 13:21] for the friend as "helper" (*'ōzēr*); 12:17 (A); 13:21 (A) for the expectation that the friend supports (*smk*) his friend.
28. Corley notices the parallel usage, citing Isa 63:5 and Ps 54:6 (*Teaching*, 147). A similar transposition is evidenced with respect to the fighting friend of Sir 37:5–6 (B, D), as I discuss ahead. In Sir 51:7 (B), Ben Sira speaks in the first person in imitation of the sufferer in the psalms of individual complaint, lamenting that aside from Yhwh, he had no "helper" (*'ōzēr*) or "supporter" (*sômēk*). Ps 22:12 expresses a similar sentiment regarding the absent "helper." In both Sir 51:7 and Ps 22:12, the "helper" or "supporter" could as easily be a family member as a friend.
29. Manuscript A reads *'āḥ tālûy*, which is opaque. Skehan and Di Lella, *Wisdom*, 204n, comment that this reading is "dubious at best." LXX *gnēsion*, "true," is the basis for Skehan and Di Lella's translation "a true brother."
30. Sir 7:12 (A) is similar: "Do not plan wrongdoing against a brother, / Or likewise against a friend or companion [*rēa' wĕḥābēr*]."
31. Corley misses this implicit shared classification, though he notes that the passage suggests that friendship is worth more than money (*Teaching*, 224). In a fragmentary context, Sir 40:23 compares a skillful wife directly to friend and companion and finds the wife superior. On this text, see my discussion ahead.
32. Sir 6:11: "When times are good for you, he is like you [*hû' kāmôkā*]"; 6:17: "For like him, so is his friend [*kāmôhû*]."
33. The reading of Hebrew manuscript B is [.........] *t ynhgw*, while the Greek reads *philos kai hetairos eis kairon apantōntes*. Segal reconstructs *'ōhēb wĕḥābēr*

lěʿē]t yinhāgû (Segal, *sēper ben sîrā' haššālēm*, 271); Corley's reconstruction is similar (*Teaching*, 221–22). This understanding seems plausible and I follow it, although I note that *rēaʿ* in place of *'ōhēb* is equally possible. Regarding *lěʿēt* as "in a timely manner," see Williams par. 274a for the lamed of manner. Skehan and Di Lella appear to reconstruct *l'Jt* as well, and with a similar understanding, translating "A friend and a neighbor are timely guides." For the subject, they appear to reconstruct *'ōhēb wěrēaʿ*, understanding *rēaʿ* as "neighbor" in this context (*Wisdom*, 463). On Qal *nāhag* with the meaning "to lead," see 1 Chr 20:1; 2 Chr 25:11. Piel *nihag* is used of Yhwh leading in a number of biblical texts and might also be used here of the friend and companion. On *nihag* with Yhwh as subject, see the next note.

34. The notion of the friend as a beneficent leader is rare in earlier materials. As with the friend as helper and supporter and the fighting friend, the idea of a friend who takes the lead might well have been derived from a common image of Yhwh in earlier biblical texts, in this instance, Yhwh as a leader of his people (e.g., Isa 49:10; 63:14; Pss 48:15; 78:52; cf. Exod 15:13; all Pi). Although the nature of the leading differs—advice versus physical guidance during travel—the verbal root used is nonetheless the same (*nhg*). Note also that Eccl 2:3 speaks of the heart guiding wisely (*wělibbî nōhēg bahokmâ*), not unlike the friend who leads in a timely manner. On the interpretation of Eccl 2:3, see Choon-Leong Seow, *Ecclesiastes: A New Translation with Introduction and Commentary* (AYB 18C; New York: Doubleday, 1997), 150. An earlier narrative portrayal of a friend functioning as a guide—in this case, nefarious—is to be found in 2 Sam 13, in which Amnon's cousin and friend Jonadab concocts a plan to bring Amnon and Tamar together, to the detriment of both.

35. Such classification is rare. Even the "woman of strength" of Prov 31:10–31, about whom much is said, is not classified with or compared to friends, even implicitly. Although the wife of Sir 7:19 is implicitly classified with the friend and brother, she is not directly compared to them.

36. The claim about the superiority of the skillful wife in Sir 40:23 is also remarkable in light of Ben Sira's attitude toward women in general, which cannot be characterized as positive (see, e.g., 7:24 [A]; 42:9–14 [B, M]).

37. A possible exception is Prov 16:7, if the enemies mentioned who are at peace are ex-friends. On this text, see my earlier discussion in Chapter 2.

38. Corley's text-critical decisions for this verse are sensible and I follow them (*Teaching*, 193–94).

39. The Greek word *loidoria* is usually used to render a *Vorlage* with *rîb or *měrîbâ, as suggested by comparison with extant Hebrew (Edwin Hatch and Henry A. Redpath, *A Concordance to the Septuagint* [3 vols.; Oxford: Clarendon, 1897], 2:887).

40. E.g., Corley, *Teaching*, 203, citing 6:9; 22:22; 27:16–21; 42:1. Earlier biblical texts also bear witness to this concern, as other scholars have pointed out (e.g., Corley, ibid., 181, citing Prov 11:13; 25:9).

41. On the expression *haśśigat yādĕkā*, "that which you possess," see the comments of Segal, *sēper ben sîrā' haššālēm*, 91.
42. Material support is rarely discussed as an obligation even of family members, though see Ruth 4:15, which speaks of Obed as a provider for Naomi in her old age (the verb is *kilkēl*).
43. The Greek reads *Pistin ktēsai en ptōcheiai meta tou plēsion*. Corley's reconstruction *sĕmōk rēʿăkā bĕdallûtô* might be correct (see *Teaching*, 193–94). Segal's reconstruction is closer to the Greek: *hēʾāmēn lĕrēʿăkā bĕʿonyô* (*sēper ben sîrā' haššālēm*, 134).
44. The Hebrew of 37:6 (B, D) reads *bišlālĕkā*, the exact meaning of which is not clear. My understanding is a guess, though it seems the most likely of several alternatives. See, similarly, Skehan and Di Lella, *Wisdom*, 425; and Georg Sauer, "Freundschaft nach Ben Sira 37,1–6," in *Freundschaft bei Ben Sira*, 125, among others. Corley's rendering "among your spoil" is difficult, as spoil is not typically abandoned; furthermore, it does not comport with Corley's own understanding of the passage: "Ben Sira urges the listener . . . to share the fruits of victory with" the friend (see *Teaching*, 67, 80). The word *zār*, "outsider," might well refer to an alien, as it often does in earlier biblical texts (see Corley, ibid., 79, for this argument).
45. A number of scholars have argued for a metaphorical understanding of the passage (e.g., Skehan and Di Lella, *Wisdom*, 432; Corley, *Teaching*, 79; though cf. Segal, *sēper ben sîrā' haššālēm*, 236). The mention of battling "the outsider" and the apparent allusion to division of spoil after a victory in battle suggests to me that a literal understanding may be most easily defended. To what would dividing spoil refer metaphorically? And why mention the outsider—presumably a foreigner—as the enemy if the passage is meant to be understood metaphorically and concern one's social circle?
46. E.g., Skehan and Di Lella, *Wisdom*, 432; Corley, *Teaching*, 80.
47. Corley argues that "the injunction to remain loyal to one's friend" in Sir 37:6b "echoes" Prov 27:10. This may be true in regard to its formulation (*ʾal-taʿăzōb*), though not with respect to its content, given the lack of a martial context in Prov 27:10 and that text's concern for the friend of one's father as well as one's own friend. Corley's suggestion that 37:6a "resonates with David's regard for Jonathan after the Philistine attack at Mount Gilboa" (1 Sam 31:1–13) is not convincing, as the statement in Sir 37:6b is rather general in its thrust, making no evident allusion to any particular narrative. For Corley's views, see *Teaching*, 80.
48. Words for female friends such as *rēʿâ* (Judg 11:37 [*qĕrê*]; 11:38; Ps 45:15) and *raʿyâ* (Judg 11:37 [*kĕtîb*]; Song 1:9, 15; 2:2, 10, 13; 4:1, 7; 5:2; 6:4) are not attested in biblical wisdom books such as Proverbs and Job.
49. Texts such as Sir 22:11–12 and 38:16–23 (B) deal with appropriate mourning practices, but neither one mentions directly a role for friends as "comforters" or even hints in any clear way at such a function. Sir 38:17 states that the mourner

should "be comforted" (*wĕhinnāḥēm*) but says nothing about who is assumed to play the comforter role. Because comforters can be kin as well as friends in earlier texts, we cannot assume that Sir 38:17 alludes to friends. The mention of providing the dead with an appropriate burial (38:16) suggests that the passage is addressed to close family members, given that it is they who have this responsibility, in contrast to friends and others, as I have discussed in Chapter 1.

50. This is a common assumption among scholars. See, e.g., Corley, *Teaching*, 213.
51. The degree and nature of the influence of Greek thought on Ben Sira has divided specialists. While some scholars are confident of Greek literary influence, others are skeptical, with some suggesting the possibility that Greek ideas and figures of speech, if discernible, were not necessarily discovered by Ben Sira in literary works (see, e.g., John J. Collins, *Jewish Wisdom in the Hellenistic Age* [OTL; Louisville, KY: Westminster John Knox, 1997], 40, on Sir 14:18 echoing *Iliad* 6.146–49, a passage that was "likely proverbial by the Hellenistic age" according to Collins). Among those who have argued for direct literary influence are Th. Middendorp, *Die Stellung Jesu Ben Siras zwischen Judentum und Hellenismus* (Leiden: Brill, 1973), 8–24, 25, 33, and Jack T. Sanders, *Ben Sira and Demotic Wisdom* (Society of Biblical Literature Monograph Series 28; Chico, CA: Scholars Press, 1983), 29, 36, 38, 58, although Sanders is only convinced that Ben Sira read and used Theognis and provides a lengthy critique of Middendorp's far more expansive and sanguine treatment. Others who are critical of those who advocate a literary dependence include Martin Hengel, *Judaism and Hellenism*, 1:149–50, and Hans Volker Kieweler, *Ben Sira zwischen Judentum und Hellenismus: Eine Auseinandersetzung mit Th. Middendorp* (Frankfurt: Peter Lang, 1992), who is cited with approbation by Schrader, "Unzuverlässige Freundschaft," 37–38. See also the reservations expressed by Beentjes, "'Ein Mensch ohne Freund,'" 15–16. Hengel sees "echoes" of Theognis as well as Euripides and others evidenced in Ben Sira, possibly to be accounted for on the basis of oral transmission (ibid., 149–50). He also speaks of the possibility of Stoic influence (ibid., 147–48).
52. The approach of Sanders is similar to mine: "When . . . a line in Ben Sira might be a paraphrase or a restating of something in the Bible, the evidence must be remarkably strong in order to make a convincing argument that Ben Sira has relied at that point on some line from Hellenic literature" (*Ben Sira and Demotic Wisdom*, 29; see also 57). Note also Hengel, *Judaism and Hellenism*, 150.
53. I shall speak only of a range of possibilities with respect to Greek influence—more likely, less likely—given the particular challenges involved in reaching confident conclusions.
54. Hebrew manuscript A reads *bsmk* in the first colon, which makes little sense in context. Corley's reconstruction *nismāk*, "is supported by," is based on the Greek *stērizetai*, and my translation reflects this understanding (see *Teaching*, 118).
55. Corley, *Teaching*, 148.
56. For the rich man's friends cast as flatterers, see my discussion ahead.

57. See Corley, *Teaching*, 148, for this citation. Corley notes that Sanders also mentions this Theognis passage (148 n. 120; Sanders, *Ben Sira and Demotic Wisdom*, 30–31). On Theognis, see, briefly, Konstan, *Friendship*, 49–52.
58. For this translation, see Michael Pakaluk, *Aristotle: Nicomachean Ethics; Books VIII and IX* (Clarendon Aristotle Series; Oxford: Oxford University Press, 1998), 5. On friendship in Aristotle, see, e.g., Konstan, *Friendship*, 67–78. Konstan's treatment at times plays down the reciprocal dimensions of friendship as it is represented in classical Athenian sources and some Roman materials (e.g., 5, 81–82, 127–28), but see also 69, 97, where expectations of reciprocity are acknowledged, although it is argued that such reciprocity is voluntary and based on generosity rather than feelings of obligation. I am not convinced by this argument. See ahead, n. 61, for Konstan's characterization of loyalty in friendship "as the obligation to come to a friend's assistance in time of crisis" (ibid., 11).
59. Needless to say, Ben Sira and earlier biblical texts do not assume Aristotle's tripartite theorization of friendship, though they do evidence friendship gradations that overlap with Aristotle to some degree (see, e.g., Deut 13:7; Prov 18:24; 19:4; Sir 6:5–17 [A; Beentjes 6:4–16]; 37:1–6 [D, partially B]). On the points of potential overlap between Aristotle and earlier biblical materials, see my discussion in Chapter 1.
60. Middendorp, *Stellung Jesu Ben Siras*, 15–16; Sanders, *Ben Sira and Demotic Wisdom*, 30–31; Corley, *Teaching*, 215, 222. Other Theognis parallels are also mentioned by Middendorp and Sanders. In addition, Corley mentions parallels in Isocrates (ibid., 51, 222 n. 17). Though Corley notices that Ben Sira's concern that friends can prove to be unreliable at times of trouble "echoes the experiences of Job and Jeremiah (Job 19:19; Jer 9:3; 20:10)" (ibid., 215), he does not mention that the theme is also prominent in the psalms of individual complaint, as I have discussed previously.
61. See the comments of Konstan, *Friendship*, 11, concerning Greek literature specifically: "Loyalty may take various forms; in Greek texts of the classical period (and also later), it is frequently interpreted as the obligation to come to a friend's assistance in time of crisis. Failure to provide such help in turn is the mark of a false friend."
62. Cicero, *On Friendship* 17; Seneca, *Epistles* 9.9.
63. *Ben Sira and Demotic Wisdom*, 30–31, 34.
64. See Corley, *Teaching*, 74, for the idea that the closest parallel to Sir 37:2 is Deut 13:7. Corley, however, prefers to follow manuscript D, which reads *rēaʿ kěnepeš*, rather than manuscript B, which reads *rēaʿ kěnapšěkā*, although manuscript B is closer in wording to Deut 13:7.
65. For Aristotle, see, e.g., *Nicomachean Ethics* 9.4 1166a 31; 9.8 1169b 7; 9.9 1170b 6; see also Plutarch, *On Having Many Friends* 90e; and Cicero, *On Friendship* 7, 21. The Plutarch citation was brought to my attention by Konstan, *Friendship*, 121.

Corley comments on the Greek idea and the biblical parallels in *Teaching*, 74; in n. 140, he provides further citations from classical sources. Corley seems to assume, however, that the Greek and biblical notions are the same: "Although Ben Sira's expression seems to mirror the Greek understanding of friendship as being μια ψυχη ("one soul") . . . he reflects several biblical phrases as well" (74). My thanks to David Konstan for calling my attention to the difference between the Greek notion of "another" or "second self" and the biblical idea of the friend who is "as yourself" or "like you" (oral communication).

66. See especially Sanders, *Ben Sira and Demotic Wisdom*, 61–106, for possible Egyptian parallels.

67. In all of the examples listed, the verb is *nsh*. A second verbal root, *bḥn*, is used similarly (e.g., Gen 42:15, 16; Jer 12:3; Mal 3:10; Ps 26:2). Such testing might have one of a number of possible goals: to determine whether the tested individual is worthy of trust (Ps 26:2); to know whether he will act as he claims he will (Mal 3:10); to establish whether he is truly present (Exod 17:7, regarding Yhwh in the midst of the people); to determine what he knows (1 Kgs 10:1). In contrast, testing the friend seems always to be connected to the issue of trustworthiness.

68. Caution regarding trusting friends and family members is a theme in earlier biblical texts such as Jer 9:3–4 and Mic 7:5–6, as I have noted, but these do not speak of testing the friend to determine his trustworthiness. Note that both Segal (*sēper ben sîrā' haššālēm*, 35) and Corley (*Teaching*, 36–37) read *bĕnissāyōn*, "with" or "through testing," in 6:7. I follow their suggestion here.

69. E.g., Corley, *Teaching*, 47–50, 182, 215–16; Collins, *Jewish Wisdom*, 74; Hengel, *Judaism and Hellenism*, 1:149; Konstan, *Friendship*, 57.

70. For Xenophon (*Memorabilia* 2.6.1), see Middendorp, *Stellung Jesu Ben Siras*, 14, and Sanders, *Ben Sira and Demotic Wisdom*, 44. For citations from the latter three writers, see Corley, *Teaching*, 49 and n. 44.

71. Sanders, *Ben Sira and Demotic Wisdom*, 44, 82. Sanders concludes that *Papyrus Insinger* 12:18 "is as close to Sir 6:7a as is Xenophon" (82). Egyptian parallels to Sir 6:7 are also discussed by Corley, *Teaching*, 48 and n. 43. Sanders notes that testing of a newly acquired friend is at issue in both Sir 6:7 and Xenophon.

72. Konstan, *Friendship*, 15, 21, 93–95, 98–103, 141. The pattern becomes quite common in the Hellenistic and Roman periods.

73. On Cicero's views of flattery in their context, see Konstan, *Friendship*, 135–36.

74. Konstan, *Friendship*, 102, for this observation and citation from Aristotle.

75. For this translation, see Pakaluk, *Aristotle: Nicomachean Ethics*, 11. Konstan quotes this text in his treatment of flatterers (*Friendship*, 95). On the flatterer as an inferior, see the discussion in Konstan, ibid., 101.

76. See Konstan, *Friendship*, 98–103, for examples in which flattery and true friendship are contrasted.

77. Others have noted the possibility of Greek influence. See, e.g., Corley, *Teaching*, 148 n. 121, where this view is implicit though clear. Corley also discusses the flattery theme on 165, including n. 40.

78. Corley, *Teaching*, 78–81, proposes various texts of influence, some more likely (e.g., Ps 35:1–2; Prov 27:10 with respect to its formulation) than others (1 Sam 31:1–13). On this, see further my discussion in n. 47.
79. Corley, *Teaching*, 78. On the *symmachos*, see, e.g., Konstan, *Friendship*, 65, 83–84, with citations.
80. Konstan, *Friendship*, 33: "Those *hetairoi* who are singled out as *philoi* belong to the most intimate circle of a man's companions and age-mates and may reasonably be regarded as friends." The context is a discussion of the use of the term in Homeric materials (ibid., 31–33). For its usage in archaic poetry, see ibid., 44–46. For the *hetairos* in the literature of classical Athens, see ibid., 59–61. For the *hetairos* in texts of the Hellenistic period, see ibid., 96.
81. Konstan, *Friendship*, 33. This is Konstan's translation of *polu philtatos hetairos*.
82. On *'anšê šālôm* as friends rather than acquaintances, see my argument in n. 6.
83. Pakaluk, *Aristotle: Nicomachean Ethics*, 40, for the rendering "ardent friend."
84. Corley, *Teaching*, 216.

Conclusion

1. On reciprocity as the foundation of biblical and early Jewish sacrifice, see Aaron Glaim, "Reciprocity, Sacrifice, and Salvation in Judean Religion at the Turn of the Era" (PhD diss., Brown University, 2014).
2. Hebrew manuscripts read *dyn* consistently. LXX *lupē* may reflect a Hebrew *Vorlage* with *dāwôn rather than *dîn*, as suggested by Moshe Zvi Segal, *sēper ben sîrā' haššālēm* (Jerusalem: Mossad Bialik, 1958), 235; Patrick W. Skehan and Alexander A. Di Lella, *The Wisdom of Ben Sira* (AYB 39; New York: Doubleday, 1987), 428; and Jeremy Corley, *Ben Sira's Teaching on Friendship* (BJS 316; Providence, RI: Brown Judaic Studies, 2002), 65, 73, and n. 135.
3. Most other texts do not credit Yhwh with disrupting friendships.
4. On the different expressions "to love *x* as oneself," a treaty idiom, and "to be as oneself," an idiom with emotional resonance, see further Chapter 1, n. 55.
5. On the idiom "to make sweet fellowship" as indicative of personal intimacy, see my discussion in the Introduction at n. 19.
6. Yet at the same time, Naomi and Ruth share the status of widow, although they are never called by this term.
7. The female lover is described as the male lover's "sister" in a number of contexts (Song 4:9, 10, 12; 5:1, 2); in 8:1, she states regarding the male lover: "Would that you were like a brother to me, one who sucks at the breast of my mother."
8. In contrast to friendships between men and women, friendships between blood relatives or in-laws of the same gender are occasionally portrayed in biblical narrative texts. Ruth and Naomi are formally in-laws, as are David and Jonathan, while Amnon and Jonadab are first cousins.
9. The termination of relations with relatives is rarely attested in biblical materials, in contrast to the ending of friendships, which is represented as commonplace. On this, see further my discussion in Chapter 2.

10. In other words, treaty relationships outside of the context of friendship.
11. Ethan J. Leib, *Friend v. Friend: The Transformation of Friendship and What the Law Has to Do with It* (New York: Oxford University Press, 2011), 32–36, on Aristotle. Leib states that "it is still necessary in modern discussions of friendship to compare one's account with Aristotle's canonical treatment of friendship in books 8 and 9 of his *Nicomachean Ethics*" (32). Leib, a law professor, speaks explicitly of his "interdisciplinary" interests on 194.
12. Ibid., 7–8 and passim, for Leib's larger arguments. Ibid., 12, for the quotation.
13. Ibid., 35.
14. Here I do not assume the work is necessarily interdisciplinary, although it is cross-cultural in its orientation.
15. Steven M. Graham and Margaret S. Clark, "Friendship," in *International Encyclopedia of the Social Sciences* (2nd. ed.; ed. William A. Darity, Jr.; Detroit: Macmillan Reference USA, 2008), 3:220–21.
16. Bettina Beer, "Friendship, Anthropology of," in *International Encyclopedia of the Social and Behavioral Sciences* (ed. Neil J. Smelser and Paul B. Baltes; Oxford: Elsevier, 2001), 9:5805.
17. Others acknowledge that the idea that friendships are necessarily informal is not supported cross-culturally. See, e.g., the discussion of Sandra Bell and Simon Coleman, "The Anthropology of Friendship: Enduring Themes and Future Possibilities," in *The Anthropology of Friendship* (ed. Sandra Bell and Simon Coleman; Oxford: Berg, 1999), 3.

Index of Passages

Hebrew Bible

Genesis

1:2	121
2:24	13, 17, 146
4:14	121
11:3	6
20:7	156
20:12	16, 19
20:13	16
22:1	98
22:2	14, 137
23:2	22
25:8	24
25:17	24
25:28	14, 15, 124, 137
27:41	22
27:43–45	134
28:20–21	144
29:14	134
31:15	146
31:23	43
33:4	73, 152
34:3	16, 17
34:19	151
35:5	43
35:20	129
35:22	128
37:3–4	14, 137
37:4	126, 136
37:34–35	22
37:35	15, 21, 133, 156
38	33, 63, 133
38:8–10	20
38:24–26	145, 146
41:40	153
42:15	168
42:16	168
43:30	15, 132
44:4	42
44:6	42
44:20	71, 110, 125
44:30	5, 121, 132, 150
44:30–31	15, 30, 70, 71, 75, 110
45:11	18
47:29	16
47:30	21, 24, 129, 130
48:5	64
49:4	128
49:29	21
49:31	21, 64
50:1–11	21
50:10	129
50:12–14	21
50:21	18
50:25–26	21

Exodus

1:10	141
4:18	124
4:22–23	12
12:4	131
13:19	21
14	48
14:4	48
14:8	43, 48

Exodus (continued)

14:9	48
15:13	164
15:25	98
16:4	98
17:2	98
17:7	98, 168
20:5–6	16, 46, 140
20:6	16, 114, 123, 126, 136
20:12	18, 23
20:20	98
21:15	139
21:17	139
32:27	28, 30, 31, 71, 105, 125, 127, 131
32:27–29	50, 51, 139
32:29	28, 51, 131
33:11	5, 7

Leviticus

7:7	133
10:3	127
18:6–7	128
18:8	128
18:9	19, 128, 158
18:10	128
18:11	128, 158
18:12	128
18:13	128
18:14	128
18:15	128
18:16	128
18:17	19
18:18	19
18:22	42
18:26	42
18:27	19, 42
18:29	42
18:30	42
19:3	18
19:17	15, 126
19:18	124, 161
19:32	18
20:7	158
20:9	19
20:10	157
20:11–12	128
20:14	19
20:17	19, 128
20:19	128
20:20	128
20:21	128
21:1–4	12, 13
21:2	21, 125, 127
21:2–3	13, 21, 26
21:2–4	13, 33, 34, 35, 133
21:3	26, 125, 127
21:10	157
21:11	13
22:11	145
22:13	145
25:25	125, 127
25:25–28	20
25:47–49	20
25:48	13, 33
26	54
26:17	139
26:33	139
26:37–38	139

Numbers

12:7	18
16:10	134
22:22	47
22:32–33	137
25:13	137
27:8	13
27:8–11	13
27:11	125, 127
35:12	20
35:19	128
35:20–21	128
35:22–28	20

Index of Passages

Deuteronomy

4:4	17
4:23	124
4:26	140
4:31	124
4:37	137
5:9–10	16, 46, 140
5:10	16, 114, 123, 126, 136
5:16	18, 23
6:5	8
6:5–9	16
7:26	42, 135
11:22	17
13:7	5, 9, 25, 26, 28, 30, 35, 36, 37, 91, 92, 97, 101, 104, 105, 106, 107, 120, 130, 160, 161, 167
13:7–12	50, 51, 71, 110
13:9	26
14:2	42
15:12	124, 134
16:15	138
17:15	134
19:1–10	20
19:11–13	128
19:14	6
20:12	138
21:18–21	50, 51
22:7	140
22:13–21	158
22:20–21	138
22:23–24	138
22:28	158
23:2–9	135
23:4–9	41, 147
23:7	123, 135
23:8–9	41
24:1	138
24:4	138
25:5–10	20, 33, 63, 133
26:14	22
27:15–26	154
27:16	19
27:22	158
28	54
28:1–14	39, 56
28:1–17	140
28:4	140
28:5	140
28:7	140
28:8	140
28:11	140
28:15–69	154
28:18	140
28:20–24	54
28:21–22	140
28:23–24	140
28:25	52, 139, 140
28:26	21, 140
28:27	140
28:28–29	140
28:31	139
28:35	140
28:36	139, 140
28:41	140
28:43–44	139
28:45	139
28:48	52
29:24	124
31:16	24, 129
32:18	41
32:50	24, 129
33:8	98
33:9	50, 51, 131, 139

Joshua

2	48
2:5	48
2:7	48
10:1	138
10:4	138
11:19	138

Joshua (*continued*)

14:11	133
20:1–9	128
22:5	17
24:6	43
24:33	21

Judges

5:11	157
9:2	134
9:3	134
11:30–31	80
11:34	80
11:34–40	94
11:35	80
11:37	9, 81, 90, 94, 112, 120, 157, 165
11:37–38	112
11:38	90, 94, 120, 157, 165
11:39	81
11:40	157
14:11	6
14:20	6, 120
15:2	6
15:6	6
16:31	21
17:1–4	138
20:11	121, 162

1 Samuel

2:30	19, 114, 128
10:1	152, 153
10:12	12
13:4	135
14:24–30	138
14:36–45	138
15:28	6, 125
16	148
17:12–31	150
17:38–39	70, 150
17:41	150
17:43	53, 54
17:48b	150
17:50	150
17:55–58	150
18:1	5, 30, 71, 73, 74, 75, 77, 90, 110, 124, 130, 132, 150, 153, 161
18:1–4	8, 69, 70, 71, 75, 76, 94, 110, 111, 149, 150, 151
18:3	30, 70, 124, 130, 150, 152
18:4	70, 150, 153
18:5	150
18:10–11	150
18:16	8
18:17–19	150
18:20	76
18:22	72, 151
18:23	86
18:27	69, 77, 149
18:28	76
18:29b–30	150
19:1	71, 72
19:1–7	69, 71, 72, 75, 151, 153
19:2	74
19:4–5	70, 71
19:10–17	149
20:1–10	69, 72, 73, 75, 86, 151
20:1–21:1	69, 72, 151
20:3	72
20:5–7	72
20:6	23
20:7	73
20:8	73, 124, 151
20:9	73, 74
20:11–17	69, 72, 73, 74, 75, 86, 151
20:12	74
20:13	73, 74, 151, 152

20:14	124, 154	2 Samuel	
20:15	73, 124, 152	1:19–26	148
20:17	152	1:19–27	10, 110
20:18	74	1:20	44
20:18–22	69, 72, 73, 75, 86, 151	1:24	45
20:21	154	1:26	76, 77, 104, 111, 113, 124, 131, 134, 148, 149, 150, 153, 154, 155
20:23	69, 72, 73, 75, 86, 151		
20:24–41	69, 72, 73, 75, 86, 151	2:6	123
		2:16	6
20:29	23	3:3	134
20:30	124, 151	3:8	6
20:39	151	3:31	21
20:40	151	3:31–37	133
20:40–41	151	5	148
20:40–42	151	5:34	155
20:41	73, 74, 75, 76, 77, 94, 106, 110, 111, 122, 149, 150, 151, 152, 153	7:12	24
		7:14	74, 144
		9:1	124, 140
		9:1–13	152
20:42	69, 72, 73, 75, 86, 151	9:3	124
		10:1–2	140
21:1	69, 72, 73, 75, 86, 151	10:1–5	81, 139
		10:1–19	49
21:7	152	10:2	16, 127, 131
22:7–8	151	10:4–5	139
22:8	151, 158	10:6	49, 135
23:14–18	69, 72, 73, 74, 75, 151	10:19	50, 138
		11:26	22
23:16–18	153	12:11	6, 125
24:12	29	12:24	157
24:17	29	13	10, 61, 81, 84, 108, 158, 164
24:17–18	12		
25:44	149	13–19	81
26:17	12	13:1	16, 82
26:19	144	13:3	132, 157
28:17	125	13:4	16, 124
29:4	47, 137	13:5	82
30:26	6, 122, 123, 131	13:13	19, 158
31:1–13	165, 169	13:15	16, 126
31:11–13	34	13:16	158

2 Samuel (*continued*)

13:22	158
13:26	158
13:28–29	82
13:31	83
13:32	82
13:32–33	82
13:33	82
13:36	22, 83
13:37	134
14:2	157
14:4–11	128
14:19	130
14:25–26	151
15:5	153
15:32–37	155
15:34	155
16:5–8	158
16:16	120, 155
16:16–19	155
16:17	124, 155, 158
16:18	155
16:19	155
16:21	135
18:18	22, 23, 34, 129
19:1	15
19:1–2	153
19:1–5	22, 158
19:4	139
19:5	15
19:6	139
19:6–7	16, 136
19:6–8	114, 153
19:6–9	46
19:13	124, 134
19:22	47
19:23	137
19:40	153
19:43	125, 127
20:2	17
20:11	72
20:16	157
21:10–11	21, 34

1 Kings

2:9	157
3:14	140
3:26	15, 132
4:5	120, 155, 158
5:15	7, 8, 12, 29, 30, 123
5:18	47
5:26	123
8	39
8:23–53	55
8:30	138
8:34	138
8:36	138
8:39	138
8:50	138
9:13	12, 29, 124
10:1	98, 168
11:1–2	16
11:2	17
11:14	47
11:23	47
11:25	47
13:29–30	34
14:11	21
20:32–33	124
20:35	6
21:26	42
22:4	133, 145
22:45	138

2 Kings

3:7	145
9:1	12
9:10	21
2 Kgs 10:11 [4 Kgs 10:11]	90, 121
2 Kgs 10:11	163
13:14	125
16:7–9	138
22:17	137

Isaiah

1:4	48
3:5	18

Index of Passages 177

7:12	98	22:10	155
20:4	139	22:18	149
22:12–14	45	29:19	137
41:8	6, 114, 123	31:4	139
47:3	139	31:33	64, 144
49:10	164	32:30	138
49:14	41	33:24	124
51:19	156	34:18–19	154
58:7	155	38:22	123
61:1–4	137	50:2–3	53
61:2–3	156		
63:5	163	Ezekiel	
63:14	164	7:18	139
63:16	51	14:5	48
66:13	157	16:8	154
		16:52	42
Jeremiah		22:7	19
2:2	16, 76, 136	24:16–17	22
2:5	40	36:28	144
2:32	41	36:29–30	139
3:1	125, 138	37:16	121, 162
3:4	8, 113	37:19	121, 162
6:26	22	42:13	127
9:2	18, 33	43:19	127
9:3	4, 9, 14, 18, 28, 33, 38, 91, 101, 104, 105, 108, 122, 161, 167	Hosea	
		1:9	144
		2:16–25	138
		2:25	64, 144, 145
9:3–4	44, 107, 108, 168	3:1	76, 125
9:4	33, 44	8:14	41
9:7	43, 88, 90, 107, 121, 126, 136	11:1	126
		Amos	
9:18	139	1:9	12, 124
9:19	142	1:11	43
11:19	90	6:8	42
12:3	168	6:9–10	21
12:6	17, 18	8:10	22
15:15	130	Obadiah	
16:4	21	1:7	120, 123
16:5	155	1:11	40
16:7	22, 34, 78	1:15	53
18:20	42	1:18	53
20:10	88, 120, 167		

178 Index of Passages

Micah		35	38, 44, 53, 54, 58, 60, 68, 84, 85, 108, 109, 129, 133, 137
6:10	130		
7:5	4, 8, 38, 85, 90, 91, 107, 108, 120, 121, 122, 160, 161	35:1–2	93, 94, 99, 169
		35:3	48
7:5–6	9, 28, 33, 44, 50, 55, 104, 105, 108, 168	35:3–4	43, 57
		35:4	48, 49, 52, 139
7:8	137	35:4–7	53, 60, 154
		35:4–8	49
Zechariah		35:5–6	54
3	138	35:10	57
3:1	47, 137	35:11	56, 60
3:1–2	47	35:11–12	47
3:8	6, 7	35:12	5, 32, 42, 52, 56, 85, 90, 96, 106, 108, 122
12:10	22		
13:9	144, 145	35:12–13	52, 59
Malachi		35:12–14	66, 74, 85, 101, 105, 106, 116
1:6	12, 18, 23, 128		
2:14	154	35:13	22
3:10	168	35:13–14	6, 30, 35, 42, 44, 78, 94, 112
Psalms			
3:6	91	35:14	22, 130, 133
6:6	135	35:15	44, 57, 60, 96
7:5	5, 42, 90, 106, 120	35:17	57
10:1	134	35:19	44, 45, 46, 49, 56, 57, 58, 60
15	105		
15:1–3	26	35:20	43, 44, 56, 88, 90, 121, 126, 136
15:2	51, 105		
15:3	38, 39, 51, 125, 127	35:22	57, 134
19:8	147	35:24	44, 57
22:12	134, 163	35:26	34, 44, 49, 52, 57, 58
22:20	134	35:26–27	108
26:2	98, 168	35:27	5, 32, 34, 44, 58, 72, 85, 90, 93, 108, 151
28	38		
28:3	43, 44, 56, 88, 90, 121, 126, 136	36:11	139
		37:17	91, 102
30	133	37:24	91, 102
31:12	121	38	38, 84, 85
32:3–7	133	38:5–6	52, 57
32:10	16	38:7	133
32:38	133	38:12	4, 17, 22, 27, 30, 32,

Index of Passages

	37, 39, 40, 46, 52, 56, 57, 89, 90, 93, 96, 101, 105, 108, 120, 121, 125, 126, 127, 137, 160, 161, 163	69:7	52
		69:8	130
		69:9	48
		69:21	34, 57, 155
		70:3	52, 151
		70:4	52
38:12–13	25	70:6	57
38:13	43, 44, 56, 57, 127, 136	71:12	40
		71:13	43, 52, 136, 138
38:14	57	71:21	57
38:17	57	71:22	40
38:19	57	71:24	52, 136
38:20	45, 46, 47, 56, 137	78:52	164
38:21	5, 17, 32, 42, 46, 56, 90, 105, 106, 121, 138	85:11	153
		88	38, 52, 60, 135
		88:5	57
38:22	134	88:5–6	135
40:15	52, 151	88:6	135
40:16	52	88:7–8	52
41:2	162	88:9	32, 39, 41, 51, 52, 56, 59, 89, 90, 108, 121, 134, 135, 163
41:8	161		
41:10	4, 88, 91, 92, 96, 97, 101, 120, 136, 161, 162, 163		
		88:13	135
		88:15	52, 60
42:10	133	88:17	52, 60
42:10–12	133	88:19	4, 30, 32, 51, 52, 59, 66, 93, 120, 121, 134, 137, 160
43:2	133		
45:8	121, 162		
45:15	165	106:40	42
48:15	164	109	46, 54, 55, 60, 126, 132, 140
54:6	91, 102, 163		
55	75, 159	109:3	53
55:14	4, 8, 90, 91, 97, 111, 120, 121, 159	109:4	46, 53, 138
		109:4–5	32, 45, 47, 127
55:14–15	8, 75, 94, 113, 159	109:5	42, 46, 56, 90, 106, 136
55:14 [LXX 54:13]	163		
55:15	5, 162	109:6	47, 138
55:21	8, 75, 84, 94, 111, 113, 120	109:6–20	52, 60
		109:8–9	53, 154
62:5	43, 44, 56	109:11–12	53, 154
69:5	137	109:12	54, 60
69:6	52, 57	109:12–22	58

Psalms (continued)

109:16	31, 46, 48, 53, 55, 57, 154	16:5	156
		16:20–21	122
109:17	72, 151	19	52
109:20	127, 138	19:2–3	78
109:22	31	19:13	22, 47, 48, 59, 121
109:24	57	19:13–14	27, 32, 40, 48, 51, 52, 78, 105, 107, 108, 141
109:29	138		
112:1	151	19:13–15	17
119:116	91	19:13–22	52
119:163	42, 135	19:14	40, 41, 59, 94, 96, 101, 121, 124, 125, 127, 161
122:8	28, 105, 127		
133:1	19		
137:4	144	19:19	30, 31, 32, 41, 46, 66, 78, 88, 89, 90, 101, 105, 106, 107, 135, 141, 161, 162, 163, 167
145:14	91		
148:14	127		

Job

1	78		
1–2	52, 138	19:21	85
1:6–12	80	19:21–22	32, 43, 48, 78
1:11	47	20:1–29	156
1:13–19	78	30:29	127
1:20	159	42:7–9	78, 79
2	78, 80	42:11	155, 157
2:1–6	80	42:11–13	80
2:7–8	78		
2:11	120, 156, 160	## Proverbs	
2:11–13	22, 34, 77, 78, 79, 81, 85, 94, 102, 112	1:29	137
		2:17	8, 154
		5:19	76
2:12	159	11:13	133, 164
4:7	79	13:20	120
4:8	155	13:24	125
5:6	155	14:20	93, 102
6:14	124, 125	16:7	50, 164
6:14–15	16, 31, 126, 140	17:17	6, 8, 12, 27, 30, 31, 66, 91, 101, 105, 120, 127, 137, 160, 163
7:3	155		
8:3–7	156		
13:4	78, 94, 102, 107, 136		
14:7	134	18:24	4, 12, 17, 24, 30, 31, 32, 35, 36, 37, 67, 71, 90, 91, 92, 99, 101, 102, 105, 106,
15:17–35	156		
15:35	155		
16:2	78, 94, 102, 107, 136		

		107, 110, 120, 137, 146, 160, 167	2:9	66	
			2:10	68, 147, 148	
19:4		35, 36, 95, 102, 106, 107, 120, 122, 159, 160, 167	2:11	68	
			2:13	147, 157	
			2:17–19	66, 69	
19:7		6, 25, 37, 39, 89, 90, 92, 93, 102, 105, 106, 107, 113, 120, 163	2:20	65, 69, 125, 127, 132, 135, 147	
			2:21	17, 66, 67, 130, 134	
			2:22	66, 67, 69	
19:14		89	2:23	17, 66, 130, 134	
20:19		133	3	133	
22:24		120	3:1	66, 67, 69, 112	
22:25		120	3:1–4	66, 69	
24:17		45	3:6	66	
25:9		164	3:9	20, 33, 66, 147, 148	
25:13		147			
27:10		5, 6, 94, 101, 124, 161, 165, 169	3:10	67, 69	
			3:11	67, 68	
31		147	3:12	13, 125, 127	
31:10		147	3:12–13	20, 33	
31:10–31		164	3:16	67	
31:11		14	3:17	66	
			3:18	66, 67	
Ruth			4	133	
1:7		147	4:1–13	21, 33	
1:8		16, 67, 125, 132, 147	4:5	63, 67, 143	
1:8–9		62	4:10	67, 143	
1:9		73, 152	4:14–15	66	
1:11		63, 147	4:15	15, 18, 69, 142, 165	
1:11–13		132			
1:14		4, 31, 62, 66, 67, 73, 90, 112, 127, 146, 152	Song of Songs		
			1:9	165	
1:15		63, 145	1:15	165	
1:16		144, 145, 146, 147	2:10	165	
1:16–17		32, 145	2:13	165	
1:16–18		63, 64	4:1	165	
1:17		133	4:7	165	
1:18–19		63	4:9	9, 169	
1:22		67, 132, 147	4:10	9, 169	
2:2		66, 67	4:12	9, 169	
2:6		147	5:1	9, 169	
2:8		17, 66, 67, 130, 134	5:2	9, 165, 169	
			5:16	8	

Song of Songs (*continued*)
6:4	165
8:1	169

Ecclesiastes
2:3	164
4:10	114, 162

Lamentations
1:2	6, 29, 30, 34, 40, 78, 123
1:8	139
1:10	135
1:11	147
1:16	34, 40, 147, 156
1:19	147
1:21	137
2:13	156
2:17	137
4:21–22	53
5:12	18

Esther
1:14	127
1:19	122
9:1	141
9:5	141
9:16	141
10:3	18, 126, 136, 153

Ezra
9:12	123

Nehemiah
2:3	23, 24
2:5	23, 24
13:1–3	147
13:4	125, 127

1 Chronicles
12:41	127
20:1	47, 164

2 Chronicles
25:11	164
28:7	153

Apocrypha

Ben Sira
6:5	160
6:5–17	167
6:6	88, 89, 100, 106, 121, 160, 161
6:7	88, 91, 98, 101, 160, 168
6:7a	168
6:8	88, 160, 161
6:8–13	91, 96, 97, 163
6:9	89, 160, 161, 164
6:9–11	107
6:10	88, 89, 90, 91, 160, 162
6:11	88, 89, 91, 97, 161, 163
6:12	88, 89, 161, 162, 163
6:13	160
6:14	160
6:14–16	89, 106
6:15	93, 160
6:16	160
6:16–17	97, 160
6:17	89, 91, 160, 163
7:12	89, 105, 107, 160, 162, 163
7:18	91, 93, 101, 105, 160
7:19	91, 92, 93, 164
7:24	164
9:10	89, 90, 160
9:14	160
9:16	90, 91
12:8	160
12:8–9	160, 161
12:9	160
12:17	90, 163
13:15–16	91, 163
13:20	163
13:21	90, 95, 160, 163
13:21–22	163

13:21–23	91
13:22	89, 94, 95, 98, 163
13:23	98
14:11	93
14:13	92, 93, 102, 160
14:18	166
21:7	163
22:11–12	165
22:20	163
22:21–22	92, 102
22:22	164
22:23	91, 93, 101, 102, 105
22:25	163
27:16–21	164
27:17	91
27:18	163
27:21	92, 102
30:18	22
31:2	160
33:20	160
35:5–6	99
37:1	160, 163
37:1–4	91, 101, 105
37:1–6	167
37:2	88, 89, 97, 106, 107, 110, 111, 130, 160, 161, 162, 167
37:4	88, 90, 91, 160, 161, 163
37:5	88, 89, 93, 99, 106, 107, 160
37:5–6	91, 93, 94, 96, 163
37:6	88, 89, 94, 101, 114, 161, 163, 165
37:6a	165
37:6b	165
38:16	166
38:16–23	165
38:17	165, 166
40:23	92, 94, 102, 162, 163, 164
42:1	164
42:9–14	164
50:27	160
51:7	163
51:20	160

Tobit

4:17	22

Rabbinic Writings

b. Ketubbot 8a	120
b. Yebamot 14b	120
y. Berakot 4	120
y. Berakot 7d	120

Ancient West Asian Texts

Ahiqar

3.48–4.49	127
4.51–52	127

Code Hammurapi

2:69	123

El Amarna Tablets

EA 17:24–26	154
EA 288	114, 123

Esarhaddon's Vassal Treaty

4.266–68	124

Gilgamesh Epic

XII.151	21

Ludlul Bel Nemeqi

BWL 32:43–46	134
BWL 34:84	134
BWL 34:92	134
BWL 34:95–98	134

Marduk Prophecy. *See* Index of Subjects

Sefire Inscriptions

I A 38–39	140
I C 16–25	139
I C 24–25	140
II A 4	140
II C 13–17	139

Sefire Inscriptions (*continued*)
III 3–4   139
III 9–14   140

Shulgi Prophecy. *See* Index of Subjects

Ugaritic Texts
CAT 1.5 VI 24–25   129
CAT 1.17 I 26   129
CAT 5.9 I 8, 10   127, 131

Other West Asian Texts

Papyrus Insinger
  12:18   168
Siloam Tunnel
  Inscription 2–4   123

Roman and Greek Authors

Aristotle, *Nicomachean Ethics*
4.6 1127a 7–10   98–99
8.3–4   3, 36, 107
8.4 1147a 21–22   98
8.4 1156b 34–35   96
8.8 1159a 15–17   99
9.4 1166a 31   167
9.8 1169b 7   167
9.9 1170b 6   167
9.10 1170b 29–
  1171a 20   100

Cicero, *On Friendship*
7   167
17   98, 167
20   98
21   167
25   98

Homer, *Iliad*
6.146–49   166
23.82–92   133

Plutarch, *On Having Many Friends*
90e   167

Seneca, *Epistles*
3.2   98
9.9   98, 167

Theognis
lines 73–75   100
lines 643–44   96
lines 697–98   96

Xenophon, *Memorabilia*
2.6.1   98, 168
2.6.27   100

Index of Subjects

abomination: aliens as, 41; treating friends as, 41, 42; treaty violation and, 42; unclean animals as, 41, 42
act as adversary toward: as act of disloyalty, 49; as rejection of friendship, 46, 47
adoption, adoption-like declaration, 64, 144; in story of Ruth and Naomi, 64
adversaries: human and divine, 47, 137, 138; legal setting of, 47
'āhēb, 14. *See also* love
Ahiqar, fraternal support in, 18
alliances, terminated, 49, 50
'allûp, 4, 5, 8, 9, 120
Amnon and Jonadab, friendship between, 81–83
angel of Yhwh, as effecting curses, 54
Aqhat epic, on responsibilities of son for dead father, 129
Aristotle: on behavioral parity in friendship, 96; and classification of friendship, 107; on flattery and friendship, 98, 99; on limiting the number of friends, 100; on reciprocity in friendship, 96; on testing friends, 98

ba'al sôd (trusted intimate), in Ben Sira, 89
Beer, Bettina, and cross-cultural theories of friendship, 116

behavioral parity: among friends, 30, 31, 36, 84–86, 95, 105, 106; and friendship, in Aristotle, 96; as norm of friendship, 101; as requirement of friends, in various biblical literary types, 105, 106; between Ruth and Naomi, 62, 66, 68, 73, 74, 85
Ben Sira: on behavioral parity in friendship, 96, 101; canonical status of, 87; ideas about friendship in, 90–94; title of book, 159; vocabulary/idioms of friendship in, 87–90, 100, 101
blessings: content of, 55, 56; loyal friends and relatives not mentioned in, 55, 56
blood relations: disloyalty of, 50, 51; disowning of, 50; ignored by Levites, 51; and marriage relations, 13, 14; termination of, 50, 51. *See also* family; relatives
"brother," and vocabulary of friendship, 7, 124
brothers: "clinging" of, 25; and exceptional friends, 25–28; political allies as, 28, 29
bṭḥ (to trust), 4, 161
burial: afterlife affected by, 128–29; not required of friends, 33; required of family members, 20, 21, 24; of Ruth and Naomi, 64, 65
burial practices, 64, 65, 133, 145. *See also* funerary practices

185

186 Index of Subjects

children, execution of, 50, 139; honor owed to parents by, 19, 21; love of parents for, 15
Cicero: on false friends, 96; on flattery and friendship, 98; on testing friends, 98
Clark, Margaret S., and cross-cultural differences in friendship, 116
"clinging": as expressing loyalty between friends, 31, 32; of Ruth and Naomi, 62, 66, 67, 68; treaty resonances of, 146; used of brothers and friends, 25
comforters, 165–66; friends as, 34, 35; and friends in non-death contexts, 34, 35; friends of Jephthah's daughter as, 81; friends of Job as, 78; as participants in mourning, 22; troubling, in story of Job, 78
commensality: as component of friendship in Ben Sira, 90, 91, 92; and friendship, 5, 90
companion (*ḥābēr*): in Ben Sira, 88, 89, 92, 93; (*hetairos*): as friend, in Greek sources, 99
curse, curses: content of, 54, 139; enmity between friends and family members not mentioned in, 54, 55, 56, 60; of lacking "one who is loyal," 54, 55
cursing: as act of an enemy, 49; of disloyal friends and allies, 52, 53, 54; of parents, 19

David, as subordinate to Jonathan, 73. *See also* Jonathan and David
dbq (to cling), 4, 5, 24, 130
dead, forgotten by Yhwh, 135
death of child, reaction of parents to, 15
death rituals, and role of family members, 20, 21. *See also* burial practices; funerary practices
deceit, speaking, against a friend, 43, 44

deity and worshipers, as intimate family members, 12
delight: in a friend's vindication, 32, 34, 44, 68, 90, 108; and loyalty of friends, 72
disloyalty: of blood relations, 50, 51, 56–58; cursing of disloyal friends, 52, 53; of friends, 48–50; result of, 49

Egyptian wisdom, and friendship in Ben Sira, 97, 98, 103
emotional bonds between male friends, 30, 71
emotions and friendship, 109, 110
Esarhaddon, binding of vassals by oath to son, 70
estrangement: of friends and family members, 47, 48; of treaty partners, 48

familial ancestral observances, 23, 129
familial language, purpose of, in story of Ruth and Naomi, 67, 68
familial rhetoric, metaphorical nature of, 9
family: death and burial requirements of, 33, 34; hierarchy of intimacy in, 12–14; respect for generational hierarchy in, 18, 19; unacceptability of sexual liaisons in, 19. *See also* blood relations; relatives
family members: and failed friends, 39, 40; as intimates, 11–14; relations between living and dead, 24
"father," and vocabulary of friendship, 7
Fischer, Alexander A., on friendship of Ruth and Naomi, 142
Fischer, Irmtraud, on Levir in story of Ruth and Naomi, 143
flatterers as false friends, 97, 98
food for the dead, 22

Index of Subjects   187

"forgetting": by relatives and friends, 40, 41; by Yhwh, 41
Frevel, Christian, on friendship of Ruth and Naomi, 142
friend/friends: anonymous and named, differences in portrayal between, 83, 84; attempting to kill, 43; as beneficent leader, 92, 164; classified with family members, in various biblical literary types, 105; as comforters, 94, 165–66; compared with family members, 24–35; denunciation of, 53; disloyal, cursing of, 154; disloyal, in Ben Sira, 96, 97; exceptional, 24–28, 31, 32, 36, 37, 106, 107; as exempt from family duties, 29; as extension of self, in Ben Sira, 97; and family members, differences between, 115; and family members, shared classifications of, 25–29; and family members, shared expectations, 29–33; fighting, 93, 94, 99; and flatterers, 97; forgotten, 40, 41; as helper, in Ben Sira, 89; hypocritical, 44; inequality of, 113, 114, 122; intimate, 35; limiting the number of, 97, 99, 100; as "lovers," 30; loving and hating, 46; loyal, as counterpart to disloyal, 58; and material generosity, in Ben Sira, 92, 93; one-dimensional presentation of, 108; as one who fights for his friends, 93, 94, 97, 99; presented with complexity/individuality, 108, 109; as providing guidance, in Ben Sira, 92; pursuing, 43; and the pursuit of one's well-being, 5; rarely as brother/sister, 28, 29; rejoicing over misfortune of, 44, 45; responsibilities in death-related rites, 34; role in ancestral cult practices, 34; as second self, in Greco-Roman discourse, 97; seeking to do harm to, 43; as superior to relatives, in Ben Sira, 92; testing of, 97, 98; unfaithful, in psalms of individual complaint, 56–58, 60; unreliable, in Ben Sira, 96; who is as oneself, 5, 26, 35, 36, 161. *See also* friendship

friendship: actions causing rejection of, 39–48; Akkadian terms for, 120, 122; of Amnon and Jonadab, 81–83; in Ben Sira, 87–103; biblical, and contemporary friendship theory, 115, 116; biblical, diachronic perspective on, 114; as bond between men, in Ben Sira, 94; causes of failure of, 51–52; classification of, in Aristotle, 107, 167; in contemporary Western culture and in ancient societies, 1, 2; and covenanting, vocabulary of, 7, 8; definition of, 1, 5; and emotions, 109, 110; failed, actions causing, 39–48; failed, divine and human role in, 51, 52; failed, in various biblical literary types, 107, 108; and family relations, vocabulary of, 7; female, 62–69, 80–81, 85, 94, 165; fictive, 29, 132; formalization of, 8; formalized through treaty, 75, 76, 111, 112; gradations of, 35, 106, 107; with homoerotic overtones, 76, 77, 111, 155; ideas about, in Ben Sira, 90–94; issues involved in research on, 1, 2, 3; of Jephthah's daughter and her companions, 80–81; of Job and his comforters, 77–80; of Jonathan and David, 69–77; modern Hebrew terms for, 120; in narrative texts, 83, 84; previous scholarship on, in Hebrew Bible, 2; representation in various biblical literary types, 104, 105, 108, 109; of Ruth and Naomi, 62–69; of Ruth and Naomi, as voluntary association, 62, 63; termination of,

188 Index of Subjects

friendship (*continued*) 49; treaty terms used in, 122–23; vocabulary and idioms of, 4–10, 120, 122; vocabulary overlap with treaties, 109, 110; and wealth, 35, 36, 159; among women, 62–69, 80–81, 85, 94, 112, 165; between women and men, 112, 113. *See also* friend/friends
funerary practices, 21, 33. *See also* burial practices

gender and inheritance, 13, 14
generational hierarchy, respect for, 18, 19
generosity to friends, in Ben Sira, 92, 93
gifts, exchange of, and treaty making, 70, 150
gods: as enforcers of treaty stipulations, 54; national, 64, 144–45
Graham, Steven M., and cross-cultural differences in friendship, 116
Greco-Roman sources on friendship, 94–100; influence on Ben Sira, 94–100, 102, 103, 166

ḥābēr (companion), used of friends in Ben Sira, 88, 89, 93
harmony, familial, 19
hating, by friends and family members, 45, 46
himtîq sôd, 5
Hiram of Tyre, as ally of David, 7, 8
honesty: and family relations, 18; among friends, 33
honor owed to parents, 19
hospitality: as component of friendship in Ben Sira, 91, 92; and friendship, 5

imprecations enforced by divine agents, 54
inheritance: and family hierarchy, 13; and gender, 13, 14

intimacy and friendship, 5, 13, 14
intimates, family members as, 11–14
'îš/'ĕnôš šālôm, 4, 7, 120, 121, 161

Jacob and Benjamin, binding together of selves, 71
Jephthah's daughter and her companions, friendship between, 80–81
Job (book), differences in prose and poetic stories, 78, 79, 80
Job and his comforters, friendship between, 77–80
Jonadab, and role of comforter, 82, 83
Jonathan: relation to David, 8; as subordinate to David, 73, 74, 151
Jonathan and David: binding together of selves, 70; covenant nature of relationship, 69, 70, 71, 72, 74, 75, 148–52; emotional bond between, 73, 152; exchange of personal items, 70, 150; friendship between, 69–77; friendship formalized through treaty, 75, 76, 111; possible erotic connection between, 76–77, 153, 155; and question of historicity, 61, 141
Jost, Renate, on friendship of Ruth and Naomi, 142

kin, responsibility to maintain family tomb, 23, 24
kinship, fictive, 28–29, 132
kinsman: maternal, 37; maternal, expectations of, 134
kissing and weeping as ritual acts, 73, 74, 77, 111, 152–53
Kugel, James, on "fixed pairs" in poetry, 27

Leib, Ethan J., on friendship theory, 116
Levir: role in familial context, 20, 21, 33; role of, not required of friends, 33; in story of Ruth and Naomi, 63, 143

Levites, and execution of family members, 50, 51
literary representations of institutions, social practices, and rites, 119
love: brotherly, 15; as expectation among friends, 29, 30; as expectation of familial relationships, 14; of father for favorite son, 71; of father for son, 14; between friends, in Ben Sira, 91, 101; of Jonathan, surpassing the love of women, 76, 155; of Jonathan and David, 71; of mother for son, 15; of parents for children, 15; sexual-emotional, 16; of suzerain and vassals, 16; in treaty/covenant contexts, 15, 16, 136; of treaty partners, 76; as treaty term, 123, 124; of Yhwh, in treaty contexts, 16
love and hate, in treaty contexts, 46
loyalty: (*dābaq*) in familial, treaty, and emotional contexts, 17; as component of loving, 8; extending beyond death, 54, 140; among friends, 30, 31; and friendship in Ben Sira, 91; (*ḥesed*) among friends, 31; (*ḥesed*) and familial relations, 16, 17, 31; of Jonathan to David, 71; and love, in treaty contexts, 16, 17, 136

Marduk Prophecy, 19, 38; on reverencing father as god, 128; social decline in, 55, 139
marriage: brother-sister, 19; as covenant, 154; and family hierarchy, 13, 14; as voluntary association, 138
mērēa', 6, 120, 121; in Ben Sira, 88
měyuddā', 4, 5, 120, 121
Moran, William L., on covenant love, 8
mourning: as duty of family members, 21, 22; gestures, 80, 81, 83; of Jephthah's daughter and friends, 81; parental, 22

mourning rites, 21, 22, 23, 35, 130: in story of Job and his comforters, 77, 78; of Tamar, 82. *See also* burial practices; funerary practices

name of father, invocation of, as mourning rite, 22
Naomi and Ruth, relationship between, 31, 32
nepeš. *See* self/selves
Nicomachean Ethics (Aristotle), types of friendship in, 3, 36, 107

oaths, in treaty settings, 70, 152
obligation, and friendship, 6
'ōhēb, 4, 6, 7, 8; in Ben Sira, 88, 160–61

parents, reverence for, after death, 128
"to pay back that which is evil," by family and friends, 42, 43
poetic parallelism as indicative of shared classification of friend and family members, 26, 27, 28
political allies: as brothers, 28, 29; as fictive kin and fictive friends, 29, 131; as friends, 131; as lovers, 30
priests and high priest, and family hierarchy, 12, 13
professionals cast as intimate family members, 12
pursuit as act of disloyalty, 48, 49

qārôb, used of kin and non-kin, 125, 127

rēa' (friend), 4, 6, 7, 8, 9, 120, 122, 149; in Ben Sira, 88, 89
reciprocity in friendship, Aristotle on, 96
reconciliation: between estranged friends, in Ben Sira, 92; of former marriage partners, 138; of friends and treaty partners, 50

redeemer: role of, in familial context, 19, 20, 21, 33; role of, not required of friends, 33
rejoicing: biblical components of, 45; inappropriate, 45; over misfortune, as act of disloyalty, 49
relatives, disloyal, in psalms of individual complaint, 56–58, 60
rich and poor, and friendship, in Ben Sira, 95
Ruth: as flawless friend, 68, 69; as ideal woman, 68, 69, 147; oath by, 64, 144
Ruth and Naomi: friendship between, 62–69, 142, 143; status as widows, 65, 66

The satan, Satan, as divine adversary, 47, 137
self/selves, binding together: of Jacob and Benjamin, 15; of Jonathan and David, 5, 30, 70, 110
Seneca, on testing friends, 98
sexual intimacy and friendship, 8, 9
sexual unions, forbidden, as abomination, 42
shaming as curse against foes, 52
Shulgi Prophecy, 38, 55
siblings and emotional intimacy, 9
šlm ṭôb (and related forms), 4–5
Smith, Mark, on covenantal language in story of Ruth and Naomi, 145
social decline: caused by conflict between friends and family members, 19, 55, 56, 60, 139; in Marduk and Shulgi prophecies, 55
Sonia, Kerry M., on ancestral cult practices, 133
sons, ancestral duties of, 34
sons of the prophets, 12
Stackert, Jeffrey, on literary institutions, social practices, and rites, 119
"standing at a distance"/"being far from": and failed friendship, 39, 40; by family members, 39, 40; by treaty partners, 40; by Yhwh, 40
stela, erection of, and mourning rites, 22, 23, 129
Stokes, Ryan, on *śṭn*, 137–38
support: for family members, 17, 18; for friends, 32
suzerains as fathers, 29

Tamar, rape of, by Amnon, 82
Theognis: on disloyal friends, 96, 97; on limiting the number of friends, 100; on rich and poor, and friendship, 95
tombs: responsibility of kin to maintain, 23, 24; ruined, 23
Toorn, Karel van der, on sacrifice of the clan, 23
treachery, speaking, against a friend, 43, 44
treaties: curses in, 53; love and hate as components of, 46; parity, 7, 77; suzerain-vassal, 53, 86, 124, 138
treaty partners: cast as intimate family members, 12; possible role in ancestral cult practices, 34; transformed into enemies, 49
treaty terms and friendship, 123–24
trustworthiness: and family relations, 18; among friends, 33

valuation of friends and family members, in Ben Sira, 93
vassals as sons, 29

wealth and friendship, 35, 159
weeping: of Jephthah's daughter, 81; and kissing (*see* kissing and weeping as ritual acts)
widows: status of Ruth and Naomi as, 65, 66; ties to husband's family, 65, 68, 145–46, 146

Index of Subjects

wife/wives: in Ben Sira, 91, 92, 164; in family hierarchy, 13, 14; as superior to friend, in Ben Sira, 92

women: and comforting, 81, 157; friendship among, 112

Xenophon, on limiting the number of friends, 100

Yhwh: as cause of friends' hostile actions, 52, 60; as cause of rejected friendship, 39; as comforter of one suffering from disloyalty, 57, 58; as forgetting the dead, 135; love of, in treaty contexts, 16; as national god, 64, 144–45

yōdēaʿ, 4, 5, 121